A Spiritual Guide to FES

First published in the UK by Beacon Books and Media Ltd
Earl Business Centre, Dowry Street, Oldham, OL8 2PF, UK.

www.beaconbooks.net

ISBN 978-1-915025-30-2 Paperback
ISBN 978-1-915025-31-9 Ebook

Cataloging-in-Publication record for this book is available from the British Library.

Cover design by Raees Mahmood Khan

Map Credits: Eric Ross

Picture Credits: See page 317.

A Spiritual Guide to FES City of Saints

Peter Dziedzic
Sam Jaffe

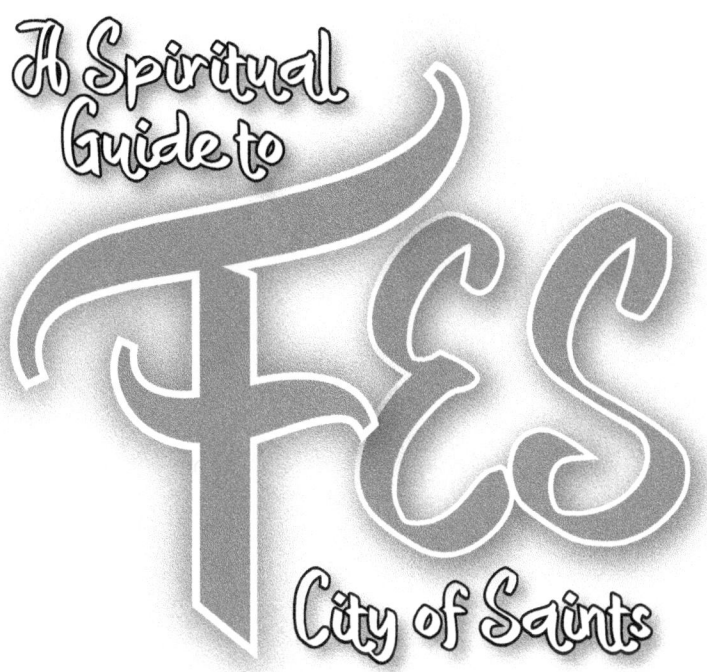

O God, in establishing this city, I want You to be worshipped, Your scripture to be recited, and Your Law and the practice of Your Prophet to be followed as long as it remains. O God, grant its people the ability to follow good and aid them therein, and protect them from their enemies and any tribulation and trial and grant them their provision with ease.

Mūlay Idrīs II

The earth of Morocco lets saints grow [in as much abundance] as grass.

Ibn Qunfūdh

Those who wish to visit the people of the Ṭarīqa in Fes should first start with visiting al-Muʿāfarī (Abū Bakr ibn al-ʿArabī) and then proceed to Sidi ʿAlī ibn Ḥirzihim, then Sidi ʿAbdullāh al-Tawdī, then Sidi Yūsuf al-Fāsī, then Sidi Muḥammad ibn ʿAbdullāh (Maʿin), then Sidi Aḥmad al-Yamanī, then [lastly my Master] Sidi ʿAlī al-Jamal.

Mūlay al-ʿArabī al-Darqāwī

Contents

Acknowledgements xi

Publisher's Note xiii

Introduction 1

Chapter 1: Fes: The Jewel of the Maghreb **5**

A brief history 5
A brief guide to life in Fes 13
Getting in and around Fes 13
Money matters 14
Finding accommodation 15
Living the Moroccan way 16
Studying Arabic in Fes 19

Chapter 2: Fes Bali: The Qarawiyyin Quarter **31**

Zawaya and Awliya **32**

Zāwiyah of Mūlay Idrīs II 32
Lella Kenza 37
Zāwiyah of ʿAbd al-Qādir al-Jīlānī 38
Zāwiyah of Mūlay al-ʿArabī al-Darqāwī 39
Zāwiyah Wazzānī of Fes Darb Houra 41
Zāwiyah Wazzāni and Rawḍat al-Khiḍr (ʿAyn al-Zlaytin) 43
Al-Majdhūb Sidi ʿAbd al-Salām al-Rakkāl 44
Sidi Aḥmad ibn ʿAlī al-Wazzānī 45
Zāwiyah of Shaykh Aḥmad al-Badawī 46
Zāwiyah ʿAbd al-Wahid al-Dabbāgh 48
Zāwiyah Nāṣiriyya of Fes 49
Zāwiyah Aḥmad al-Tijānī 50
Zāwiyah Naqshbandiyya 53
Zāwiyah Kattāniyya (ʿAbd al-Qādir al-Kattānī and Muḥammad) al-Qandūsī 54
Ḍarīḥ Sidi Qāsim ibn Rahmūn 56

Ḍarīḥ ʿUmar al-Saqalī 58
Zāwiyah Aḥmad al-Saqalī 59
Ḍarīḥ Badr al-Dīn al-Hamūmī 63
Ḍarīḥ Sidi Muḥammad Mayyāra 64
Ḍarīḥ Sidi Muḥammad al-Bunānī (ʿAbd al-ʿAziz al-Tujībī) 65
Zāwiyah Shaykh Tawdī ibn Sūda 65
Ḍarīḥ Shaykh Aḥmad al-Shāwī 67
Ḍarīḥ Muḥammad ibn Faqīh 69
Zāwiyah Sidi Aḥmad Mansūr 70
Zāwiyah ʿAbd al-Qādir al-Fāsī 71
Zāwiyah Būtchīchiyya 73

Masajid **74**
Masjid al-Qarawiyyin 74
Masjid Bāb al-Gheesa 76
Masjid Rcif 77
Masjid Bāb Bujlud 77
Masjid Sharabliyn 77
Masjid al-Azhar (Ibn Arabi Khalwa) 78

Madaris **79**
Madrasa Bu Inaniya 79
Madrasa Mesbahiya 80
Madrasa al-Sharatayn 80
Madrasa al-Atarayn 80
Madrasa al-Sefarayn 81

Typical Neighbourhood Elements **82**
Hamam 83
Quranic Madrasa 84
Hanut 84
Fountain 84
Bakery 85

Places of Interest in Fes Bali **85**
Bāb Bujlud 85
Talaʿa Saghira 86
Talaʿa Kabira 86
Funduq Tazi 87
Batha Museum 87
The Center for Training and Qualification in Craftsmanship, Fes 88
Bāb al-Gheesa 89
Bāb Mahruq and Suq 89
Suq Ayn Alu 89
Henna Suq 90
Suq al-Atarayn 90

Suq al-Ashabayn 91
Rcif Suq 92
Jamai Palace 92
Kaysariya al-Kafah 92
Al-Najareen Square 93
Al-Sefarayn Square 93
Dar al-Muwaqit 94
Mnebhi Palace 94
Tanneries 95
House of Shaykh Aḥmad al-Tijānī 95
Shop of the Prophet ﷺ 97
House of Ibn Khaldūn 97
House of Maimonides 98

Chapter 3: The Andalusian Quarter **109**

Zawaya and Awliya **110**
Sidi ʿAlī al-ʿImrānī al-Jamal (the Camel) 110
Zāwiyah Muḥammad ibn Jaʿfar al-Kattānī 113
Ḍarīḥ Sidi ʿAlī ibn Abū Ghālib al-Sārīwī 115
Zāwiyah Makhfiyya Abī Maḥāsin Yūsuf al-Fāsī 117

Masajid **118**
Masjid al-Anwar 118
Masjid al-Andalus 118
Mosque of Sidi Darrās 119

Madaris **119**
Madrasa Sabaʿyn 119
Madrasa Sahrij 120

Places of Interest in the Andalusian Quarter **121**
Zinqa Seffah 121
Metalworkers' Area 121
Gazīrah Street: Sandal of the Prophet ﷺ 121
Authenticity of the Sandal 122

Chapter 4: Fes Jdid and the Mellah **131**
Fes Jdid: The Medieval New City of the Merinids 131
The Mellah and the Jewish Community of Fes 132
Important Sights of the Mellah 132

Awliya and Tzidiqim **133**
Rabbi Abner Ha-Tsarfati 133
Lalla Sol Ha-Tseddiqa 134
Rabbi Yehuda Ben-Attar 135

Ḍarīḥ **136**
Ḍarīḥ Mūlay Abū Bakr ibn Arabi 136

Masajid **138**
Masjid al-Ḥamrā᾽ 138

Synagogues **139**
Synagogue al-Fasiyinem, "Salat al-Fasiyine" 139
Synagogue Ibn Danan 140

Places of Interest in Fes Jdid and the Mellah **141**
The House of Charles de Foucauld 141
The Jewish Cemetery of Fes: Bayt al-Khayam 141
The Tzidiqim 143
Old City Walls 144
Bāb Sammarine 144
Royal Palace Gates 145
Suq Fes Jdid 145
Garden Jnan Sabil 146
Kasbah Shararda 146
Borj Nord 146
The Merinid Tombs 147

Moroccan Judaism **147**
Early History: "The Golden Age" 147
The Jews of Morocco: A History of a People 149
Origins of the Mellah: Persecution and Survival 152
The Present Day: Emigration and Memory 155

Chapter 5: La Ville Nouvelle: The French New City **165**

Lafayette **166**

Zawaya and Awliya **167**
Zāwiyah Shādhiliyya Darqāwiyya ʿAlawiyya 167

Masajid **169**
Masjid Hayy Fadila 169
Masjid Imam Mālik 169

Chapter 6: Bab al-Futuh Cemetery **173**

Zawaya and Awliya **175**
Maḥmad ibn Ibrāhīm ibn ʿAbbād al-Nafzī al-Rondī 175
Muḥammad ibn Muḥammad ibn Dāwūd ibn Ājurrūm 177
ʿAbd al-ʿAzīz ibn Masʿūd al-Dabbāgh 178
Darrās ibn Ismaʿīl 181

Sidi Yūsuf Abū al-Maḥāsin al-Fāsī al-Fihrī 181
'Abd al-Raḥmān ibn Muḥammad al-Fāsī 183
The Seven Shuhadā': The Qubbah of the "Seven Men" 185
Qāsim ibn Qāsim al-Khaṣāṣī 186
Maḥmad ibn Maḥmad ibn 'Abdullāh Ma'an 188
Aḥmad ibn Maḥmad ibn 'Abdullāh Ma'an 190
Al-'Arabī ibn Aḥmad ibn 'Abdullāh 191
Sidi 'Alī ibn Isma'īl ibn Ḥirzihim 193
Sidi Muḥammad ibn 'Alī Ibn Ḥarāzim 196
'Alī ibn Muḥammad Humāmūsh 197
Sidi al-'Arabī ibn Aḥmad al-Fashtālī 197
Majdhūb Sidi 'Alī ibn Aḥmad al-Dawwār al-Ṣinhājī 198
Sayyida Āminah bint Aḥmad ibn 'Alī Ibn al-Qāḍī 200
'Ārif Murrabī Sidi 'Abd al-Wahhāb al-Tāzī 201
'Abd al-Wāḥid ibn Aḥmad ibn 'Āshir al-Anṣārī 202
Sidi 'Abd al-Raḥmān ibn Idrīs al-Manjarah 203
Sharīf Sidi Aḥmad al-Yamanī 204
Sidi Riḍwān ibn 'Abdullāh al-Janawī 206

Chapter 7: Visiting Outside of Fes **211**

Sidi 'Abd al-Salām ibn Mashīsh al-Ḥassanī al-Idrīssī 213
Sidi Aḥmad Zarrūq 219
Mūlay Idrīs al-Akbar 222
Mūlay 'Abdullāh Sharīf al-Wazzānī and The Seven Quṭbs of Wazzān 225
Sidi 'Abd al-Raḥmān al-Majdhūb 229
Shaykh al-Kāmil Sidi Muḥammad ibn 'Īsā 230
Mūlay Isma'īl, Second 'Alawite Sultan of Morocco 231
Mūlay al-'Arabī al-Darqāwī 233
The Imam Abū Ya'zā al-Hazmīrī 236

Chapter 8: Ziyarah **243**

Visiting the Saints: What to Expect 243

Rulings on Visiting the Saints by al-Kattani 248

The Benefits of Visiting the Tombs of the Righteous 257

Etiquettes of Ziyarah 259

How to perform Ziyarah 269

On gifting the reward for recitation to the deceased 273

Itineraries and gatherings 282

Index of Gatherings 284

Litanies and Supplications of the Moroccan Tradition **288**
The General Litany of Mūlay al-ʿArabi al-Darqāwī 288
The General Wird of the Wazzānī Ṭarīqa 289
Litany of the Tijāniyya Ṭarīqa 290
Ṣalāt al-Mashīshīyah 291
Dua Nāṣirīyah 294
Jawharat al-Kamal 301
Dalāʾil al-Khayrāt 302
Ḥizb al-Baḥr 302
Glossary **309**
Bibliography **313**
Photo Credits **317**

Acknowledgements

I would like to thank the Fulbright US Student program and the Moroccan-American Commission for Educational and Cultural Exchange for their support in the development of this project. Without it, this project could not have been realized. I would also like to thank Dr. Aziz Idrīssī el-Kobaitī of the International Center for Sufi and Aesthetic Studies for his research support, guidance, and friendship. I also want to thank the Friedmann family in Fes for welcoming me into their home, to Farhana Singh for her advice on the scope of this book, and Eric Ross for creating the useful maps for this text.

Peter Dziedzic

I would like to thank my father and my shaykh, Sidi Muḥammad al-Jamāl of Jerusalem, who passed away before the publication of this series, for inspiring me to move to Fes and opening the doors for me to become a student of its ancient spiritual tradition and to experience the luminosity of its hallowed grounds. I owe abundant thanks to my dearly cherished grandfather, Alfred Deetjen, with whom I always had a home. I am grateful as well to all of the Ṣāliḥīn working at the CLC in Murrākesh who made my enterprise in Morocco possible. Lastly, I am grateful to my co-collaboraters, Peter Dziedzic and Jamil Chishti, and our editor Siema Rafiq. May God preserve them all.

Sam Jaffe

Publisher's Note

A Spiritual Guide to Fes is the first book in a series of travel guides created with the spiritual seeker in mind. These books are unique in that they focus on the shrines, sacred sites, places of worship, and religious gatherings in major cities across the Muslim world.

This book is designed to be a companion on your journey through Fes, with up-to-date information regarding travel and availability. As a result, some of the details may no longer be applicable during your stay. If you notice any information that is incorrect or obsolete, please contact us through our website at www.beaconbooks.net, so we can endeavour to make future editions as accurate as possible.

We would like to thank the authors Peter Dziedzic and Sam Jaffe for their patience and dedication, as well as Eric Ross for his diligent work in mapping the city of Fes for the purpose of this book. We would also like to thank Andrew Idris Watts for his advice and his contribution to the chapter on visiting the tombs of saints. This project has been a labour of love for all involved.

Introduction

Fes is a city of mythic proportions. It is a city with over a thousand years of history, where the narrow alleys are still clogged with mule-drawn carts and fresh fruit stands, where ancient *masājid* still provide havens of prayerful retreat for rich and poor alike, and where secret gardens and fountains still invite weary travellers to pause and admire the city that was home to dynasties, luminaries, and thousands of saints. In a world of increasing uncertainty and conflict, where many of the greatest centres of Islamic civilization have been lost or destroyed, the city of Fes stands as an enduring exception to the great cultural and historical losses we face in our times. It is a city still very much accessible to the visitor seeking a taste of a unique spiritual heritage of humanity.

The city of Fes is abundantly rich—culturally, intellectually, and spiritually. Fes has been home to some of the greatest religious scholars, spiritual masters, writers, scientists, and teachers of the Islamic world, from Leo Africanus and Ibn Khaldūn to Ibn al-ʿArabi and Maimonides. They walked these streets, visited these mosques, studied in these schools, and shopped in these *suqs*. Known as 'the city of saints', Fes is where many Sufi spiritual guides were trained, inspired, or taught. The graves of hundreds of friends of God, *awliyāʾ Allah*, fill every corner of this city. Many of them are still visited and sought for their *baraka*, their blessedness. Many more are lost or forgotten, their graves defaced and their *zāwiyahs* crumbling. It is a city known for its cultural production throughout the ages, for its goods and craftsmanship—leather, herbs, metalworking, carpentry, and much more. It is also renowned for its stunning art—geometrical zillij patterns, intuitive symmetry, and rich plaster flourishes. The artistic culture of Fes fulfills the perennial mission of Islamic art: to mirror the beauty and harmony of the Heavens.

There are a growing number of visitors to Fes, and the tourist industry is continually expanding. While there are many tourists who come to taste Moroccan culture, there is also a growing number of *zuwār*—spiritually inclined individuals visiting Fes to taste its rich religious and spiritual history—seeking the many awliyāʾ of the city to take their baraka, to visit the places they lived, taught, or are buried, and to sit among the contemporary Sufis of Fes in circles of *dhikr* (remembrance and Divine praise). Despite this, there is often very little information provided or guidance offered for those visiting the many sacred sites of Fes. Most guidebooks will outline the most important sites, such as the Masjid al-Qarawiyyin and the zāwiyah of Shaykh Aḥmad al-Tijānī. This only scratches the surface. A city as ancient and as important as Fes has produced thousands of awliyāʾ and mystics, and they have left their indelible mark on the city.

This book intends to be a resource for the *zaʾir*, the spiritual visitor of Fes, someone seeking to encounter the religious, intellectual, and cultural history and life of the city of saints. This is the first practical resource written in English for such visitors. This text is intended to be simple and user-friendly. We do not wish to overburden the reader with historical and academic details. While these are important and must necessarily be studied, translated and preserved, that is not the goal of this particular text. It offers information on the major sites of spiritual interest in Fes—the zāwiyahs and tombs, the religious schools, the mosques, the suqs, and other sites of interest.

Using the *Salwat al-Anfās* of Muhammad ibn Jaʿfar al-Kattānī, the biographies of the awliyāʾ are offered, along with short histories, useful information on visiting, and practical maps. Also included is an index of the religious gatherings of Fes occurring throughout the week, various important litanies and religious texts of the Moroccan Sufi tradition, and proposed itineraries.

Salwat al-Anfas

Much of the source material for this guidebook comes from *Salwat al-Anfās wa Muḥadathāt al-Akyās Miman ʿUqbira Min al-ʿUlumā wa al-Ṣuluḥā bi Fās*, a three-volume encyclopaedic guide to the saints of Fes by Muhammad ibn Jaʿfar al-Kattānī (1858–1927). A descendant of the famous *sharīf* family of scholars and saints who were prominent in Fes' religious circles (until their persecution and subsequent migration in the 20th century), at the time al-Kattānī was writing the entire spiritual scene of Fes as it had been known for over a millennium was rapidly shifting. Scouring the ancient libraries of Fes for every remaining manuscript of biographical (and frequently, hagiographical) literature remaining, al-Kattānī ambitiously combined these texts in an attempt to immortalise the spiritual legacy of Fes. He was able to compile the biographies of over three thousand of the city's saints before passing away himself and becoming part of the sacred tradition he dedicated his life to. His zāwiyah and tomb, arguably the most recently established in Fes medina, still stands today.

Here in this guidebook, some of this priceless legacy has been translated into English for the first time.

Structure

The text is organized into six sections—the Qarawiyyin Quarter, the Andalusian Quarter, Bāb al-Futūḥ Cemetery, Fes al-Jdid, the Ville Nouvelle, and Outside of Fes. This is meant to logically divide the city's important sites into already delineated geographical areas, allowing visitors to explore part or all of a given area as they like. We hope this text will be a useful resource for all of those interested in encountering the baraka of Fes, its saints, its rich history, and its contemporary life. All mistakes in this text are ours, and all thanks belong to God.

1 Fes: The Jewel of the Maghreb

A brief history

The history of Fes is long, rich, and often confusing. Fes, like the wider Maghreb, has faced centuries of rapid political and cultural shifts. It is through this history, however, that Fes has become a city of synthesis, a city of the crossroads, and it is where we come to discover the many important places that await the modern visitor. Fes has been built over generations, and its culture developed over time to become one of the most refined—culturally and intellectually—in the Islamic world. It has come to be called endearingly by admirers as the "Makka of the West" and the "Athens of Africa." The city, once steeped in the wisdom of Sufism, Quran studies, religious law and traditional arts, is still a vibrant, pulsing medina. It is a UNESCO World Heritage Site, and one of the largest vehicle-free cities in the world.

The city of Fes dates back to the 8th century, when Idrīs ibn ʿAbdullāh, also known as Mūlay Idrīs, fled westward from Abbasid repression in 788 CE after an attempted and partially successful assassination attempt on his family. As the great-grandson of Ḥassan, son of Fāṭima, Idrīs ibn ʿAbdullah is a close descendant of the Prophet Muḥammad ﷺ. He fled to northwest Africa and arrived in the Roman city of Volubilis, near the modern-day city of Meknes, in 789 CE. He was welcomed by the local Amazigh people and became one of their leaders. He soon began building his own settlement in the hills above Volubilis with the support and partnership of the local Awraba tribe. Mūlay Idrīs grew in power and eventually founded the Idrīssīd dynasty of Morocco, which was the second polity after al-Andalus to break with and declare independence from the Abbasid Caliphs of Baghdad.

Berber vs. Amazigh: The native populations of Morocco and North Africa have traditionally been called Berbers, which is originally derived from the Greek "barbaros", a term used to describe all speakers of foreign languages. It was not initially considered pejorative in its context but throughout the course of history, the term developed a derogatory meaning. There is a movement among some "Berbers" seeking to change the narrative and adopt the term "Amazigh" as a self-referential term. Amazigh, in local languages, is often translated to "free person." While this is still a term which has not yet been universally adopted, this text seeks to respect the legacy of the Amazigh people and as such will use the term "Amazigh" to refer to the native populations of Morocco.

Idrīs eventually conquered large areas of northern Morocco and began construction of a new capital—Fes. Established in a fertile valley with rich freshwater supplies and excellent trade and military potential, Mūlay Idrīs set the foundations for the new Idrīssīd capital. With its sweet water, clear air, and fertile soil, Fes was destined to be a vibrant and well-resourced city. Surrounded by dense woods and plentiful gardens, the bounties of Fes soon became legend. The water was claimed to be good for curing gallstones, softening skin, and getting rid of lice. Mūlay Idrīs II was tasked with transforming this valley into the new Idrīssīd capital.

There are different legends surrounding the naming of Fes. One claims that an old monk from a local Christian tribe approached Mūlay Idrīs and asked his intentions. When Mūlay Idrīs offered his intention to establish a city where God would be worshipped and where His scriptures and laws would be maintained, the monk blessed Mūlay Idrīs, and claimed that on the foundations of Fes stood a city hundreds of years ago, named Saf. It was foretold that a righteous man of Prophetic descent would restore it to its former glory. The name was transformed to Fes, the inverse of Saf.

Another legend states that when the foundations of the city were being dug, a gold and silver pickaxe was discovered in the earth. The foundations of the city were completed with this, and thus the city took on the Arabic name for axe, Fes. Others say that the name is derived from the Arabic word for horse, *fāris*, because of the Iraqi horsemen who pledged allegiance to Mūlay Idrīs. The legends unite, however, in relating that Mūlay Idrīs, before commencing his work, lifted his hands up in prayer and asked for God's blessing upon the city and its people:

> O God, in establishing this city I want You to be worshipped, Your scripture to be recited, and Your Law and the practice of Your prophet to be followed as long as it remains. O God, grant its people the ability to follow good and aid them therein, and protect them from their enemies and any tribulation and trial and grant them their provision with ease.

Thus the city of Fes was born. Despite these legends, historical records do not indicate the use of the name "Fes" to refer to the urban area until 1070 CE, when the two sides of the river were united into a single entity. Before these, the two often competing areas were known as Fes el-Bali, founded by Mūlay Idrīs, and al-ʿAlīya, founded by his son, Mūlay Idrīs II. Al-ʿAlīya became the new Idrīssīd capital in 808 CE.

Mūlay Idrīs was assassinated in 791 CE on the orders of the Abbasid Caliph of Baghdad, Harūn al-Rashīd. Mūlay Idrīs II was raised under the protection of the Waraba tribe at Volubilis and moved to Fes in 809 CE. He continued and concluded the work of his father in establishing Fes. In the early 9th century between 815 and 825, thousands of families were exiled from al-Andalus and Tunisia, particularly the city of Qayrawan. These migrants brought many skills and trades with them, which allowed for Fes' rise as a major city and the Idrīssīd capital. Most of the families from Qayrawan settled on the left bank of the river, the modern day al-Qarawiyyin quarter, and the Andalusi families settled on the right bank, the modern day al-Andalus quarter. This is also where the two most important mosques of Fes, the Masjid al-Qarawiyyin and the Masjid al-Andalus, get their names. This also allowed Fes to develop with heavy Arab influence from its early foundations. After the death of Mūlay Idrīs II in 828 CE, the kingdom was divided, weakening the dynasty politically and socially.

After Mūlay Idrīs II inherited Fes, it continued to grow under his descendants. Later in the 9th century, both Masjid al-Qarawiyyin and Masjid al-Andalus, eventually to be the most important religious centres of Fes, were founded by a pair of sisters: Fāṭima al-Fihri and Maryam al-Fihri. The Idrīssīds were expelled as the rulers of Fes in the 10th century when an expanding Fatimid Caliphate briefly conquered Fes. The Fatimids were quickly displaced by Zenata Amazigh tribes allied with the Caliphate in Cordoba. Under their rule, Masjid al-Qarawiyyin was expanded, and the two areas of Fes expanded into each other.

The Idrīssīd dynasty was central to the development and institutionalization of Sufism in Morocco. ʿAbd al-Salām ibn Mashīsh, often seen as the father of Sufism in Morocco and the second "pole" of Islam, inherited his mystical wisdom from Sidi ʿAlī ibn Ḥirzihim and Abū Madyan in Fes, and passed it on to the renowned Sufi shaykh ʿAbd al-Ḥassan as-Shādhilī, founder of the indigenous and now globally influential Shādhilī Sufi order. After the fall of the Idrīssīd dynasty, many Idrīssīd Shurufāʾ became involved in the circles of early Moroccan Sufism.

The city of Fes was united in 1070 CE under the Almoravids, who conquered a vast swath of territory from the Sahara to al-Andalus. Though the capital of the dynasty was moved to Murrākesh, Fes was established as a centre of religious knowledge and a centre of commerce. Under the Almoravids, there was great architectural and cultural expansion in Fes, particularly with a new wave of Andalusian influence. Masjid al-Qarawiyyin underwent a massive renovation and restoration, taking on its current shape.

The Almoravids soon fell to Ibn Tumart, leader of the new Almohad dynasty in the 12th century. The Almohads conquered Fes, which continued to expand under their rule. They gave the Fes medina its current shape, and the medina walls still standing are attributed to them. Under Almohad rule, Fes grew to become the largest city in the world with a population of roughly

200,000. Despite not being a capital city, Fes thrived culturally and economically.

Under the succeeding Merinid dynasty, Fes became the capital of Morocco once more. The Merinids founded Fes al-Jdid as a new military and political centre. Merinid rule in Fes is often considered a "Golden Age" for a number of reasons. Under the Merinids, religious scholarship was heavily sponsored, and Fes soon came to be known as an intellectual capital. The famous *madāris* of Fes were founded, and they sponsored new architectural and public works programs, transforming Fes into a thriving urban centre. In 1438 CE, the Jewish Mellah of Fes was founded near Fes al-Jdid. This provided political protection to the often-persecuted Jewish minority of Fes. With the influx of Sephardic Jews escaping the Spanish Reconquista in the 15th century, Fes became a vibrant centre of Jewish life in Morocco.

The prominence of Shurufāʾ, descendants of the Prophet Muḥammad ﷺ, took on a more prominent role in Merinid society. This was the first resurgence of the Shurufāʾ since the Idrīssīd dynasty. After the Merinids, the political dynasties of Morocco were centred on claims of Shurifian lineage. This is the historical root of the importance of Shurufāʾ in Morocco, which continues to this day. The dynastic successors to the Merinids and the Wattisids continued many of the same urban policies in Fes. During Wattisid rule, Morocco was struggling politically with Portuguese and Turkish incursions as well as political instability in the countryside with the rise of influential Sufi leaders and rural, politically active awliyāʾ. Under the Saadian dynasty, the capital was moved south to Murrākesh. Through the Saadian dynasty and after their fall, Fes declined in importance but remained an active trading centre.

Under the Saadians, the concept of the right to rule of the Shurufāʾ was solidified and legitimized. Though this was an already established tradition since the Idrīssīd dynasty, this legitimization was spread through the activities of Sufi communities in rural areas who relied on them as political and social leaders. Their importance stemmed from a long-standing tradition of Moroccan religious and social thought. During this time, the important role of the Shurufā' and Sufism converged in Shaykh Muḥammad ibn Sulaymān al-Jazūlī, who was seen as a reviver of the Shādhilī Ṭarīqa in Morocco. Through his popular work, *Dalā'il al-Khayrāt*, a collection of blessings and prayers upon the Prophet ﷺ and a spiritual tradition of Prophetic praise, the status of the Shurufā' was raised, which was to have lasting implications in Moroccan religious and political thought. It is through Shaykh al-Jazūlī that many modern Moroccan Sufi orders trace their lineage.

The 'Alawī dynasty also embellished the city with a number of monuments. Under the 'Alawī sultans, Fes regained its status as capital. Many important monuments were constructed in Fes, such as the Bujlud Palace. Following centuries of gradual European economic and military incursion into Morocco, the French Protectorate was established over most of Morocco in 1912, following the Treaty of Fes. Under the French, there was a scheme of urban protection, and they built the Ville Nouvelle—the modern new city of Fes—in an effort to maintain the character and culture of the old medina. This was a policy of cultural preservation adopted by the French administration across the Protectorate and led to the phenomenon of a "dual city"—a French *ville nouvelle* and the traditional medina—in most major Moroccan cities. Fes was the capital of Morocco until 1925, when the capital was moved to Rabāt where it remains today. The French Protectorate lasted until 1956.

After independence, Fes maintained a reputation as one of Morocco's most important cities. It is a thriving university city with a large student population. The masjid and university al-Qarawiyyin still draws many students from around the world, and more so now given Morocco's efforts to promote moderate Islam globally. Many students from West Africa and as far away as Malaysia and Indonesia are sponsored in Morocco. The medina remains on the UNESCO World Heritage Site list, though preservation efforts are hindered by lack of funding and an ever-expanding population. Fes is also a booming tourist city and is becoming one of the largest tourist centres in Morocco.

The documentary "Fez: City of Saints" produced by the Britain-based NGO Radical Middle Way, offers a brief account of the spiritual history of Fes while following the ziyārah of several prominent shuyūkh. Watching the documentary is an excellent way to become acquainted with the city and its global importance in Sufism.

The spiritual history of the city, however, is something that is often missed among large tour groups. For the individual visitors—for Muslims, Sufis, and spiritual seekers—it is the essence of Fes, a city which is host to hundreds of important awliyāʾ—some who are famed around the globe, and others known only in local neighbourhoods. From these sites—the tombs of the saints, their zāwiyahs, and their centres of activity—a rich tradition of ziyārah has developed (visitation of the tombs of saints). This practice of ziyārah still attracts Muslims from around the world today, from as far as Brazil and Indonesia. It is a culture which has developed over the centuries, though it is the centre of Sufi life in Fes today. Experiencing this is experiencing a history of Fes often hidden to most tourists, backpackers, and travellers. It is an experience waiting to be had.

A brief guide to life in Fes

So you have moved to Fes. Or at least, you are planning to. It is hard to guess your personal motivation but some likely scenarios come to mind. Perhaps you have come to the ancient city temporarily in order to study Arabic at the American Language Center in Fes, drawn to the international reputation of the institute. Or perhaps you have moved to Morocco seeking to study the traditional Islamic sciences and gain your *ijāza* in Mālikī fiqh. Or perhaps you have already visited the city and were inexplicably drawn to it, overwhelmed by its unique charisma to such an extent that when you returned home you simply couldn't stop thinking about it. Now, months or years later, the seed that was planted has sprouted and you are planning against all odds and reason to make your move.

During my time in Morocco, I met people who had moved to Fes for all three of the aforementioned reasons. A number of people arranged a homestay for their trip, some stayed in the American Center dorms, while others purchased full-blown riads in the old city, even undertaking the task of renovating them from a state of utter collapse. Whatever one's motivation for moving to Fes, the reality of the journey is that it is not an easy one. Barriers, both linguistic and cultural, pave the road that leads to Fes. Overcoming these can be a severe challenge, as I myself learned when I first moved there at the tender age of seventeen. To aid others in the same process, I have written a simple guide to life in Fes, replete with simple tips and factoids from my own experience when undertaking the move.

Getting in and around Fes

I will start at the beginning. The first challenge that one likely faces on this journey is physically arriving in Fes. From my own experience, there are two good ways to do this. One is to fly directly into the Fes international airport. The other option, generally slightly cheaper, is to fly into the Casablanca airport and just walk downstairs to the train station inside the airport. Trains from Casablanca lead directly to the Fes train station, where one can catch a small taxi to their hotel or address.

As for departing the airport in Fes, the first experience that may frustrate a new traveller is haggling with the taxi drivers. For many, haggling in general will be a new experience; the aggressive mannerisms of some Moroccans (who may want to take advantage of unwary tourists) can be stressful. A taxi ride from the airport should cost between 100–200 dirhams, and if one feels that the first taxi driver they speak to is offering them a raw deal, it is important to know that it is perfectly acceptable to either ask for a lower price or simply walk away and choose another taxi. Remember that, by law, the taxi meter must be turned on.

That first hassle overcome, one will hopefully arrive at their new address. One will probably note that navigating the streets of Morocco is a bit challenging—the cars drive far more erratically than in Western countries; many of the streets have no obvious street signs or names; and if one is living in the old city then they are literally faced with a labyrinth to navigate. Unfortunately, the chaos is just part of the experience and with time it is not so difficult to memorise the names of streets and neighbourhoods. In the meantime, if you get lost, simply speak to a native. You will be surprised at how helpful they can be (although don't be too surprised if a minority of them ask for a "donation" afterwards—20 dirhams is plenty, if they really insist).

Money matters

After settling into one's hotel or home, it may dawn on the new traveller to question just exactly how to measure the appropriate cost for goods and services in Morocco, especially when the prices are so often inflated. The answer is actually quite simple. Ten Moroccan dirhams equal about one dollar, and the costs for all services including taxis, menial and skilled labour, etc. follows a general paradigm of costing about one tenth of what it would in the U.S. or Europe (or in other words, the equivalent price but in dirhams rather than dollars). So a plumber that might cost $150 in the U.S. will likely cost about 150 dirhams in Morocco. For my large unfurnished two bedroom apartment in the new city I paid 2,250 dirhams a month—about $225. The cost of food, however, is more like half what it would be in the West, so take note of that exception.

In terms of work, when you move to Morocco the only job you are likely to find that pays anywhere near the wages one is used to back home is teaching English. Native speakers are in high demand in Morocco. There are many institutes and as a full-time teacher one can expect generous compensation nearing up to $2,000 a month. As a foreigner, becoming a language instructor is really the best (if not the only) option available to you.

Finding accommodation

When goods and services cater directly to tourists they tend to cost considerably closer to what they would in the West, as this is a special market. For this reason, a lot of apartments in the old medina which are generally marketed to foreigners looking for the immersion experience can cost upwards of $500 a month just for a bedroom in a shared space. Arabic tutoring at established institutes will also not be cheap. This is why it is wise to avoid arranging one's affairs via tourist agencies as much as possible. Doing so in the beginning will likely be impossible since you are unfamiliar with the terrain, so be prepared for some surprising expenses at the beginning of your journey.

If you are at all able to speak Arabic or French, or have contacts in the country, then by utilizing those assets you can seek your very own sarsār, or real estate agent. With their help you can rent directly from actual Moroccans who aren't expecting to charge you a premium for the rent. In this case the sarsār expects a commission of about one month's rent. The employees at your hotel may be able to refer you to someone, and these sorts of agents are generally just friendly neighbourhood characters advertising their services through word of mouth.

As for choosing accommodation, living in the old city is generally attractive to most. It may be enjoyable at first but the reality is that many foreigners find it overwhelming after just a few months. Aside from the noise and raw way of life, the old medina is rife with trash, ghettos, pickpockets, scammers, and drugs just as much as it is overflowing with cultural and religious treasures and hospitable people, and until one has a good grasp of the old city's structure, the local culture, and the language, finding more of the latter rather than the former may not be so easy. Ideally if one wishes to live in the old city, accommodation should be sought in Bathā—a district near Bāb Bujlud that is extremely decent by comparison. Otherwise, it may be worth considering living nearby in the new city, even if that seems a bit dull and beside the point.

Living the Moroccan way

Within a few weeks in your hotel you will ideally have been able to arrange a homestead through your sarsār, contacts, or a local institution. From this point onwards, life in Morocco will steadily become much easier. Scammers in the country are very sensitive to the inexperienced tourist—they can tell when a person is completely new to the city and more easy to prey on. After one begins to simply feel and act more comfortable in the city, however, that confidence is daunting to scammers. If you learn the names of districts and a little Moroccan Arabic you may quickly find that most people leave you in peace, and that your interactions increasingly begin to reflect the true nature of Morocco: unparalleled hospitality, kindness, and a charming easygoingness. Taxis will simply turn on their meters when you enter the car and stop trying to invent exorbitant rates, and the experience gradually becomes more and more natural.

Of course, one important habit to hold to no matter how long one lives in the city is to try not to engage with or even make eye contact with strangers who rudely call out to you in the street, be they a vendor, a passerby, or otherwise. Just keep walking and they will leave you alone; but if you engage at all they may continue their harassment for quite some time, leading to considerable consternation.

From this point on it is really up to you whether the experience succeeds or fails. In general what I can share is that the successful Moroccan enterprise founds itself on one critical thing above all else: a sincere attempt at integration. If you want to live in Morocco, don't stay in your room or selectively stick to a circle of other expatriates. In Moroccan culture, lives intertwine in an elaborate social network, and survival without community is impossible. By the same token it is a mistake to try and only study classical or Modern Standard Arabic while neglecting the local dialect, *darījah*. Learn the language. Make friends. Learn and adopt the customs, until Moroccans see you as just another Moroccan. Memorise the terms Moroccans use to get around and the hotspots where grand taxis congregate, as well as the routes they take, so that you are better able to get around. If you can do this then life in Morocco presents limitless opportunities and wonder.

By contrast, those that fail to integrate generally fail to enjoy their sojourn for too long. After a few months or years of culture shock and clash these expatriates tend to find themselves returning home, frustrated, hurt, and most likely never having truly understood the country they so enthusiastically came to in the beginning. It is hard to imagine a greater tragedy than that.

Indeed, many aspects of Moroccan culture can shock or take getting used to at first. Locals never eat with utensils for instance, and always share food from the same large dish. In fact it is considered extremely rude in Morocco not to share your food if you are eating in public, so don't be surprised if a rider next to you expects some sharing if you pop open a bag of chips in the taxi. Mint tea is the lifeblood of the Moroccans and appears at every ceremony and interval of life in the Maghreb.

Modesty is also an important part of the culture and locals will frequently tell you to just pay whatever you want when asking for the price of a service. That doesn't mean they won't get offended if you pay less than what is due, and sometimes it is important or even expected for you to force a payment against their (false) objections. Along the same lines, if a local does a favour for you they may come calling for a favour of their own in the future, so beware of accepting too much generosity unless you are willing to pay it back somewhere down the line.

Most of all, Moroccans are kind, hospitable, and fun-loving people. If you are a guest in their home they will lavish you with food, gifts, and affection, even more so if you protest. Similarly, if a local family takes a liking to you, you may be surprised at the extent to which they will attempt to adopt you into their day-to-day life, as if you were a long lost son or daughter returning home after many years. Generosity towards strangers abounds in Morocco, to an extent that is hard to even imagine in most Western countries.

I could go on about the infinite number of unique and rich customs of this country, but I think this small taster is enough to suffice for the purpose of this guidebook. It would be impossible to encompass the breadth of Moroccan culture in an article of any size. This is just a glimpse of what you will experience in the first few months of moving to Morocco. It is sufficient here just to offer a few examples, encouraging you, the reader, to discover the rest for yourself, and wishing you the best of luck in your Moroccan endeavour.

Studying Arabic in Fes

In recent years, Morocco has become one of the most important centres for studying the Arabic language in the world, due to global events and the impossibility or risk of studying in the once-great centres of Iraq, Syria, and Egypt. Morocco, along with Jordan, has become one of the most accessible options for Arabic and Islamic studies. Many come to Fes to pursue these studies due to its history as a rich centre of higher studies and spirituality, and to benefit from reputable study centres. In choosing to study Arabic in Fes, you will join a rich and diverse community of foreign students studying the language for a variety of reasons—Islamic practice, diplomatic service, academic research, or cultural interests. Not only does this create a rich support network of other students, but it allows you to engage with people from different backgrounds and to journey on your linguistic quest together.

There are a variety of official and unofficial channels for studying Arabic. Your options will depend on the type of support you have and your particular focus. Are you coming with a university cohort? Are you taking a year off to memorise Quran? Are you interested in studying Mālikī fiqh and hadith sciences? Are you coming as a young bachelor, or an established family with a spouse and children? All of these considerations will shape your plan of studies. Thankfully, there are a variety of options to fit a range of students.

Moroccan Arabic or Modern Standard? This is an enduring question in Arabic studies. Should you focus on the dialect, or Modern Standard Arabic? Studying Moroccan Arabic will allow you access to deep engagements with locals, and is useful if you plan to live long-term or build a career in Morocco. Modern Standard Arabic is good as a basis for further Islamic studies, media studies, and for using Arabic in other countries. You will likely use Modern Standard Arabic more than Moroccan Arabic abroad. Thus, you must assess how important it is to you.

The two most popular centres for Arabic study are the American Language Center in Fez (ALIF) and Subul Assalam Centre for the Arabic Language (SACAL). There are also several other, smaller institutes such as the Ibn Ghazi Institute (IGI) and the International Institute for Languages and Cultures (INLAC). All of these institutes have functioning websites. ALIF and SACAL, however, have an enduring reputation and have trained generations of Arabic language students. ALIF is based in the Ville Nouvelle near the Institut Français and the Fes Youth Hostel. This institute has many exchange programs with universities in the US, UK, and Europe. They also host many scholarship students, such as Fulbright and FLAS grantees. ALIF provides a range of classes in varying levels of Modern Standard Arabic, Moroccan Arabic, Media Arabic, and Readings in Islamic Texts. There is also private tuition offered for single or pairs of students, and the students can choose the curriculum and hours of the tutoring sessions. ALIF also offers a range of cultural and tourist excursions, film screenings, academic presentations, and a range of other activities for students. SACAL is located in the Fes medina, in the Rcif neighbourhood. SACAL offers a variety of courses in Modern Standard Arabic, Moroccan Arabic, and Islamic Studies. There is also excellent support for private tutoring in the above subjects as well as French and Amazigh. The hours and course topics are flexible.

Tip: It is cheaper to pursue private tutoring at centres if you study with a friend. Try to plan for private tutoring with a friend to save costs and focus on the topics you find most interesting.

Studying Arabic at these official centres often suits study-abroad students, university students, academic researchers, and those on a gap year. While there is not a large focus on Quranic studies, studying Arabic in a modern context will still provide you with an understanding of the basics, constructs, and grammar of the language which can be deepened with further studies. There are many benefits to formal study, including receiving formal transcripts and transferable credits for studies back home, being surrounded by a community of other foreign students, and the presence of teachers who also speak and can explain in English. Unfortunately, the cost of these studies can be prohibitive and a barrier for many students. A six-week group course will easily cost over $1000, and private tutoring is usually no cheaper than $25 an hour. This often makes Arabic studies impossible for self-funded students.

Outside of the formal language centres, there are other options. It is possible to seek out local Fessis as informal language tutors. Fes is a major university city, and there are many college students who would benefit from the teaching experience, extra money, and chance to engage with foreigners. Moroccan college students are also more likely to speak English and to understand and communicate in Modern Standard Arabic. Asking around in your community—with foreign friends, among host families, and at local cafés, for example—will help you seek out tutors. It is generally acceptable to ask for a sample tutoring session before committing. This is a very flexible option and demands personal initiative. This option may be frustrating as it could take some time to find a tutor you work well with. If seeking an independent private tutor, it is important to stick to your interests, goals, and commitments. Rates do not usually fall below $10 per hour, though group sessions are cheaper. This is a good option for self-starters, independent students, and those on a budget. The downsides are a lack of formal certification, transcripts, and certified instructors.

Morocco is an excellent destination for Quranic studies. Moroccans are committed to Quranic study and recitation, and it is an enduring feature of the country. A hizb of the Quran is recited in most major mosques after fajr and after maghrib prayers. For those who are interested in studying Quran, tajwīd, and Quranic Arabic, there are many Quran teachers in Fes. While it is rare to find a teacher who can teach *hafs*, the Moroccan *warsh* style is widespread. There are several madrasas in Fes dedicated specifically to Quran study. While these usually focus on providing services for children, foreigners have studied here before. There is no pre-registration process, and this demands visiting the school in person. Locals will have the best insight into options near your home. Masjid Hafsa in the Montfloure neighbourhood of the new city has extensive experience with foreign students, including a regular cohort of Spanish exchange students. Otherwise, each neighbourhood usually has a Dar al-Quran where locals come to refresh or expand their tajwīd and memorisation skills. These are usually women-friendly and provide spaces for women to improve their skills. The Dar al-Quran in the Batha neighbourhood of the medina also has extensive experience working with foreigners. While this is not strictly Arabic language study, it is a central activity for foreign students of knowledge in Fes. Teachers do not usually charge a price for Quranic studies, though it is assumed you will offer some payment in exchange for their time and services. This is a good option for those seeking to pursue a taste of classical Islamic life in Morocco.

For those interested in other Islamic studies, one often turns to the Qarawiyyin university. While most classes have moved to a recently established centre in the Ville Nouvelle, and although the structure of the classical Islamic education has drastically changed and arguably declined over the past century, there are still opportunities for engaging with the traditional Islamic intellectual tradition. Several classes are still taught in the old mosque, and they are taught in the traditional style, with the students gathering around a seated shaykh. The classes are often offered in a mix of *fusha* and *darījah* dialects, and with prior permission from masjid officials, it is possible to sit in on some of the classes. For those seeking formal enrollment in the Qarawiyyin, the entrance standards for foreigners are lower than for Moroccans or native Arabic speakers. For foreigners, a *juz* of the Quran, along with memorisation of the *Matn al-Ajrūmiyya* in grammar and *Matn ibn ʿĀshir* in Mālikī fiqh is usually a prerequisite, as well as the ability to understand Arabic. Outside of this, there are several Qarawiyyin students who are willing to teach basic Islamic texts such as the *Ajrūmiyya* and *Ibn ʿĀshir* in their free time. It is best to negotiate the terms of financial reimbursement before beginning. It is possible, with dedication, to study the basic texts in one year with the anticipation of enrolling in the Qarawiyyin the following year. This requires dedication, long-term vision, and financial support. This is best for those who already have an advanced level of Arabic and are looking to deepen their religious knowledge. The cost of enrollment is not high, though one needs enough to support living costs. Al-Zawiyah al-Fassiyyah is also working on opening a comprehensive program to teach Arabic (for non-native speakers) through Islamic studies and culture.

The best option for language study, in any case, is immersion with locals. Try to speak and listen to as little English as possible. Surrounding yourself with Moroccans will encourage you to use your language skills and become a confident Arabic speaker. While it is good to develop a strong network of foreign friends, do not miss the chance to fully immerse yourself in the culture. This is best achieved through homestay programs, which can be arranged through the language institutes. Use your Arabic in the markets, restaurants, and when travelling across the country.

Fes is what you make of it. It can be a city of many opportunities, and it can be a city of many frustrations. Remember your goals and your motivations for studying Arabic, and let these guide you on this long, and rewarding odyssey into one of the world's most beautiful languages.

▲ Taxis waiting for fares on a busy Fes road.

▼ The train station in Fes Ville Nouvelle.

▲ Students learning the art of Arabic calligraphy.

▼ Arabic Language Institute in Fes (ALIF).

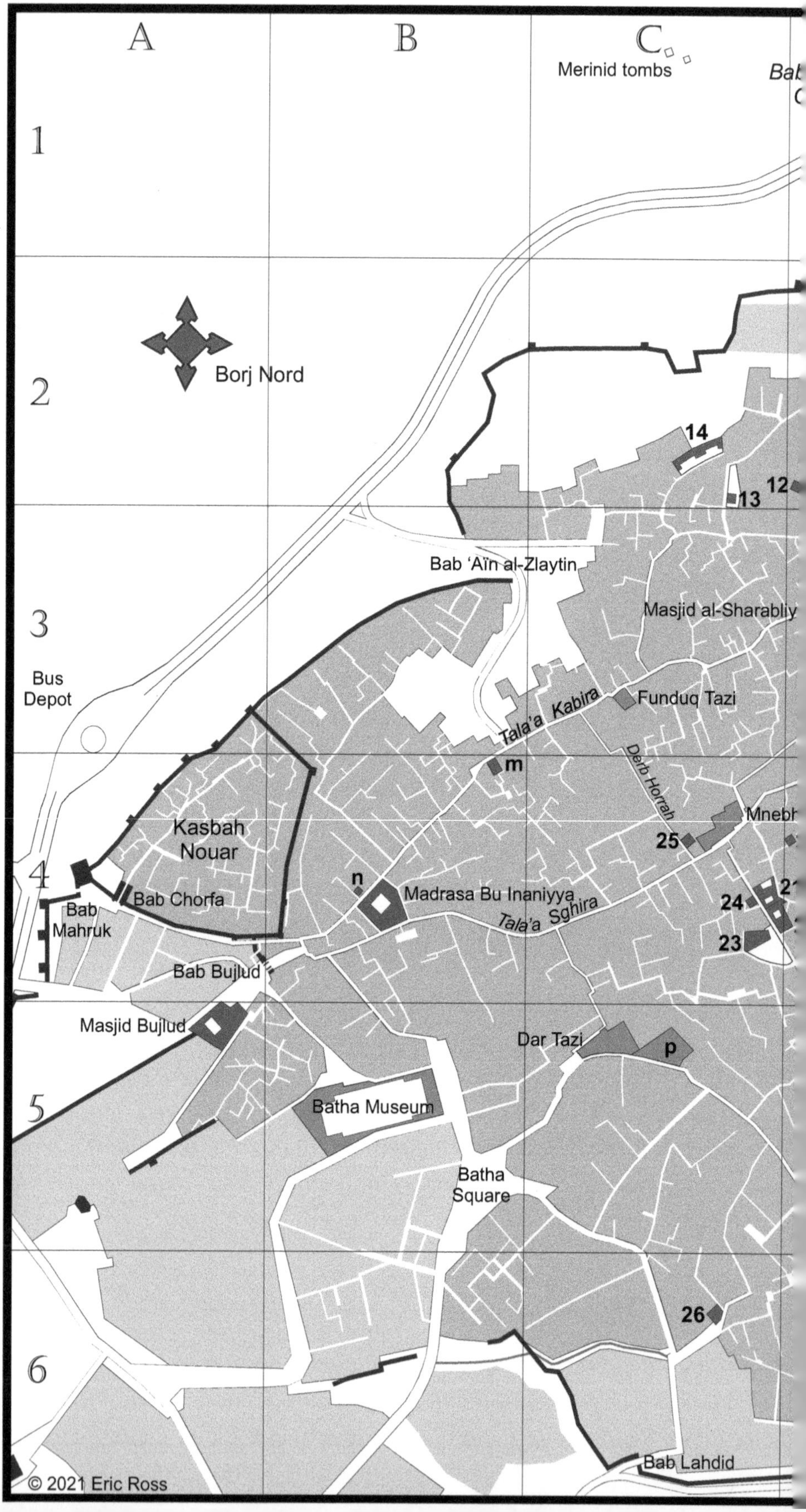
A
B
C
Merinid tombs
1
2
3
4
5
6
Borj Nord
14
12
13
Bab 'Aïn al-Zlaytin
Masjid al-Sharabliy
Bus Depot
Funduq Tazi
Tala'a Kabira
Derb Horrah
m
Kasbah Nouar
25
Mnebh
n
Madrasa Bu Inaniyya
24
23
Bab Mahruk
Bab Chorfa
Tala'a Sghira
Bab Bujlud
Masjid Bujlud
Dar Tazi
p
Batha Museum
Batha Square
26
Bab Lahdid
© 2021 Eric Ross

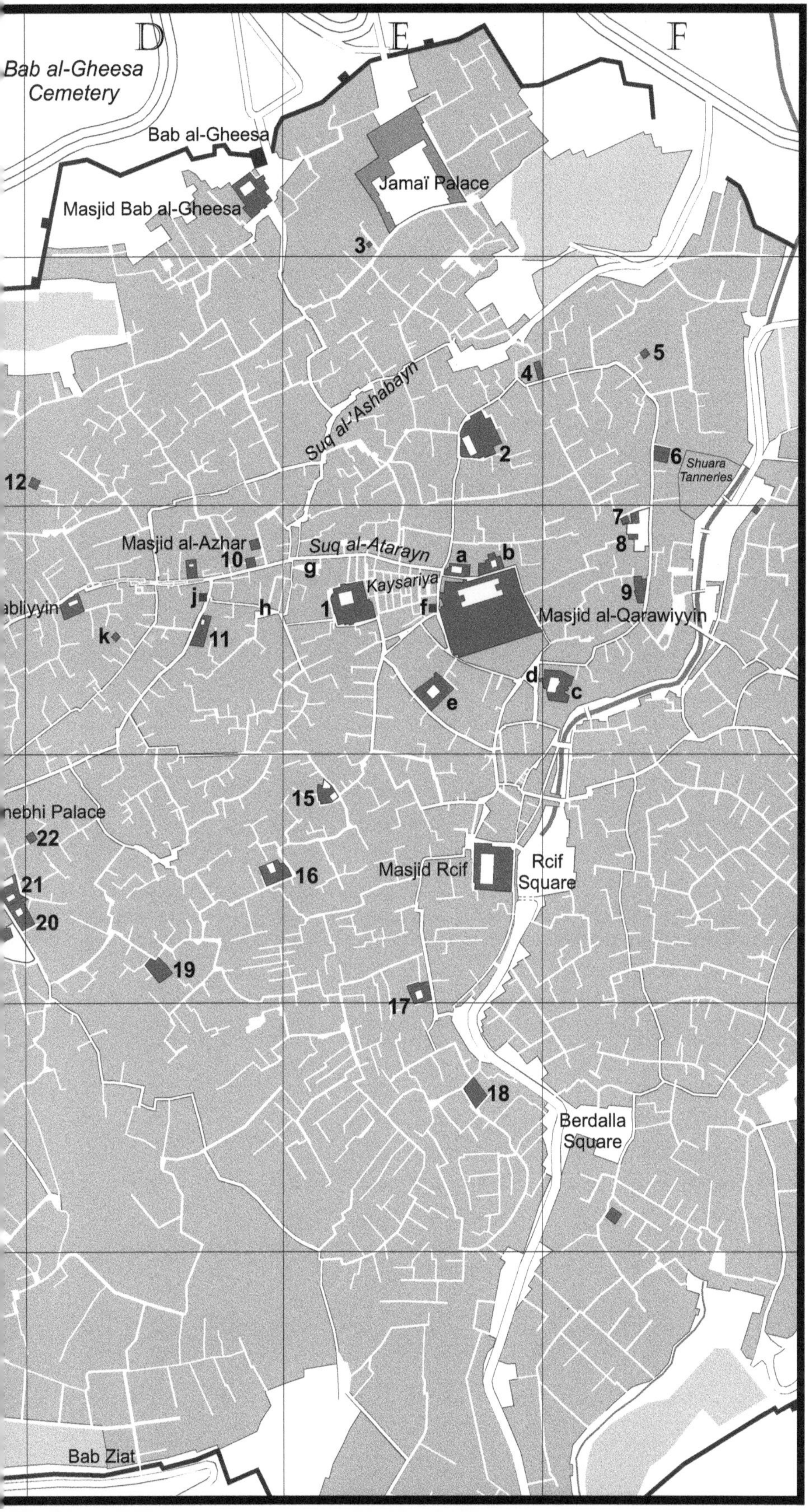
D
E
F
Bab al-Gheesa Cemetery
Bab al-Gheesa
Masjid Bab al-Gheesa
Jamaï Palace
3
4
5
Suq al-'Ashabayn
2
6
Shuara Tanneries
12
7
8
Masjid al-Azhar
10
Suq al-Atarayn
g
a
b
Kaysariya
9
j
h
1
f
Masjid al-Qarawiyyin
abliyyin
k
11
d
c
e
15
nebhi Palace
22
16
Masjid Rcif
Rcif Square
21
20
19
17
18
Berdalla Square
Bab Ziat

MAP LEGEND

Qarawiyyin

1. Zāwiyah of Mūlay Idrīs II
2. Zāwiyah of Aḥmad al-Tijānī
3. Zāwiyah of Sidi Aḥmed Mansūr
4. Ḍarīḥ of Sidi Allāl ibn al-Tuhāmī al-Hamūmī (Badr al-Dīn)
5. Zāwiyah of Mūlay al-ʿArabi al-Darqāwī
6. Ḍarīḥ of Sidi Muḥammad ibn Ṭayyeb al-Ṣaqalī/ʿUmar al-Ṣaqalī
7. Ḍarīḥ of Sidi Muḥammad al-Bunānī (ʿAbdul ʿAziz al-Tujibi)
8. Ḍarīḥ of Sidi Maḥmad ibn Aḥmad Mayyāra
9. Zāwiyah of Mūlay Aḥmed ibn Muḥammad al-Ṣaqalī
10. Zāwiyah of ʿAbd al-Qādir al-Jīlānī
11. Zāwiyah of Ibn Raḥmān (Ḍarīḥ of Sidi Qāsim ibn Muḥammad ibn Raḥmūn)
12. Zāwiyah of Sidi Aḥmed ibn ʿAlī al-Wazzānī
13. Rawḍat al-Khidr
14. Zāwiyah of Sidi Muḥammad ibn al-Tuhāmī al-Wazzānī
15. Kattāniyya Zāwiyah
16. Zāwiyah of Sidi Muḥammad al-Tawdī ibn al-Ṭālib ibn Sūda al-Murī
17. Ḍarīḥ of Sidi Maḥmad ibn al-Faqīh al-ʿUmarī al-Zajānī
18. Zāwiyah of Sidi ʿAbd al-Qādir ibn ʿAlī al-Fāsī al-Fahrī
19. Ḍarīḥ of Sidi Aḥmed ibn Muḥammad al-Shāwī
20. Zāwiyah Nasiriyya Sidi Maḥmad ibn Nāṣir al-Darʿi
21. Zāwiyah of Shaykh Aḥmed al-Badawī
22. Naqshbandiyya Zāwiyah
23. Ḍarīḥ of Muḥammad al-Ḥajj
24. Zāwiyah of ʿAbdul Wāḥid al-Dabbāgh
25. Zāwiyah of Muḥammad ibn ʿAlī al-Wazzānī
26. Būtchīchiyya Zāwiyah

Other places of interest

a. Madrasa al-Attarayn
b. Madrasa Mesbahiya
c. Madrasa al-Sefarayn
d. Sefarayn Square
e. Madrasa al-Sharatayn
f. Dar al-Muwaqit (astronomical tower)
g. Henna Suq
h. Al-Najareen Square
j. Shop of the Prophet
k. Dar al-Maraya (House of Sheikh Ahmad al-Tijani)
m. House of ibn Khaldūn
n. House of Maimonides
p. Center for Training and Qualification in Craftsmanship

2

Fes Bali: The Qarawiyyin Quarter

The Adwat al-Qarawiyyin, or the Qarawiyyin Quarter, is where the majority of Fes' cultural and spiritual treasures are located. It is also the quarter with the most tourist activity and accessibility, with a variety of dining and accommodation options on offer.

The book *Bāb to Bāb,* which offers a detailed and engaging map of Fes, is great if you would like to do extensive exploration on foot. While this book provides maps detailed enough to be used as a guide, some may prefer a colorful and engaging fold-out map (but be wary—walking around the medina with a large unfolded map may make you a target for hawkers and salesmen!).

The expansion of the Qarawiyyin Quarter was accelerated in the 9th century. Following an attempted rebellion in Qayrawan in Tunisia, over 2,000 Arab families were expelled westward. They ended up settling in Fes. Most of the families expelled from Tunisia settled on this side of the riverbank, and families expelled from al-Andalus settled on the other side—thus, this quarter came to be known as the Qarawiyyin Quarter.

These two quarters developed as distinct polities with a separating wall. However, this wall, along with a good portion of the city of Fes, was destroyed in 1069 CE under the Almoravids. This allowed for the integration of the local communities into a singular urban centre, divided by the Wad Bukakareb.

Today, the Qarawiyyin Quarter is the best starting point to explore Fes' history, culture, and contemporary life. It is also where many of the city's greatest saints lived, taught and were buried.

Zawaya and Awliya

The Zāwiyah of Mūlay Idrīs II (E3)

The Imam Mūlay Idrīs al-Anwār: Founder of Fes (d. 213 AH)

Some of the names the people of Morocco gave to Mūlay Idrīs II were al-Anwār (the Most Luminous), al-Azhār (the Radiant), al-Muthanā (the Praised), and al-Fāsī (he of the city Fes). Mūlay Idrīs' father was also called Mūlay Idrīs, and for that reason they are often distinguished by the names Mūlay Idrīs al-Akbar (the older/senior) and al-Aṣghar (the younger/junior).

It is reported that this was merely his name in the material realm, and that among the awliyā ʾ and the Divine Assembly he was known as Faḍl (the Blessed). His father Mūlay Idrīs al-Akbar was the son of Mūlay ʿAbdullāh al-Kāmil, who was the son of Ḥassan al-Muthanā, the son of al-Ḥassan, son of the fourth rightly guided Caliph ʿAlī, may God be pleased with them all.

His father came to Morocco in the aftermath of the famous historical event known as al-Fakh, in which some of the family of the Prophet ﷺ attempted to reclaim the caliphate from Harūn al-Rashīd only to have their rebellion swiftly crushed. Mūlay Idrīs was forced to flee and eventually arrived at the Roman ruins of Walīlī at the foot of Jabal Zorhūn, where the local Amazighs received him. Most of the people of Morocco at that time were polytheists, Jews or Christians, but the Amazighs soon accepted Islam and swore loyalty to him as the leader of a new, nascent Islamic state in the West.

Unfortunately he died soon thereafter, leaving behind (according to the most reliable accounts) only a pregnant Amazigh slave girl named Kenza, but according to other accounts two sons, one named Imrān and the other Idrīs. Three months after his passing his wife Kenza gave birth to Mūlay Idrīs al-Aṣghar, in the year 177 AH.

Until the young prince was old enough to assume leadership of the new community, his father's trusted servant Abū al-Saʿd Sidi Rashīd Mansah al-ʿŪrūbī took the position of leadership, all the while raising Mūlay Idrīs to be king. Sidi Rashīd taught Mūlay Idrīs the art of horseback riding, archery, politics and warfare, as well as fiqh, hadith, Arabic, grammar and even poetry. Mūlay Idrīs memorised the Quran by seven or eight years old, and his genius was such that Sidi Rāshīd and the Amazigh community swore loyalty to him and ushered him into leadership when he was merely ten or eleven years old, according to historians.

This was in the year 188 AH, and thereafter all of the Amazigh tribes swore loyalty to Mūlay Idrīs as their new king. According to Ibn Khaldūn, however, this was in fact the fourth time they had given Mūlay Idrīs their oath, the first being when he was in the womb, the second when he was still nursing, and the third after he was weaned.

Mūlay Idrīs, in spite of his young age, was a just and righteous king who ruled according to the Quran and Sunnah and under whose reign Islam became firmly established throughout Morocco. Many tribes entered Islam voluntarily in response to his *daʿwā* (missionary) efforts, and still others succumbed to his armies and entered under his banner as protectorates (*dhimmis*), until he had built a well-sized country.

His mother Kenza was a pious woman, and as has already been stated, was an Amazigh slave woman of his father. Some theories abound, however, that she was in fact the descendant of ʿAbd al-Majīd, the Emir of Europe. As for Mūlay Idrīs himself, he was described as a man white of colour, tinged with red, with black eyes, curly hair and broad shoulders.

He was also an eloquent poet and speaker, as well as a profoundly knowledgeable and intelligent man. Imam Suyūṭī wrote regarding him that he achieved all of the excellent Muḥammadan character traits and learned twelve sciences while he was still just a youth at twelve years old, and that he was a courageous warrior knowledgeable in all the ways of war.

He was a very modest, forbearing and forgiving man who acted justly and accepted the excuses of those who had done wrong with ease. He collected the zakāt according to the precise rules of the sharīʿah and would dispense it to those who had a right to it: widows, orphans and the needy. Indeed, he ruled according to the sharīʿah in its entirety.

In the year 192 AH he established the city of Fes with his own blessed hands, and upon its establishment he supplicated to God, saying:

> O God, in establishing this city, I want You to be worshipped, Your scripture to be recited, and Your Law and the practice of Your prophet to be followed as long as it remains. O God, grant its people the ability to follow good and aid them therein, and protect them from their enemies and any tribulation and trial and grant them their provision with ease.

The awliyā' of Fes regarded Mūlay Idrīs in the highest esteem. All of the characteristics of his grandfather ﷺ which were divided up at that time between his various descendants were gathered together in his character. 'Abd al-Qādir al-Fāsī wrote that it had been revealed through the inner vision of the saints of Fes that Mūlay Idrīs was both indeed buried in the grave attributed to him and also among the elect of the awliyā'. Various others attributed to Mūlay Idrīs the station of the quṭbāniyya and Aḥmad Tijānī said regarding him, "If only the people of Fes knew the value of Mūlay Idrīs, they would sacrifice their children over him." He said also, "If it was permitted for there to be a prophet after the Prophet ﷺ then Mūlay Idrīs would have been so," and, "Mūlay Idrīs is the Adam of the awliyā'."

Other biographers described Mūlay Idrīs as the Sultan of the awliyā', and that the maqām (rank) in which he began is the maqām that is the end affair of most, for he united three mighty qualities: the Prophetic lineage, sainthood, and knowledge.

Mūlay Idrīs died in the year 213 AH and was buried in Masjid al-Shurafā'. His mosque there became a very famous pilgrimage site as well as a destination for prayer gatherings, recitation of the Quran, prayers on the Prophet ﷺ, and all other forms of worship. It is also reported that occasionally a beautiful scent, neither of musk nor amber nor any other known perfume, would waft from his grave and flow out the doors of his mosque into the streets beyond.

Though it was believed that Mūlay Idrīs was buried in his mosque in Fes, this was not confirmed until nearly six hundred years later, upon the destruction of one of the walls of the mosque. Behind it they found his tomb, which had crumbled away to nearly nothing, revealing his corpse, which had not aged nor rotted in all those years.

The zāwiyah of Mūlay Idrīs II is the spiritual and physical heart of the city. It is, unarguably, the most important zāwiyah of Fes. It is also one of the most beautiful, having been restored and reopened in 2015. The zāwiyah is an excellent place to relax during the week as there is a calm, welcoming atmosphere. It is a good place to write, journal, or reflect. The zāwiyah is maintained by the descendants of Mūlay Idrīs, and it is still an active graveyard, with Idrīssīd Shurufāʾ still being buried in the zāwiyah to this day.

Note: There is a rich tradition of Quranic recitation in Morocco. Across the country, there is a hizb recited in the morning and in the evening in most major masājid. This is a long-rooted tradition, and goes back to the strong tradition of memorisation in religious education which was the fame and glory of the greater Maghreb. Moroccans, due to their extensive study and recitation of the Quran, became known as the "preservers of the Quran." This culture of engagement with the Quran continues to this day. It is common to see shopowners break from their work to recite a hizb, or to play audio recordings of the Quran while working. For this reason, Moroccans remain known as the "preservers of the Quran."

The zāwiyah opens around 8am every day, and there is no fajr prayer there. The other four prayers, however, are offered. There are often special gatherings held in the zāwiyah during Rabiʿ

al-Awwal, Ramaḍan, and Muḥarram. The moussem/ʿurs of Mūlay Idrīs II is hosted annually during the month of Rabiʿ al-Awwal. There is a big festival at the zāwiyah and a parade through the city, where the new ghatiya, which will adorn the darbūz of the Shaykh for the rest of the year, is paraded through town, usually from Bāb Bujlud to the zāwiyah.

Gatherings: On Fridays after ʿasr, the *Dalāʾil al-Khayrāt* is read in full.

Lella Kenza

Her full name is Lella (Lady) Zaynab, daughter of al-Sayyed al-Sharīf, the famous and lofty Mūlay Idrīs ibn Mūlay ʿAlī al-Ḥassanī al-Idrīssī al-Tounsī.

She was, may Allah have mercy on her, according to accounts, an ascetic servant (of Allah) and a blessed saint. It is narrated about her that one night she went out with her paternal uncle's daughter for a visit to the Idrīssī sanctuary and passed by a shop (which she is buried in now), and said, "Look at this house my Lord has given me!" On account of this, upon her death she was buried there, and this is counted as being among her miracles.

Today, there is little known about her or her death, except that it was in the middle of the second century after 1000 AH (and Allah knows best). Furthermore, she was still living in Rajab (the Hijri month) of the year of her death, at least twenty years after 1100 AH, and her mausoleum is in the shop in the Idrīssī sanctuary facing Dār al-Qaytūn.

People visit her even today seeking baraka, although now she is known as Lella Kenza. Some of those with no knowledge of history and genealogy believe that she is Sayyida Kenza, the mother of Mūlay Idrīs, the founder of Fes. Yet her noble (*ashrāf*) relatives, who have more information about her and also have the right of disposal over her tomb, maintain that her name is Zaynab, and that she was the daughter of someone as mentioned, and that her husband was the Sharīf Mūlay ʿAbd al-Allāh ibn Mūlay Aḥmad al-Ḥassanī al-Idrīssī al-Jūtī.

The Zāwiyah of ʿAbd al-Qādir al-Jīlānī

Among the pilgrimage sites of Fes is a room attributed to Shaykh ʿAbd al-Qādir al-Jīlānī inside the Qarawiyyin from the entrance of the Seven Wilāyah. This site has been known to the people of Fes since ancient times, and it is popularly attributed to the famous shaykh as a site wherein he supposedly performed a period of *khalwa* (meditative seclusion). However, it is without a doubt that Shaykh ʿAbd al-Qādir al-Jīlānī never once travelled westward to Fes and so these legends are nothing but a fabrication.

In addition, there is also a building called the khalwa of ʿAbd al-Qādir al-Jīlānī which has the same legend attributed to it. This building, however, was in fact constructed for Quran students by the Merinid sultan Ibrāhīm Abū Salīm al-Mustaʿīn Billāh. Later, it became a gathering place of members of the Qadiriyya Ṭarīqa in Fes, and so it is possible that on this account the legend developed as it did and that the people of Fes took to visiting the building for blessings, giving in charity to the descendants of Shaykh ʿAbd al-Qādir al-Jīlānī.

This zāwiyah is located on Talaʿa Kabira, close to the major suqs. There are varying legends about it. It is popularly attributed to be the tomb of Shaykh ʿAbd al-Qadir al-Jīlānī, the famed Sufi master of Baghdad; however, his tomb is located in Baghdad. Some say the tomb is empty, and others that it is the tomb of an important student of the Shaykh who came to Morocco and settled in Fes. Other legends indicate that it gained its fame due to people merely having seen visions of ʿAbd al-Qādir al-Jīlānī there in their sleep. Explanations such as this are possible.

Regardless, this remains a popular spiritual site and many locals, especially women, visit the zāwiyah for the healing baraka of the Shaykh. It is common for visitors to bring and leave a lock at the tomb, signifying one's trust in the walī's baraka.

The tomb is open during the day, though it is not open on Fridays after jumʿa.

The Zāwiyah of Mūlay al-ʿArabī al-Darqāwī

Mūlay ʿAlī ibn al-Shaykh Mūlay al-ʿArabī al-Darqāwī (d.1239 CE)

Buried in this humble little zāwiyah, which was founded by one of the world's greatest spiritual teachers, is the tomb of his no less noble son Mūlay ʿAlī, whom the Shaykh left in charge of the affairs of the Ṭarīqa in Fes upon his death. It was Mūlay ʿAlī who became the new "Shaykh al-Murabbī" (the fully matured spiritual guide and teacher who takes the hand of the seeker and leads him on the path to God) to the fuqarā of Fes.

The Shaykh spent his life and died in the city of Fes in the year 1239 CE. During his lifetime, he was able to travel to Makka, perform the Hajj, and visit the tomb of the Prophet ﷺ in Medina. One of his companions on this journey related on authority of one of the ashrāf who accompanied him, that he (the sharīf) once fell sick, and Mūlay ʿAlī was not aware. He related, "When Mūlay ʿAlī did not see me for some time, he asked after me, and was told that I had fallen ill. He replied angrily, 'And you did not inform me of this?! If one of our companions should fall sick, then tell me about him!' Then he summoned me, and asked for a pitcher of water. They brought it, and he recited something simple over it, then ordered me to drink it. By God: through nothing more than drinking it my disease molted like hairs of wheat and I became healthy right there and then, as if there had never been anything wrong with me at all."

This zāwiyah, located in the Bledia neighbourhood, opened in the 13th century AH and was the first zāwiyah established by Shaykh al- 'Arabī al-Darqāwī as well as the first zāwiyah in which he taught. Today, there are hundreds of Darqāwī zāwiyahs across Morocco and internationally. The present zāwiyah was renovated in 2006.

Mūlay al- 'Arabī al-Darqāwī is one of the central figures of Moroccan Sufism, and his branch of the Shādhilī tradition has been blessed with many awliyā ʾ over the past two centuries. While Mūlay al- 'Arabī al-Darqāwī had three sons, Mūlay Ṭayyib, Mūlay Muḥammad, and Mūlay ʿAlī, only the latter, Mūlay ʿAlī, and his descendants are buried here. His living descendants maintain the zāwiyah. The zāwiyah is also a Quran school for children, with lessons on Sunday mornings.

The current muqaddam of the zāwiyah is Dr. Muḥammad al-Darqāwī, though the guardian, Sidi Tajul Deen, is often at the zāwiyah to welcome visitors. The zāwiyah is often open for maghrib and ʿisha prayers, and there is an annual gathering during Rabīʿ al-Awwal for mawlid. Tajul Deen, or others at the zāwiyah, can offer more information on specific dates for mawlid gatherings.

Gatherings: After dhuhr on Wednesdays, portions of the *Dalāʾil al-Khayrāt* are read until ʿasr. After ʿisha on Thursdays, there is often a dhikr gathering of Darqāwī fuqarā. Usually, Surah al-Kahf is read, followed by the litany of Mūlay al-ʿArabi al-Darqāwī,[1] and various qaṣāʾid. Occasionally, the fuqarā do not come to the zāwiyah, and you will find the door closed.

1 See index.

Zāwiyah Wazzānī of Fes Darb Houra

Muḥammad ibn ʿAlī al-Wazzānī

For a detailed biography of the founding saint of this ṭarīqa, Mūlay ʿAbdullāh Sharīf in Wazzān, see the chapter "Visiting Outside of Fes".

His full name was Abū ʿAbdullāh Sidi Muḥammad, son of the great saint Abū al-Ḥassan Sidi ʿAlī, son of the quṭb Mūlay Tuhāmī, grandson of the quṭb Mūlay Muḥammad and great-grandson of the great quṭb and founder of the Wazzānī Ṭarīqa Mūlay ʿAbdullāh Sharīf.

He took the Sufi way from his father Mūlay ʿAlī and from his father's paternal uncle Mūlay al-Ṭayyib. He also took by way of baraka from the Wazzānī majdhūb Sidi ʿAbd al-Salām al-Rakkāl, and when this noble saint died it was Abū ʿAbdullāh who carried the body to his house and washed it. His house was an important gathering place for the Wazzānī Ṭarīqa in Fes, and when delegations of the Ṭarīqa would come to Fes from Wazzān, Abū ʿAbdullāh would put them up at his house, feed them and take care of them. He was a highly respected saint, well-known to the people of Fes, and lived a longer life than his brother Aḥmad ibn ʿAlī, who is buried in the Wazzānī zāwiyah in the Sharshūr district of Fes. Upon his death he was buried in the zāwiyah in the Darb Houra, to the right of the mihrāb, and a darbūz was constructed upon his grave.

Buried in this zāwiyah is his son Sidi ʿAllāl (1314 AH) who was also among the saints of Fes. His grave is in the open courtyard outside of the qubbah, by the pillar to the left of the entrance. In the courtyard to the left of the entrance at the right-most pillar underneath a plaque of marble lies the grave of his grandson al-Rāḍī ibn Aḥmad (1304 AH), who was also a famous saint and majdhūb of the Wazzānī Ṭarīqa.

This is one of two Wazzānī zawāya in Fes located on Darb Houra, a main thoroughfare connecting Tala'a Kabira and Tala'a Saghira, near the Swaqt ben Safi neighbourhood. The other zāwiyah is located in the 'Ayn al-Zlaytin neighbourhood.

The Wazzāniyya, also known as the Tayibiyya Ṭarīqa, originated in the city of Wazzān in the north of Fes. Wazzān emerged as a spiritual capital of Morocco in the 17th century due to the work and influence of Mūlay 'Abdallah al-Sharīf (1596–1678 CE), an Idrīssī sharīf. The Wazzāniyya is a branch of the Shādhilī-Jazūlī Ṭarīqa. This Ṭarīqa was founded during the ascension of the new 'Alawī dynasty from the south of Morocco. An alliance was formed between the shurufā' of Wazzānī and the new 'Alawī sultans. This solidified the power and influence of the Wazzāniyya over northern Morocco and parts of Algeria. The shurufā' of Wazzān eventually established a political entity separate from the 'Alawī sultans and cooperated with the French during the 19th century. Post-independence, the Wazzāniyya remained an influential ṭarīqa across Morocco, and their zawāya are still active in many cities and regions of Morocco. All of the tombs in the zāwiyah on the Darb Houra complex belong to Wazzānī shurufā'.

The zāwiyah is closed except for Thursday nights. It occasionally opens for special gatherings and holidays, such as mawlid or the annual moussem of Mūlay Idrīs.

Gatherings: Thursday evenings. Dhikr is recited on Thursday after the 'isha prayer. The samā' mainly consists of communal recitation of a ḥizb of the Quran and a portion of the *Dalā'il al-Khayrāt*, followed by a variety of qaṣā'id and, occasionally, a ḥaḍra. Tea is usually served.

Zāwiyah Wazzāni and Rawḍat al-Khiḍr (ʿAyn al-Zlaytin) (C2)

Sidi Muḥammad ibn al-Tuhāmī al-Wazzānī (d.1150 AH)

His full name was Abū ʿAbdullāh Sidi Muḥammad, son of the Quṭb Mūlay Tuhāmī, who was the brother of the Quṭb Mūlay al-Ṭayyib, both of whom were the sons of the Quṭb Mūlay Muḥammad and the grandsons of the great Quṭb and founder of the Wazzānī Ṭarīqa Mūlay ʿAbdullāh Sharīf al-Ḥassanī al-ʿIlmī al-Yamlaḥī.

He descended, may God be pleased with him, from a noble and blessed household. Nothing could deter him from performing good works for the sake of Allah, from feeding the poor and the orphans to guiding people to the path of God. He took the Sufi way from his father Mūlay Tuhāmī, who raised him to perfection in its way, taught him the awrād of the ṭarīqa, and gave him permission to pass on that knowledge and awrād to those who were intelligent enough to receive them. He at first lived in a place called Zakār which was half a day's journey from Wazzān, and would only visit Fes once a week to attend the Friday prayer and visit his father. However, upon his visits he began to build up a following of murīds, to the extent that he eventually requested and received permission from his father to migrate to Fes permanently. He then bought a house in front of his holy grandfather's zāwiyah, which in time became a major spiritual centre in Fes that whole delegations would visit, and he himself became one of the famous saints of the city.

He, his father's companions and their muqaddam used to sit every morning and evening in the zāwiyah of his grandfather Mūlay Muḥammad to recite the wird of the ṭarīqa and their ahzāb. They would then perform a dars (lesson) in which they would discuss works such as the *Qūt al-Qulūb* of al-Makkī, the *Iḥyāʾ* of Imam Ghazālī, the *Qawāʿid* of Imam Zarrūq and other important works.

It was reported by the author of *al-Nashr* that he heard from multiple people that the Shaykh was one of the four Quṭbs to sit under the leadership of the Quṭb al-Jāmiʿ, to which he remarked that he considered this very likely as the Shaykh had been a God-fearing man who respected the limits set by God, in addition to being descended from a long line of Quṭbs.

He died in the year 1150 AH and was buried in a house in front of the house in which he used to live in the Sharshūr district of Fes. Later, a qubbah was constructed over this and transformed into a burial ground. His own grave is in the centre of this house and has a small structure built over it.

Buried directly in front of him and linked to his grave are the graves of his sons, the sharīf Sidi Aḥmad al-Khiḍr ibn Muḥammad al-Wazzānī (1160 AH) and Mūlay al-Ṭayyib ibn Muḥammad al-Wazzānī (date of birth and death unknown).

Al-Majdhūb Sidi ʿAbd al-Salām al-Rakkāl (d. 1172)

Buried just outside and touching the small qubbah of his shaykh in the open courtyard beyond isʿAbd al-Salām Abū Muḥammad al-Rakkāl, the inheritor of Shaykh Mūlay Muḥammad al-Wazzānī.

This shaykh was once a very rich and materialistic man who used to delight in wearing expensive clothes and eating fine foods. Then, he became a student of Mūlay Muḥammad al-Wazzānī, and abandoned all of these things to become a poor mendicant of the Sufi path. Upon inheriting his Shaykh's secret he became overwhelmed by stations of *jadhb* (divine attraction) until eventually he turned out to be a spectacular majdhūb who felt neither thirst nor hunger, heat nor cold, divested himself of all clothing except for what sufficed to cover his nudity, and took to living in the oven of the bath house in ʿAyn ʿUlūn, very rarely speaking to anyone and never marrying.

The Sharīf and Akhbārī Sidi Aḥmad ibn ʿAlī al-Wazzānī (d. 1231 AH) (D2)

Buried in his own zāwiyah near the Wazzānī zāwiyah, facing the entrance to the small darb that leads to the zāwiyah of Mūlay Tuhāmī, in the first bilāt within it and at the base of the first pillar to the right of the mihrāb, is Shaykh Abū al-ʿAbbās Sidi Aḥmad, son of the famous saint Mūlay ʿAlī and grandson of the famous Quṭb Mūlay al-Tuhāmī.

Sidi Aḥmad ibn ʿAlī was well-known for his business of copying and selling books, and was also the grandson of the great Shaykh al-Ḥajj al-Khayyāṭ from his mother's side. He is known to have taken the Sufi way from his father Mūlay ʿAlī, and it is also likely that he took from his father's paternal uncle, the Quṭb Mūlay al-Ṭayyib.

Also buried in his zāwiyah are his descendants, ʿAbdullāh ibn Muḥammad (1274 AH), Ṭāhir ibn Muḥammad (1301 AH) and Aḥmad ibn Muḥammad (1311 AH). This is one of two Wazzānī zāwiyahs in Fes. The other one is located in Darb Houra near the neighbourhood Swaqt ben Safi. Like the other zāwiyah, this is a cemetery complex. Burials still occur and locals regularly visit the graves of family and friends.

All of the tombs in the zāwiyah complex belong to Wazzānī Shurufāʾ. The Wazzānī complex extends across the alley to include two other cemetery complexes: the Rawḍat al-Khiḍr and the zāwiyah of Aḥmad ibn ʿAlī. This zāwiyah is home to an important Wazzānī walī of Fes, Sidi al-Khayyat.

The zāwiyah is closed except for Thursday afternoons, when the *Dalāʾil al-Khayrāt* is read, and Friday mornings from 8am to 12pm, when locals come to visit the graves of their ancestors. The current muqaddam, ʿAbd al-ʿAlī, is friendly and happy to allow visitors inside. A donation is expected, though not required.

Housed in the main qubbah of Rawḍat al-Khiḍr is Sidi al-Khiḍr. The door is usually locked, though the guardian ʿAbd al-ʿAlī can help you access the tomb.

Gatherings: After ʿasr prayer on Thursdays, portions of the *Dalāʾil al-Khayrāt* are read in the main qubbah at the top of the hill. This gathering lasts until maghrib prayer. Tea and bread are usually served.

The Zāwiyah of Shaykh Aḥmad al-Badawī (C4)

Shaykh al-Murabbī Sidi Aḥmad al-Badawī Zaytūn (d. 1275 CE)

His name was Aḥmad al-Badawī and he was a student of the great Shaykh Mūlay al-ʿArabī al-Darqāwī.

He in fact held a very high position among the students of Mūlay al-ʿArabī al-Darqāwī, and upon his death there were a good many of the Darqāwā of the belief that it was he who in truth inherited his secret and his station. One of his (Aḥmad al-Badawī's) students wrote a biography of his shaykh upon his death, wherein he went as far as to attribute the station of not only the quṭbāniyya but of ghawth to his late master, saying, "And whoever sees his writings on the various sciences—particularly that of the Divine Realities and Truth (al-Ḥaqāʾiq)—can have no doubt that he was the Quṭb of his time. For the qualities by which the people of the Way have described the Quṭb, and the (secret) knowledge said to be unique to him, were all to be found in the Shaykh, may God be pleased with him."

As for the Shaykh's origins, he began as a simple merchant in the Atarine market, in which he owned a small shop. Eventually, he decided to leave it to pursue knowledge of the religion, and he took up studying with some of the shuyūkh of Fes. He did not attend extensively to these outer sciences, however, and after learning just enough to become sound in his religious practice he abandoned the pursuit of material sciences in lieu of inner knowledge (*ʿilm al-bāṭin*). After obtaining what he needed of the religious sciences, he became the imam at a mosque in the Sharablayn and then set out in search of someone to guide him on the path to God.

This search would lead him to the great Shaykh Mūlay al-ʿArabī al-Darqāwī, and he soon became one of his foremost students. Upon the Shaykh's death, Aḥmad al-Badawī would become the spiritual guide for many of the murīds of the Ṭarīqa in Fes, and produce numerous spiritually mature guides in his own right.

As for how he got the name "Badawī" (meaning, from the countryside) when he lived his life in the city of Fes, it is said that it derives from a promise his father made during his pilgrimage to Makka. Along the course of his Hajj, he stopped by the grave of a famous saint named Aḥmad al-Badawī and begged Allah to grant him a son, promising that if he did so he would name him after that holy saint. He hoped in doing so that Allah would grant his son something of the saint's blessed station, and indeed not long after a son was born to him, who would go on to become as blessed a saint as any.

Today, there is a family living in the zāwiyah and they are almost always available. There is a doorbell on the left side of the arch which visitors should ring. The zāwiyah is in need of repair. A donation is not usually expected, though appreciated by the family.

Zāwiyah ʿAbd al-Wāḥid al-Dabbāgh (C4)

The Shaykh, the Murabbī and Sharīf ʿAbd al-Wāḥid ibn ʿAllāl al-Dabbāgh (d.1271 AH)

His full name was Sidi ʿAbd al-Wāḥid ibn ʿAllāl ibn Idrīs al-Dabbāgh, and he was a Sharīf of Idrīssī-Ḥassanī descent.

ʿAbd al-Wāḥid ibn al-Dabbāgh was a prominent shaykh of tarbiyya in Fes and took from a number of saints. His first guide in the Sufi way was the shaykh Sidi Muḥammad Ibn Bakkār, who was a student of his brother Mūlay Idrīs Abū al-ʿAlā, and upon his death he took from another of his brother's students, ʿAbd al-Qādir ibn Abī Jaydah al-Fāsī. After his death, he took from Maḥmad ibn Ibrāhīm, who was the Muqaddam and Khalīfa of the grand Shaykh Mūlay al-ʿArabī al-Darqāwī, and eventually the great Shaykh himself came to visit Fes. ʿAbd al-Wāḥid received the wird of the Ṭarīqa from him directly and completed his training under the Shaykh. Thereafter, he garnered a large following and became a prominent shaykh of the Ṭarīqa, much like his brother in the Ṭarīqa Aḥmad al-Badawī, who is buried across from him in his zāwiyah. When ʿAbd al-Wāḥid died he was at first buried in the zāwiyah of his Shaykh's Shaykh, ʿAlī al-Jamal, and was later moved to a zāwiyah that was prepared for him in the darb he remains in today, with a large darbūz over his grave.

ʿAbd al-Wāḥid was a very forthright and outspoken man who never feared to say what he thought to be right. Nothing upset the Shaykh more than lies, and he would become outraged on account of them. The Shaykh frequently sought the counsel of those around him, and would often recite the hadith that "Religion is *naṣīḥah* (counsel)". ʿAbd al-Wāḥid would also speak frequently in the form of *ishārāt* (mystical allusions) and said, "All of our speech about the Sufi way is allusions (*ishārāt*), and if ever it becomes *ʿibārāt* (forthright speech) then its true meaning becomes hidden!"

Some of his companions mention in a book they wrote of the Shaykh's life that he reached the quṭbāniyya before his death, and that his entry into that station was in the year 1269 AH (three years before his passing).

Today, there is a family living in this zāwiyah, and they are almost always available. Visitors need to knock. The zāwiyah is not well-maintained and is in need of repair. The family expects a donation for the visit.

Zāwiyah Nāṣiriyya of Fes (D4)

The Imam Sidi Mahmad ibn Nāṣir al-Darʿi (b. 1085)

The Nāṣiriyya of Fes sits directly next to the zāwiyah of Sidi Aḥmad al-Badawī and contains the final resting places of numerous shuyūkh of the Nāṣirī lineage. The zāwiyah is most famously attributed to Shaykh Abū al-ʿAbbās, the son of Sidi Mahmed and his inheritor, who was more well-known than his father. However, in truth, the zāwiyah originally belonged to Sidi Mahmad, and was built for him by his student Muḥammad ibn Ibrāhīm al-Khayyāṭī, buried not far away in the Darb Houra.

Sidi Mahmad was a scholar of the Islamic sciences as well as tasawwuf and studied under numerous teachers, including those he encountered during a journey to the East. In the Sufi way, however, his teachers were the Quṭb Sidi 'Abdullāh ibn Ḥussayn al-Tamakrūtī al-Darʿī al-Raqī, Aḥmad ibn ʿAlī al-Darʿī and Sidi al-Ghāzī. He also had numerous students, such as the scholar al-Alussī, who wrote a very famous madh called *Dāliyya* in praise of the shaykhs Abū al-Ḥassan al-Shādhilī and Abū al-ʿAbbās al-Mursī.

As previously mentioned, after his death the Ṭarīqa was led by his son Abū al-ʿAbbās, who developed a large following throughout all of Morocco. Additionally, it was said that he had between twenty and twenty-three thousand followers from among the believing djinn. He died in the year 1129 and was buried in the zāwiyah of his father and shuyūkh of the Dar'ī Ṭarīqa. It was said that the cause of his death was the excessive swarming upon him of his followers from among the djinn.

Today, there is a family living in the Zāwiyah Nāṣiriyya. Visitors need to knock, and the family is often amenable to guests. Sometimes the family is not available. It is best to visit in the mornings, when the door is occasionally left open. The family often expects a donation for the visit.

There is an annual mawlid gathering during Rabī' al-Awwal. The date changes every year, but members of other zāwiyahs can help you with this.

Zāwiyah Aḥmad al-Tijānī (E2)

Mūlay Aḥmad ibn Muḥammad at-Tijānī (d. 1230 AH)

His full name was Abū al-'Abbās Aḥmad ibn Muḥammad al-Tijānī, Abī 'Abdullāh Muḥammad ibn al-Mukhtār. His father, Abī 'Abdullāh Muḥammad ibn al-Mukhtār, was a renowned saint in his own right, and both of them purportedly trace their lineage to the famous Muḥammad Nafs al-Zakiyya.

He was born in the year 1150 AH in the village of 'Ayn al-Māḍī, and it is there he grew up. By the age of seven he memorised the whole of the Quran, after which he committed himself to the pursuit of knowledge. He studied there under Shaykh Sidi Mabrūk ibn Bu'āfiyya al-Māḍawī al-Tijānī, until the year 1171 AH when he migrated to Fes. At that time he was no more than twenty-one years old.

The first great shaykh he met there was Mūlay at-Ṭayyib al-Wazzāni, from whom he took the wird of the Wazzāni Ṭarīqa. He also met the Quṭb Aḥmad al-Ṣaqalī at that time but neither spoke nor took anything from him. Another teacher from whom he received blessings was the great Shādhilī shaykh Sidi al-ʿArabī ibn ʿAbdullāh Maʿin, the teacher of Sidi ʿAlī al-Jamal, who in turn was the guide of Mūlay al-ʿArabi al-Darqāwī, his contemporary and also a contender for the title of Quṭb. Both shuyūkh considered themselves to be the Quṭb, as well as their respective ṭarīqas—and God knows best the stations of his awliyāʾ.

From this point, Aḥmad Tijānī would go on to encounter a number of turbulent years in both his worldly and spiritual life, as he passed through various ṭarīqas and countries. After leaving Fes, he would spend five years in the Sahara desert near the tomb of Sidi al-Shaykh, throughout which he would revisit his homeland of ʿAyn al-Māḍī, then travel to live for a time in the city of Tilimsān. It is here that he had his first great spiritual opening.

After this, he dedicated himself to performing the Hajj. Throughout his journey to the East he sought knowledge and baraka from whomever he could along the way and met with a great many shuyūkh. It is also along this journey that, after briefly taking up then abandoning in quick succession the Qadirī and Nāsirī Ṭarīqa, the Ṭarīqa of Aḥmad al-Habīb al-Sijilmāsī, and the Ṭarīqa of Abī ʿAbbās Aḥmad al-Tawwāsh, that he committed to what was to be his final Ṭarīqa before he abandoned the established brotherhoods altogether and formed his own Tijānīyya Order: the Shādhilī Khalwatī Order, at the hands of Abū ʿAbdallāh Maḥmad ibn ʿAbd al-Raḥmān al-Azharī. In addition to al-Azharī, there existed a number of famous shuyūkh and awliyāʾ from whom he would seek blessings, correspond, or take their awrād and aḥzāb both throughout that journey and after.

He returned to Tilimsān in the year 1188 AH. What followed would be another turbulent period of travel and study at the hands of various shuyūkh, until eventually he settled in the desert village of the Quṭb Abū Samghūn. It was there, in the beginning of the twelfth century, that he would finally achieve his greatest spiritual opening. Not long after, in the year 1214 AH, he would settle at last in the great city of Fes and achieve the great station of the Quṭbāniyya.

It is a hallmark of the Tijānī Ṭarīqa that Shaykh Aḥmad Tijānī was not granted the title of Sufi shaykh by any living shaykh but rather, according to Aḥmad Tijānī, directly by the Prophet ﷺ himself in a spiritual vision. Regardless, the ijāzas and wirds given to him by various shuyūkh were numerous by the time he felt compelled to break away and establish his own brotherhood, and this unique characteristic did not obstruct him from obtaining a huge following upon his return to Fes.

He remained in Fes, teaching and instructing students in the way of God until his death in the year 1230 AH. His burial was a major event, and great throngs of people swarmed over his funeral bier seeking his baraka, in such numbers that they broke the wood around it. He was laid to rest in his zāwiyah, which remains as previously described.

The Tijānī zāwiyah of Fes was established in the early 19th century and became the main zāwiyah of the community after the gathering in the Shaykh's private home on Zqaq Rwah. Since this time, the zāwiyah has been the beating heart of the global Tijānī Ṭarīqa. The Tijānī Wazīfa is read communally daily after ʿasr and at other times throughout the day by groups of Tijānī fuqarā. The zāwiyah often provides basic lodging to visitors who cannot afford other options, a common practice of many zāwiyahs.

Gatherings: The Tijānī zāwiyah is open during the day for those wanting to visit the tomb of Shaykh Aḥmad Tijānī, his living descendants who maintain the zāwiyah, and for recitations of the wazīfa. Daily after ʿasr, there is a lively communal reading of the wazīfa. On Fridays after ʿasr, the wazīfa is extended to include the Tijānī ḥaḍra.

Zāwiyah Naqshbandiyya (D4)

The Naqshbandī zāwiyah is located in a private home in a beautifully restored traditional dār in the Swaqt ben Safi neighbourhood. The zāwiyah follows the way and teachings of Shaykh Nāzim of Cyprus and Shaykh Hishām al-Kabbānī, and it is one of the newest and most lively zāwiyahs in Fes. It is an especially accessible gathering as there are many foreigners and the ṣuḥba is offered in English and/or French. Often the famous munshid Sidi Anouar Berrada of the Burda Ensemble and a number of other munshids grace the gatherings with their rich and beautiful Qaṣāʾid. If you would like a private meeting with Sidi Husayn, the Naqshbandī muqaddam of Fes, it is best to contact him via email at *rumi.todd@gmail.com*. The muqaddam has the following poem of Rumi attached to the door, and says it is the guiding spirit of the zāwiyah:

> Come, come, whoever you are.
>
> Wanderer, worshipper, lover of leaving.
>
> It doesn't matter.
>
> Ours is not a caravan of despair.
>
> Come, even if you have broken your vows a thousand times.
>
> Come, yet again, come, come.

Gatherings: On Thursday evenings after ʿisha, there is a ṣuḥba offered by the Naqshbandī muqaddam (except when he is out of town), followed by the communal Naqshbandī wird and several Qaṣāʾid. Tea is often served along with a meal following the dhikr. There are also occasionally shorter gatherings on Saturday nights after maghrib.

Zāwiyah Kattāniyya (ʿAbd al-Qādir al-Kattānī and Muḥammad) al-Qandūsī (E4)

This zāwiyah, located on Zqaq al-Bghal in the Kattāniyyin district, was the first Kattānī zāwiyah in Fes. The main saint of the zāwiyah is Shaykh ʿAbd al-Kabīr al-Kattānī, the father of the famous Sufi shaykh of the 19th century, Muḥammad al-Kattānī.

This zāwiyah was established in the 19th century, and was formerly a garden before being purchased by the al-Kattānīs, a very influential elite local family. The Kattānī Ṭarīqa was part of a wave of mystical revival which swept Morocco in the late 18th and early 19th centuries. Shaykh ʿAbd al-Kabīr was a renowned Sufi shaykh and instructed his students, including his son, on the texts of al-Suhrawardī, Ibn al-ʿArabī, and al-Tirmidhī. Shaykh ʿAbd al-Kabir's son Muḥammad al-Kattānī was an important advocate of Islamic revival and anti-colonial resistance. Muḥammad al-Kattānī was eventually stifled and charged by the ʿAlawite dynasty for challenging their claim to authority.

Although the story of the al-Kattānī family has disappeared from discussions on Sufism in Morocco, it has a rich history that deserves to be better known.

Want to know more about the al-Kattānī family? Read Dr. Sahar Bazzaz's *Forgotten Saints: History, Power, and Politics in the Making of Modern Morocco*, published by Harvard University Press.

There are two graves under the darbūz of Shaykh ʿAbd al-Kabir al-Kattānī. Most believe that it is the tomb of Shaykh Muḥammad al-Qandūsī. Others believe it is an empty grave that was intended for Sidi ʿAbd al-Hayy al-Kattānī, ʿAbd al-Kabīr's brother who was later buried in France. In any event, both ʿAbd al-Kabīr al-Kattānī and Muḥammad al-Qandūsī are buried next to each other in this zāwiyah. And God knows best.

Shaykh Muḥammad al-Qandūsī, a 19th century Algerian saint who moved to Fes and was connected to the Nāṣirī and Qādirī Ṭarīqas, is also buried in this zāwiyah. Shaykh al-Qandūsī is the author of *The Drink of the People of Purity* and is credited with writing the Supreme Name of God in the unique script on the wall of the zāwiyah of Mūlay Idrīs II. This has become ubiquitous throughout Morocco.

A state of disrepair: Many of the zāwiyahs in the Fes medina are in a state of disrepair and in danger of being lost. While there are several organizations committed to their restoration, and government support has been expressed, there has been a lack of concrete construction efforts in most zāwiyahs. There is now a constant stream of reconstruction and expansion activity across Fes—from the tanneries to Masjid al-Qarawiyyin to the madrasas of the Andalusian Quarter—yet many of the zāwiyahs have yet to benefit from these initiatives.

Today, the intricate, ancient central doors of the zāwiyah are permanently closed. If you are facing the doors, turn right and there will be a small door on your left. Knock, and Sidi Muḥammad, the caretaker, will let you in and provide you with a warm glass of mint tea which he is always able to produce at a moment's notice. There are no regular gatherings, though there are dhikr gatherings during the month of mawlid.

Ḍarīḥ Sidi Qāsim ibn Rahmūn (D3)

Sidi Qāsim ibn Muḥammad ibn Raḥmūn (d. 1146)

The full name of the shaykh was Abū Muḥammad Mūlay Qāsim ibn Muḥammad, Ḥammu ibn ʿUmar ibn Raḥmān al-Zorhūnī al-Fāsī. The Shaykh's father emigrated with him to Fes from Jabal Zorhūn when he was still a boy. He belonged to a tribe nearby that were known as the "Ibn Raḥmūn", not far from the tribe of Maṣmūda and the Wazzāniyya. The members of this tribe were Ḥussaynī shurufāʾ, meaning they were descendants of the Prophet ﷺ from his grandson Ḥussayn's lineage, though this matter remains under some contention today. They also claimed to have emigrated originally from the city of Sicily, Italy, near the end of the fifth century.

In the beginning of his spiritual seeking Sidi Raḥmūn accompanied Shaykh al-Ḥājj al-Khayyāṭ (the tailor), buried in Sharshūr. He accompanied the Shaykh for nearly sixteen years before he was guided at his hands to the Shaykh Mūlay 'Abdullāh. After his death he followed his son Mūlay Tuhāmī, then finally his brother Mūlay at-Ṭayyib until at last he died within his (Mūlay at-Ṭayyib's) own lifetime.

Ibn Raḥmūn said regarding his shaykh, "I served Sidi al-Khayyāt for nearly sixteen years. I never used to say anything to him, and if I sat before him I would fold my knees like a child. If I needed something I would merely consult him on the matter in my heart (without saying anything), and my Lord (by the grace of the Shaykh) would inspire me with an understanding of that matter." He used to at first work for a weaving business, sometimes performing physical labour and at other times he would use his talents to advertise their wares. Whichever of those two tasks he performed, his tongue was always busy remembering God, be it day or night, until God sent for him someone to take his hand (and guide him on the spiritual path).

Sidi Ibn Raḥmūn used to enter frequently into a state of *wajd* during his dhikr, a state which would flow through him to affect the rest of his followers (according to their capacity), of which he had many. He and his followers would sit every day from dhuhr till they gathered for the ʿasr prayers at the repository between the Bāb Hafat of the Qarawiyyin and the Bāb al-Shuhūd al-Kubrā. He would face the qiblah with his back to his students, and all of them would sit facing the qiblah with their prayer beads, quietly absorbed in dhikr and not saying a word to one another.

Sidi Raḥmūn died on a Monday of Dhul Ḥijjah in his house at the end of the Darb al-Mina, in the year 1149. There he was buried, and there he remains today. His tomb continues to be a famous mazār in Fes, particularly to followers of his beloved Wazzānī order.

Gatherings: This zāwiyah does not have regular gatherings; there are sporadic gatherings throughout the year and during mawlid. Sidi Ḥassan al-Amrani, the old caretaker, is usually inside the ḍarīḥ from 9am to maghrib. If you knock, he will be happy to let you in and show you around. There are two doors to the zāwiyah—one uphill and one further downhill, before the masjid. He is usually at the lower door. You need to be patient as he is rather old and needs time to walk.

Ḍarīḥ ʿUmar al-Saqalī (F2)

Sidi Muḥammad ibn Ṭayyib al-Ṣaqalī and his son ʿUmar al-Ṣaqalī

On the right side of the balīda, very close to the tanneries, lies the zāwiyah of ʿUmar al-Ṣaqalī and his father Muḥammad ibn Ṭayyib al-Ṣaqalī. The zāwiyah was founded by Sidi Muḥammad, although according to the plaque outside the entrance it is the zāwiyah of Sidi ʿUmar, who inherited it upon his father's passing.

All that is related of Sidi ʿUmar is that he was a man of knowledge, of holy descent, and that he inherited from his father after his passing in the year 1107 AH. Thereafter, he was buried in the zāwiyah of his father. As for Sidi Muḥammad, he performed the Hajj during his lifetime and along the way took the Ṭarīqa Khalwatiyya from the Ghawth Sidi Fatḥ Allāh, who took it from Shaykh Sidi Aḥmad al-Ṣāwī, from the Quṭb Sidi Aḥmad al-Dardīr, may God be pleased with them. This Shaykh granted him ijāza.

He wrote a treatise on tasawwuf which he called *Al-Ilāhiyya* (The Excellent Qualities of the Divine Secrets). In it, he frequently records what was revealed to him directly from the Prophet ﷺ during waking visions and without an intermediary. Among them is the good news which the Prophet ﷺ shared with him, that none of his companions would die except that the Prophet ﷺ was present at the departure of his soul, and that none of them would die except upon a perfect Islam.

He had unrivalled knowledge of al-saqar, and in the beginning of his affair he allegedly took part in some criminal behaviour on account of which the Sultan ʿAbd al-Raḥmān al-ʿAlawī had him incarcerated in a prison outside of Fes. He remained as such for over two years with a metal chain fastened around his neck until his step-relation Sidi Ṣāliḥ al-Bunānī interceded on his behalf. The Sultan then released him and even granted him a generous pension from the state fund for religious causes (al-Ḥabus).

It was during his time in prison that he first achieved his spiritual opening and began his journey on the Sufi path. Thereafter he became a great saint with a large following and many reported miracles, among them that one day he was walking in the garden of Hajar Farah in the Ramīla district with a qawwāl (musician) and some of his companions. The Shaykh loved samāʿ and so he requested the qawwāl to sing something for them but he declined, saying that it was a time of great drought and hardship for the people of Fes and so he felt it was an inappropriate time to sing. Sidi Muḥammad then told him to sing, and swore that they would not depart from that garden except amidst rain. Thus, the qawwāl began to perform. When he began it was still the morning, and by the afternoon fierce winds began to blow from every direction and in their trail a great downpour of rain followed. They exited the garden together but the flooding had already begun. They were unable to continue except by taking off their sandals so they all left their sandals behind and continued forward, plunging barefoot through the water. The Shaykh then turned to the qawwāl and said, "Have I not been vindicated as to my oath?" The qawwāl replied, "Yes indeed, o Sidi!"

Sidi Muḥammad died in the early morning on a Saturday, in the year 1270 or 1271 AH, and was buried in his zāwiyah. Currently, the zāwiyah is closed and is in need of renovation.

Zāwiyah Aḥmad al-Saqalī (F3)

Aḥmad ibn Muḥammad al-Ṣaqalī

His name was Abū ʿAbbās Aḥmad, son of the righteous walī and divine blessing Mūlay Muḥammad ibn Aḥmad ibn Ibrāhīm al-Saqalī al-Ḥussaynī al-ʿUraydī. He was from the lineage of Sidi ʿAlī al-ʿUraydī ibn Jaʿfar al-Ṣādiq.

He was born in the year 1112 AH and grew up in nobility and virtuousness. He memorised the Quran and beautified its inscriptions through tajwīd recitation, and dedicated himself to reciting it morning and evening. He studied the fiqh under the scholars of his age, and in his education he clung to learning what would set right the rites of his religion in both their public and private aspect.

He then divested himself of bad actions in order that he might be victorious in what he hoped for. He began to fast some of the days and stand some of the nights in prayer, and to recite what he could of the Quran. He began to seek the Sufi way and to read the books of its people, in particular Ibn ʿAbbād al-Rondī's *Sharḥ* (commentary) of Ibn ʿAtāʾAllāh's *Ḥikam*. Indeed, he would not part from this book by night or by day. He owned a perfume shop in the greater perfume market in Fes from the side of the madrasa, and he was never seen there except poring over the aforementioned *Sharḥ*, and he would not go out for any occasion except that he had it with him, tucked under his arm. He was, on account of this, soft, easygoing and kind—indeed of a very noble and beautiful character altogether. He would spend long periods in silence and contemplation, busying himself with what concerned him and leaving what did not concern him.

He had a strong bond of brotherhood with the erudite faqīh and Sufi Abū Muḥammad Sidi ʿAbd al-Majīd al-Manālī, known as Zibādī. He would frequently stay over at his home, he visited the maqām of Mūlay ʿAbd al-Salām ibn Mashīsh with him, and they performed the Hajj together with the same group of pilgrims in the year 1158. Travelling by caravan in the year following that, en route to Egypt they met Shaykh Abū ʿAbdullāh Maḥmad ibn Sālim al-Ḥafnāwī al-Miṣrī al-Shāfiʿī, and together they took from him the tarīq and the idhn of the Shādhilīyya Khalwatiyya.

When he returned from Hajj, the news of his great affair and sublime secret spread through the land and people sought him out to take from him. He then announced his own affair and began to call people to Allah, in both public and secret. He established his house as a zāwiyah and those related to him yielded their affairs to him and came to him from all over, such that the legacy of the Khalwatiyya Ṭarīqa in Morocco today is entirely due to him.

There manifested to him many miracles, some of which were mentioned by Sidi al-Tawdī ibn Sūda al-Marī in his autobiography, and others by the author of *Sulūk al-Ṭarīq al-Wariyya.* The news of his quṭbāniyya spread through the land and the expanses were illumined by his Gnosis. Among the accounts of him are that he would say of his residence which was a house in the Zinqa (street) al-Ḥajāmāt in Fes,[2] "The maqām of this, my house, is like the maqām of Ibrāhīm (in Makka); whosoever enters it is secure (āmīn)." Furthermore, the people once saw him in Makka and the house was circulating around him![3]

The Rabbānī Quṭb Sidi Aḥmad Tijānī met with him when he came to Fes for the first time in the year 1171, except that he did not take anything from him and in fact did not even speak to him. Some of his companions mentioned in some of their books that: "After it opened to him what he had his opening to, and he was bestowed of the distinguishing secret what was bestowed upon him, he would very often talk about him (Aḥmad al-Ṣaqalī) and inform the people about the truth of his affair (i.e. his quṭbāniyya), and elevate him above the heads of all the witnesses (of the truth) by the loftiness of his rank, and the brilliance of his

2 The location where he is buried today.

3 Of that, al-Suyūṭī (the famous scholar) mentions in his books, "the sayings are clear in the permissibility and conceivability of the racing (of the Ka'ba around) the Walī." Indeed, there are a large number of saints that bore witness to the Ka'ba circulating around them.

glory. He would speak openly about how he (Mūlay Aḥmad) had reached the greatest quṭbāniyya and imāma over the people of his time, and how he had been buried in the city of Fes in a reclusive corner of the city, which was perfumed (by the essence) of he who had left the stain of his breath upon it."

Al-Tijānī used to say: "No Quṭb was buried within the walls of the city of Fes other than Aḥmad al-Ṣaqalī." Furthermore, the Shaykh Sidi al-Tawdī said near the end of his life, "Mūlay Aḥmad has gone from our hands and not one knew his value."

His affair remained ever increasing, his counsel spreading in urban and rural places, until he died. In *Ghayat al-Āminah* it states: "(This was) after ʿasr on Saturday on the seventh of Ramadan, and he was buried the next day at dhuhr after the prayer upon him in the Qarawiyyin, in a house which is in the furthest end of the Sabaʿa Wilāyāt (a street by the Qarawiyyin), where they built his blessed zāwiyah, and that was the year 1177."

There are an additional seven saints buried in the zāwiyah alongside the Master. They are:

- Abū ʿAlaʿa Idrīs ibn Muḥammad al-ʿIrāqī (a great hadith scholar)
- Sidi Muḥammad ibn ʿAlī al-Ṣaqalī (who was first a student of Sidi ʿAlī al-Jamal)
- Mūlay Aḥmad ibn Muḥammad al-Ṣaqalī (first grandson of Aḥmad al-Ṣaqalī)
- Mūlay Hādī ibn Aḥmad al-Ṣaqalī (son of the previous)
- Mūlay Ibrāhīm ibn Muḥammad al-Ṣaqalī (second grandson of Aḥmad al-Ṣaqalī)
- Sidi al-Māhī ibn Ibrāhīm ibn Muḥammad al-Ṣaqalī (son of the previous)
- Muḥammad ibn Aḥmad al-Ṣaqalī (the son of the subject of this biography)

Gatherings: This zāwiyah is usually open between ʿasr and maghrib throughout the week, though it is occasionally found to be closed. Between this time, there may be some Quran reading or reading of *Dalāʾil al-Khayrāt*, though there is no formal gathering.

Ḍarīḥ Badr al-Dīn al-Hamūmī (E2)

The Faqīh and Sharīf Sidi ʿAllāl ibn al-Tuhāmī al-Hamūmī

His full name was Abū Ḥassan Sidi ʿAlī ʿAllāl ibn Abū ʿAbdullāh Sidi Muḥammad al-Tuhāmī ibn Abū al-ʿAbbās Sidi Aḥmad ibn al-Ḥassan ibn Maḥmad ibn al-Ḥassan al-Hamūmī. His grandfather Abū al-ʿAbbās was a famous saint, and the entire Hamūmī family was one of the famed and blessed families of Fes, who combined mastery of the outer and inner sciences. Sidi ʿAllāl was a student in the Sufi way of the Shaykh of both his father Mūlay al-Tuhāmī and the Shaykh Aḥmad ibn al-Tawdī ibn Sūda al-Murī.

The Shaykh died in the year 1250 AH and was buried in his zāwiyah, which is in the Balīda district between the mosque of Sidi Sulaymān al-Ghumārī and the public oven of the district. Buried next to him is his inheritor and son, al-Ḥussayn, and the son of al-Ḥussayn's paternal uncle Sidi Badr al-Dīn ibn al-Shādhilī al-Hamūmī.

The zāwiyah was originally built by the Shaykh and was used as a Quranic madrasa. It is usually open for dhuhr and ʿasr prayer only. Outside of these times, the owner of the shop across the way, Sidi ʿAbdullāh, owns the key and is willing to let visitors in upon request. The Shaykh and his wife are buried in the corner of the zāwiyah, under the carpets.

Ḍarīḥ Sidi Muḥammad Mayyāra (F3)

The Imam and Faqīh Sidi Maḥmad ibn Aḥmad Mayyāra

His full name was Abū ʿAbdullāh Sidi Maḥmad ibn Aḥmad ibn Muḥammad, but he was known as al-Mayyāra. He was born, raised, and died in the city of Fes.

The Shaykh Sidi Mayyāra was a prominent student of the great Shaykh ʿAbd al-Wāḥid ibn ʿĀshir, author of the great matn on Mālikī fiqh and Junaydī Sufism called *Murshid al-Muʿīn* (The Guiding Helper), and made his greatest contribution to knowledge in the form of two commentaries on his Shaykh's matn which became famous and well-regarded. These he called the *Mayyāra al-Kabīr* (The Greater Commentary) and the *Mayyāra al-Ṣaghīr* (The Lesser Commentary). In addition to these he authored numerous other works such as a *Ḥāshiyya* of Bukhari and a commentary on the *Lāmiyya*. For this contribution, and due to his overall mastery, he was considered one of the flag-bearers of the Mālikī madhab in his time.

Commenting on his Shaykh, Ibn ʿĀshir, Sidi al-Mayyāra once said, "I used to sit in the teaching circle of the muqrī (reciter of the Quran) and taking knowledge from him was always clear and easy. But when I sat in the teaching circles of Ibn ʿĀshir, I found it all confounding." This was because the muqrī was just one who had memorised knowledge, whereas Ibn ʿĀshir was highly critical of the knowledge he possessed, and used to dig into the matter at hand until he unearthed insights that confounded others.

He died in the year 1072 and was buried in a house at the end of the Darb al-Ṭawīl, which afterwards became a burial ground and was expanded to include an open square. A qubbah was built over his grave, and it became a popular pilgrimage site.

This tomb is often open throughout the day, although it is closed in the evenings and on Friday afternoons.

Ḍarīḥ Sidi Muḥammad al-Bunānī (ʿAbd al-ʿAziz al-Tujībī) (F3)

The owner of the textile shop across the way, Sidi Muḥammad, has the key and is willing to let visitors into the Ḍarīḥ. Sidi ʿAbd al-ʿAziz al-Tujībī is buried in a patch of earth on private property next to this Ḍarīḥ. His tomb is not maintained and is being forgotten.

Zāwiyah Shaykh Tawdī ibn Sūda (D4)

Shaykh al-Islam Sidi Muḥammad al-Tawdī ibn al-Ṭālib ibn Sūda al-Murī (d. 1209)

Sidi Muḥammad al-Tawdī ibn Sūda al-Murī was not only one of the most famous saints but also one of the most famous scholars of twelfth century Fes. The name "Tawdī" was given by the people of Fes to a certain tribe from the nearby countryside, and it is a name that came to be associated with good omens to the Moroccans due to the large number of godly men that sprung from that region.

Rather than take from one primary shaykh, as was the practice of most Sufis and scholars, Muḥammad al-Tawdī attached himself to a great and unusual number of instructors in both the spiritual and religious sciences. The total number of shaykhs he recorded exceeds well over a dozen, and he mentions teachers in both the East and the West of the Islamic world. Some of them included: Abū ʿAbdullāh Muḥammad ibn Aḥmad ibn Jilūn, Abū ʿAbbās

Aḥmad ibn ʿAlī al-Wijārī and Abū ʿAbbās Aḥmad ibn Aḥmad al-Shidādī. It might be said that the one he relied on most, however, was Shaykh Abū ʿAbbās Aḥmad ibn Mubārak al-Sijilmāsī al-Lamatī.

It might even be said that the shaykh he seemed to rely on most in life was one already taken by death—the great Quṭb of Morocco, Sidi ʿAbd al-Salām ibn Mashīsh. It is said that Ibn Sūda visited ʿAbd al-Salām over seventy times throughout his lifetime, and never failed to make a journey at least once a year until his death at about 84 years old. It is said that on his last journey, upon visiting the tomb he recited the following verses of poetry:

> I have come to you in old age, in maturity and in youth /
> And always and still I seek your abundant favors
>
> And so here am I, stretching out my tent in your *fanā* /
> Weakness and inability have overridden me
>
> So do not turn me away without granting me the overflowing waters of your oceans /
> And do not forbid from me the greatest divine Bestowals.

When he returned from that visit Allah granted his request and unveiled to him the greatest of unveilings and revealed to him the loftiest of secrets. The weight of these secrets was so strong that for a whole year he fell gravely sick. He fell into such a profound state of *ghayba* (absent-mindedness) in that time that he seemed to be asleep. At the end of that year he recovered to the extent that he awoke from his state of ghayba, and his spirit strengthened so that he was able to carry out what had been entrusted to him.

However, his overall state of ill health continued until his death at ʿasr time on Thursday 29th of Dhul Hijjah in the year 1209. He was prayed over in the Qarawiyyin Mosque and then buried in his zāwiyah in the Ziqāq al-Baghl, which became a mosque in which the five daily prayers were performed. Today, it has fallen into great ruin and decay, but one can still gain access to it, or they can learn about the Shaykh in his numerous famous publications, such as his commentary on the *Tuḥfah* of Ibn ʿĀsim or his *Ḥashiyya* of *Sahīh al-Bukhārī*.

Buried with him are a number of prominent shuyūkh from among his offspring, relatives and tutelage.

Ḍarīḥ Shaykh Aḥmad al-Shāwī (D4)

Al-Imam al-Murabbī Sidi Aḥmad ibn Muḥammad al-Shāwī (d. 1014)

His full name was Abū ʿAbbās Aḥmad ibn Muḥammad al-Shāwī. His lineage was of the al-Shāwiyya Arabs in the Hijāz. For various reasons which are mentioned by the great historian Ibn Khaldūn, this tribe was expelled first from their homeland to the land of Egypt, and then from Egypt westward to Algeria, then Morocco, where the Sultan Yaʿqūb al-Manṣūr admitted them into his protection.

Sidi Aḥmad was among those of his tribe who migrated to the city of Fes from their homeland and upon his arrival, he attached himself to the care of the Sufi shaykh and Malāmatī Aḥmad ibn Yaḥyā al-Hawārī, who is buried in the Qarawiyyin district of Fes. Sidi Aḥmad entrusted his affair entirely to Sidi Yaḥyā and threw himself upon him, standing for long hours at the door of his house to cater to his Shaykh's every need, be it merely to purchase some meat, to transport his flour and dough, or to look after his mare. Then, the Shaykh married him to one of the girls of his household and put him in a house behind the door of his own home, so that Sidi Aḥmad's wife worked inside the house and he worked outside of it.

The Shaykh used to greatly care for Sidi Aḥmad, and perhaps he wished to conceal that from those around them, for he would severely scold him and make it appear as if he had rejected Sidi Aḥmad while in reality, in the inner spiritual dimension, he was supporting him.

When the Shaykh was on his deathbed, he fainted, and when he regained consciousness he asked, "Who is at the door?" to which those around him responded, "Al-Shāwī." Sidi Yaḥyā then replied, "Lā ilāha illallāh—God wants only al-Shāwī." He then passed away, and it was Sidi Aḥmad who inherited his secret.

Sidi Aḥmad then took to guiding spiritual seekers on the Sufi way. He also achieved a fair deal of success in agriculture and livestock, so that he had large sums of money available that he spent in the Way of God. Sidi Aḥmad arranged so many waqfs that sheerly on account of his contributions the number of ḥabus skyrocketed. He also donated to various restoration projects, such as repairing the water flowing through the Andalus Mosque from the Bāb al-Ḥadīd and the arch over the door of the Bāb al-Jadīd.

He established five zāwiyahs, each of which was filled with students of the Sufi way and dispensed free food in charity. His Sufi way, all in all, could be described as one of giving and taking, such that he used to say to some of the tribes associated with them, "Whenever you raise a piece of meat in your hands then give one bone of it to al-Shāwī [himself]." His fame and following soon became very great, until eventually he was considered one of the greatest and most influential saints in the history of Fes.

Sidi Aḥmad died in the year 1014. He was buried in his zāwiyah in the Fes al-Qarawiyyin district, and all—not only in Fes but the regions surrounding Fes—came to attend the funeral of this great shaykh.

Sidi Aḥmad left behind him four pious widows, two of whom were Malāmatī Majdhūbs (Sayyida Fāṭima al-Ḍaḥakiyya [the smiling] and Sayyida Āmina al-Dakmasiyya) and three of whom moved into a house next to the Shaykh's zāwiyah and continued his work of feeding the poor and helping all those who came to them, without ever remarrying, until their death. Upon the death of these three, they were then buried in the Rawḍa of the Shaykh.

This zāwiyah is unfortunately closed and is in dire need of repair.

Ḍarīḥ Muḥammad ibn Faqīh (E4)

Sidi Maḥmad ibn al-Faqīh,ʿUmarī al-Zajanī (d. 1136)

The famous Shaykh, the great Ghawth, the complete gnostic, Abū ʿAbdullāh Sidi Maḥmad was also known as Ibn al-Faqīh. Zajanī by house, Fāsī by travels and pilgrimage, he was the son of Sidi Muḥammad, who was the son of the faqīh and teacher Sidi Muḥammad ibn ʿĪsā al-Zāhid (the ascetic), who was himself the great-grandson of the clear Quṭb Aḥmad ibn ʿUmar, buried in the village of Azajan of the Maṣmūda tribe.

He took from the Quṭb Mūlay ʿAbdullāh al-Wazzānī who instructed him from an early age. He would come to Mūlay ʿAbdullāh from the village of Azajan to Wazzān. Then he would pray Salat al-Fajr with him, and remain with him until the final prayer before returning to his home. Ibn al-Faqīh remained in his service, along with Sidi Khayyāṭ al-Ruqʿī, until the death of the Shaykh, at which point his son, Sidi Muḥammad, took over. Sidi al-Khayyāṭ continued to follow his son, but Sidi Maḥmad discontinued his apprenticeship at this point and from then on would say, "The Shaykh Mūlay ʿAbdullāh did not die until he had split his secret in half between me and his son, Sidi Muḥammad."

When he came to Fes his renown increased so that the people began to gather around him. He made an attempt to build a zāwiyah when Shaykh ʿAbd al-Qādir al-Fāsī became aware of him. He sent for Ibn al-Faqīh to come visit him in order that he might exchange blessings with him, and Shaykh ʿAbd al-Qādir was delighted by him. They wandered around deep in conversation, and Shaykh al-Fāsī began to ask him about the stations and the Ṭarīq (the Way) and the various stages (in the wayfaring), station by station and stage by stage, and he (Ibn al-Faqīh) would answer him, "I am above that." This happened repeatedly until Shaykh al-Fāsī asked him as to what is in the Heavens and the Earths, and the seas and what is in them, and Ibn al-Faqīh answered him saying, "I am one of the abdāls," and another time, "I am one of the ajrās," and another time, "I am the Quṭb," and another time, "I am the Ghawth."

This proceeded until al-Fāsī asked him, "Have you seen the sea of the blind (*al-baḥr al-makfūf*)?" To which he replied, "Yes." So al-Fāsī asked him, "And are there fish in it?" In response, Ibn al-Faqīh drew his head and his hands into his qishāba (a traditional Moroccan article of clothing), and remained there for the measure of time it took to read Sūrah Ikhlās three times, then he removed his head and hands from the qishāba and said, "There are no fish in it; however, there are some frogs in it, like this one." Al-Fāsī looked, and there before him, running across the shoulders of Ibn al-Faqīh, was a little green frog. After a moment green frogs began to descend from his shoulder like rain, to the astonishment of al-Fāsī.

This zāwiyah is unfortunately closed, though it has been repaired and may soon open pending ministry approval.

Zāwiyah Sidi Aḥmad Mansūr (E1)

This small zāwiyah is located in the Bāb al-Gheesa neighbourhood, off "Znqa Dundq al-Yahudi." While it is also used as a masjid, the main gathering is the Saturday afternoon reading of the entire *Dalā'il al-Khayrāt*. This is an enduring spiritual practice of the people of Fes and the text is read in its entirety six days a week. There is a group of very dedicated old fuqarā who gather daily at various locations across the city to read the text communally. Many have memorised the text. This is the largest weekly gathering for reading the *Dalā'il al-Khayrāt*.

Gatherings: On Saturday afternoons, between ʿasr and ʿisha, the entire *Dalā'il al-Khayrāt* is recited communally.

Zāwiyah Abd al-Qādir al-Fāsī (E5)

Shaykh al-Islam, ʿAbd al-Qādir ibn ʿAlī al-Fāsī al-Fihrī (d. 1091)

The full name of the Shaykh was Abū Muḥammad (and Abū Saʿūd) Sidi ʿAbd al-Qādir al-Fāsī ibn Abū al-Ḥassan Sidi ʿAlī, who was a jurist and the son of the equally great and venerated master buried outside of the Bāb al-Futūḥ, Sidi Yūsuf Abū al-Maḥāsin al-Fāsī. Indeed, for their innumerable contributions to the spiritual tradition of the city it is perhaps only fitting that the family as a whole should come to be known as the "al-Fāsī"—meaning, those of Fes.

The Shaykh was born in Kasr al-Kabīr on a Monday on the second of Ramadan, and it was there he grew up. In the year 1025, when ʿAbd al-Qādir was eighteen and his father was still alive, he decided to travel to Fes with the aim of completing his education in the traditional centre of scholarship in Morocco. Here, he engaged in his studies with such eagerness that within only a few short years he was able to achieve the highest rank amongst scholars. It is related in *Nashr al-Mithānī* that it was commonly said among the people that were it not for three, knowledge would have disappeared altogether from Morocco in the tenth century due to the widespread catastrophes that appeared. They are: Sidi Maḥmad ibn Naṣr in Darīa, Sidi Muḥammad ibn Abū Bakr al-Dilāʿī in Dilāʿ, and Sidi ʿAbd al-Qādir al-Fāsī in Fes. It is also mentioned that some used to say that he was to the people of Fes as Ḥassan al-Baṣrī was to the people of Basra. It is also said that there was not to be found a single scholar or student in all of Morocco and Africa except that he was either his student or a student of one of his students.

As for the Sufi way, he took it from his father's uncle ʿAbd al-Raḥmān al-Fāsī, who had inherited the mantle of the Ṭarīqa after the death of his brother, Yūsuf al-Fāsī. When he died, he took from Muḥammad ibn ʿAbdullāh Maʿin, the inheritor of ʿAbd al-Raḥmān.

ʿAbd al-Qādir al-Fāsī was particularly well-known for his asceticism, and in spite of his vast knowledge and fame and the many gifts imparted to him because of it, he refused all charity and subsisted solely on the wages he earned from transcribing—by his own hand—copies of al-Bukhārī. He would sell these copies and people would rush to buy them for the baraka perceived to have been transmitted through them by him.

It is recorded that the Sultan Mūlay Rashīd once offered to provide material support for him as well, but the Shaykh merely replied, "Tell him to concern himself with others, for He who has provided for me since the cradle until my beard whitened, He provides for me (still)."

It eventually began to be said of him that he had reached the station of Quṭb, and the Shaykh himself did not object to their saying that. It was also said of him that he was among the rare few to reach the level of Abū al-ʿAbbās al-Mursī and encompass what he had encompassed of secret knowledge. Among the miraculous events ascribed to the Shaykh was that among those who used to regularly attend the morning prayer in his mosque was none other than al-Khiḍr عليه السلام.

The Zāwiyah ʿAbd al-Qadir al-Fāsī is located just off of the main road leading to Rcif Square. It continues to be a very important zāwiyah school in Fes, offering classes and weekly dhikr gatherings.

Zāwiyah Būtchīchiyya (C6)

The Zāwiyah Būtchīchiyya is the hub of the Qādirī-Būtchīchī Ṭarīqa in Fes. It is located between the Batha and Bāb Ziat neighbourhoods in the old medina.

The Ṭarīqa Qādiriyya-Būtchīchiyya is currently one of the largest, most active, and influential Sufi orders in Morocco. The current shaykh of the Ṭarīqa is Sidi Ḥamza al-Būtchīchī, who lives in Nyima in eastern Morocco near the Algerian border. Sidi Ḥamza is one of the most important living Moroccan Sufi teachers, and the Qādirī-Būtchīchī Ṭarīqa has spread throughout Morocco, Europe, and North America during his lifetime. Though the Ṭarīqa is primarily a branch of the Qādirī Ṭarīqa, Sidi Ḥamza's silsila include transmissions from Darqāwī, ʿAlawī, and Tijānī shuyūkh. The Ṭarīqa has a large following among university students, government officials and upper class families. The main Qādirī-Būtchīchī zāwiyah is located in Madagh in eastern Morocco, and there are usually lively gatherings during mawlid and Ramadan.

The gatherings of the Qādiriyya-Būtchīchiyya in Fes are rather private, and outsiders are not usually expected to join without receiving an invitation or the permission of a Qādirī-Būtchīchī muqaddam. While you would not necessarily be turned away, it would be considered poor adab (manners).

Gatherings: Every night after maghrib, there is a gathering where the wazīfa and various qaṣāʾid are recited. Often, a ḥaḍra is performed. A meal is usually served at the end. The main gathering of the week is on Saturday night, when a dars is offered in the zāwiyah.

Masajid

Masjid al-Qarawiyyin (F3)

The Masjid al-Qarawiyyin is arguably the most important masjid in Fes and is considered among the world's most historically important masājid. The masjid was constructed in 857–859 CE by Fātima al-Fihrī, the sister of Maryam al-Fihrī who founded the Masjid al-Andalus across the river. She was a pious woman and a native of Qayrawan in Tunisia. The original masjid was very modest, and the current structure is the result of over one thousand years of transformations, additions, renovations, and expansions. The masjid, which also developed into a university, is often considered to be one of the oldest institutions of higher learning in the world. The Merinids, however, are the ones credited with transforming Masjid al-Qarawiyyin into a university after the introduction of the madrasa system. The masjid has hosted most of the luminous figures who lived in or visited the city of Fes. From Imam al-Jazūlī and Shaykh Aḥmad al-Tijānī to Ibn Khaldūn and Muḥyuddīn Ibn al-ʿArabī, to Shaykh Ḥabīb ʿAlī al-Jifrī and King Muḥammad VI, this place has hosted many of the greatest scholars and Sufis of the Maghreb and the Islamic world of both distant and recent past.

The Almoravids, who ruled Fes in the 11th and 12th centuries, are credited with providing the Masjid al-Qarawiyyin its basic orientation by employing artisans from Spain. It is a masterful repository of Almoravid art. According to local legend, at the time of the Almohad conquest, the people of Fes covered the most elaborate Almoravid decorations with plaster. This was done out of fear that the Almoravids might destroy the beautiful work. This legend was proven true, as restorers uncovered these in the 1950s. The Merinids expanded the role of the Qarawiyyin as an institution of learning through the introduction of the madrasa system, which allowed students from across the country to study there. It also assisted in the formalisation of religious creed in Morocco and furthered the spread of the study of Mālikī law.

Crooked qibla? You may be startled to find that the people in the Qarawiyyin, and many ancient mosques around Fes, pray slightly turned away from the supposed qibla. This is because the calculations under both the Almoravids and the Almohads were later found to be inaccurate. This was discovered at a later date, and it is now common for people to turn slightly.

The Masjid al-Qarawiyyin is a visually stunning structure which could occupy the visitor for hours: the ornate mihrāb with stained glass windows, the intricate Almoravid domes, the arches and colonnades, the precious wood minbar, and the huge chandeliers in the nave. The two flanking pavilions, ablution fountains designed under the Saadians, are modeled on the Lion Court of the Alhambra in Granada. In the southeastern corner of the masjid is an old khalwa room that was purportedly used by Shaykh Aḥmad al-Tijānī, and has been given the name "Bāb Shaykh Aḥmad al-Tijānī."

The Qarawiyyin library, which is attached to the Qarawiyyin Masjid complex, is also a historically important hub of intellectual life in the city of Fes. The Merinid Sultan Abū Inan is credited with establishing the library, and it soon became home to a vast and definitive collection of documents and books. The rulers of the Saadian dynasty enriched these collections with additional texts and rare manuscripts. The collection exceeded 320,000 volumes by 1613. This was the meeting point of many of Fes' important teachers, eager students, and visiting scholars. The Qarawiyyin library has undergone important renovations in recent years and is now open to students. External visitors may need to enquire about access.

Interested in studying at the Qarawiyyin? Please see the section "Studying Arabic in Fes" for more information.

The Masjid al-Qarawiyyin is considered the hub of religious life in Fes, and many masājid base their adhān off of its adhān. The Qarawiyyin university is still an active centre of learning. While most of the classes have moved to a new centre in the Ville Nouvelle, the masjid still hosts a variety of beginning and advanced classes throughout the day. The traditional learning style, where students gather at the feet of a seated teacher, is still employed. The masjid is also rather lively during Ramadan, when it is packed for tarawīh prayers.

Bunani's bookstore, which is situated in an ancient funduq next to Masjid al-Qarawiyyin, is often listed as the best bookstore in Fes. It is a resource for most students of the Qarawiyyin and those looking for rare texts.

Masjid Bāb al-Gheesa (D1)

Masjid Bāb al-Gheesa is the first structure that visitors encounter upon entering the medina through Bāb al-Gheesa. The masjid was built, along with the adjacent madrasa, in 1760 by the ʿAlawite Sultan Muhamad III. After falling into disrepair, it was restored by Sultan Muhamad IV between 1859 and 1873. It is the central masjid of the area.

The adjacent madrasa currently houses contemporary students of the Qarawiyyin who are Fes natives and who cannot afford their own rooms. These students are given a free room and stipend to further their religious studies at the Qarawiyyin.

Masjid Rcif (E4)

It is known as the Rcif (Rasif) Mosque or the Great Mosque of Rasif. Traditionally, Friday prayer was solely prayed here in this area of the city. It also gets it name from the marketplace nearby known as Rasif. It was built by Sulaymān b. Muḥammad al-ʿAlawī in the 13th century. It has the tallest minaret in the city and holds a sundial in the courtyard. Many famous scholars such as Jaʿfar al-Kattānī undertook their primary studies in a school just below Uqbah ibn Sawal, where they would attend for prayer.

The area where Rcif Mosque is today was originally just an area where prayer was performed but in the 19th century Mūlay Sulaymān established it as a mosque and expanded its structure.

Masjid Bāb Bujlud (A5)

Masjid Bāb Bujlud is located just outside of Bāb Bujlud. The masjid is a very active community centre and serves as the religious hub for this economically active area of the city. It is a popular place to go to read a hizb of the Quran after fajr or maghrib, to pray jumʿa, or tarawīh prayers during Ramadan.

Masjid Sharabliyn (D3)

It was built in the 13th century and renovated in the 18th to 19th century. Sidi Abū Bakr b. Muḥammad al-Tawdī bin Sūda delivered the sermons there in 1215. It is famous for the design of its minaret.

Masjid al-Azhar (Ibn Arabi Khalwa) (D3)

This mosque is where the Sufi master Muḥyuddīn Ibn al-ʿArabī al-Ḥātimī al-Andalūsī obtained spiritual enlightenment in 1197 CE, which he describes as follows: "I obtained this station [Abode of Light] in 593 AH at Fes, during the ʿasr prayer at the al-Azhar Mosque in the ʿAyn al-Khail. It appeared to me in the form of a light that was if anything more visible than what was in front of me. Also, when I saw this light the status of the direction 'behind' ceased for me. I no longer had a back or nape of a neck, and while the vision lasted I could no longer distinguish between different sides of myself. I was like a sphere; I was no longer aware of myself as having any 'side' except as the result of a mental process—not an experienced reality." (Futûhât, 2/486).

In a little masjid located just off of Talaʿa Kabira on "Rue Ain Lkhil," the famed Sufi master Muḥyuddīn ibn al-ʿArabī spent forty days in khalwa. It is popularly known as the ʿAyn al-Khail masjid, named after the district that it is located in. It is the only masjid on the street, and is on the left. It is said that Shaykh Ibn al-ʿArabī, after spending his forty days in khalwa, received a spiritual opening during the ʿasr prayer, and his spiritual vision was greatly expanded. Shaykh Ibn al-ʿArabī spent several years in Fes and his spiritual mentor was Muḥammad ibn Qāsim al-Tamīmī.

Unfortunately, the story is not well-known today and the masjid has no commemoration for Shaykh Ibn al-ʿArabī's khalwa. The mosque is open for the five daily prayers, and one can visit for the baraka of the Shaykh. A clear sign for the turn to "Rue Ain Lkhil" is visible from Talaʿa Kabira.

Typical of Almohad mosques, the al-Azhar comprises a prayer hall with horseshoe arches supported on columns, a courtyard with a fountain, and an octagonal minaret. If you are alone or a couple, the imam may invite you to climb the ancient minaret for a spectacular vista of the city from above.

Madaris

Madrasa Bu Inaniya (B4)

According to legend, when the Merinid Sultan Abū ʿInan commissioned the building of Madrasa Bu Inaniya and was confronted by its large price, he said, "Whatever is beautiful cannot be expensive at any price. What is enthralling can never be too costly." Abū Inan then tore apart the ledger of expenses presented to him and threw it into the river without even looking at it.

The Madrasa Bu Inaniya is one of the most well-known madrasas in Fes and is a top tourist destination of the medina. Its construction was commissioned between 1350 and 1356 CE. The madrasa is actually a combined madrasa and masjid, which is unusual and makes it rather unique. The Madrasa Bu Inaniya was the last madrasa to be built by the Merinids, crowning a long era of artisanship and scholarly patronage.

The madrasa has undergone extensive restoration in recent years. The mosque is notable for its graceful and well-preserved mihrāb, the onyx marble columns, and an elegant minaret. The courtyard is decorated with zillij tile work, cedar wood trims, Arabic calligraphy, and carved stucco that is typical of most Moroccan madrasas. Separating the courtyard from the masjid is an empty channel where the waters of the Wad Bukharareb used to flow, allowing Muslims to make their ablutions.

Across from the madrasa is a unique element—an ancient water clock, also known as the Magana. It once signalled the hour of the day by releasing metal balls from 12 small doors into brass bowls. It no longer functions, but represents the great cultural initiatives of the period.

Madrasa Mesbahiya (E3)

Built in 1346 CE by Sultan Abū Ḥassan, the Madrasa Mesbahiya was also known as al-Rokham and al-Khossa, for "marble" and "basin". These names are derived from both the quantity of marble used to decorate the madrasa and the central basin, which was brought over from a masjid in Andalusia. This madrasa was once one of the largest in Fes. It is composed of a ground floor and three upper levels, though the upper floor was destroyed in the last century. The madrasa lies directly across from the northern face of the Qarawiyyin.

Madrasa al-Sharatayn (E3)

The Madrasa al-Sharatayn, named after the local rope makers, was built by the ʿAlawite sultan Mūlay Rashīd in 1670 CE. It had the capacity to house 130 students, making it one of the most spacious and accommodating of the Fes madāris. The madrasa students attended the Qarawiyyin university.

Madrasa al-Atarayn (E3)

The Madrasa al-Atarayn was built in 1323 CE by Sultan Abū Sayd Uthmān and bears the name of the local suq, which was famous as a spice market. The madrasa was considered a marvel for its time and is considered to be one of the best decorated and well-preserved madrasas in Morocco. It housed between 50 to 60 students from the north of Morocco—in particular, Tangier, Larache, and Kasr al-Kabīr. It was used as an active student dormitory until the early 20th century and was attached to the Qarawiyyin university. The madrasa has hosted many famous religious scholars and spiritual figures. Shaykh ʿAbd al-Azīz al-Tebba, one of the most important students of Imam al-Jazūlī, gave lectures on Sufism at this madrasa and led recitations of the *Dalāʾil al-Khayrāt* for its students.

The madrasa is a masterpiece of Moroccan architecture. The courtyard, bordered by two narrow galleries, is paved with square zillij mosaic. The inner prayer room is decorated by a carved glass wood dome and windows with coloured Iraqi glass. A 14th century bronze chandelier adorns the room. Its carved marble capitals, intricate calligraphy, arches in carved wood and plaster, refined mosaic, and Kufic scripts are excellent examples of Moroccan-Andalusian infusion. Restoration of the madrasa was carried out by the Arab Fund for Economic and Social Development. Today, the madrasa is one of the most popular tourist destinations of the city.

Madrasa al-Sefarayn (F3)

The Madrasa al-Sefarayn is one of the oldest of the Merinid madrasas in Fes. It was constructed in 1270 CE by the Merinid Sultan Abū Yūsuf Yaʿqūb and bears the name of the neighbourhood it graces. It was also known by some as the Yaqūbiyya madrasa, in honour of its founder. In spite of the irregularities of design, the Madrasa Sefarayn is organised around a courtyard with a central fountain and student rooms encircling it on the ground and first floors. The madrasa once housed a very important collection of manuscripts, and it is distinguished for having the oldest extant mihrāb in Fes. Little is left of the original design.

The madrasa was made famous as the former school of the highly influential Imam al-Jazūlī, who was an important Shādhilī Moroccan shaykh and the author of *Dalāʾil al-Khayrāt*. He wrote the religious classic within the walls of the madrasa. Imam al-Jazūlī met and was influenced by Shaykh Aḥmad Zarrūq while studying at the Qarawiyyin. The madrasa is also supposed to house the stone which al-Jazūlī brought back from Hajj to make dry ablutions.

A popular legend, displaying Imam al-Jazūlī's piety, has arisen about the Shaykh's time as a student. Imam Jazūlī apparently closed himself in his room often, avoiding food and locking his door. Many thought he was hoarding something valuable. As rumours spread, his father visited the school and forced himself into his son's room. He entered and found the word "death" written all over the walls. From this moment, his father knew that his son possessed a strong spiritual destiny.

Legend of Dalāʾil al-Khayrāt: One day, Shaykh al-Jazūlī awoke late for the fajr prayer. He stirred and hurriedly began looking for a source of pure water to make his ablutions, though none could be found. While searching, the Shaykh encountered a young girl, who questioned him. The young girl, aware of the Shaykh's conundrum, spat into a well, which began to overflow with pure, fresh water. Shaykh al-Jazūlī, astounded, inquired how the young girl attained such a high spiritual station. The young girl replied, with beautiful simplicity, "By making constant prayer to God to bless the best of creation ﷺ."

Typical Neighbourhood Elements

The Fes medina is a unique case of urban design and organisation, heralding back to traditional designs of the Islamic world. Because the Fes medina has been remarkably preserved, many of the traditional fixtures of the medina can be encountered. A neighbourhood often consists of several important elements, such as a masjid, a Quranic madrasa, a hamam, a fountain, a hanut, and a bakery. With the rapid development of the Fes medina over the past few decades, and with the continuing population expansion in the medina, a neighbourhood is no longer strictly defined by these elements, and many of the traditional elements of medina neighbourhoods have changed. Despite this, you will encounter many important fixtures as you travel. It is good to be aware of them, as you will spot them throughout your journeys in a range of conditions—from crumbling and defunct to renovated and in use to this day.

Hamam

While hamams today are a big tourist attraction and are often seen as a way to relax and treat oneself, the hamams were traditionally used as a primary bathing centre. Some Moroccan families today still do not have running water or shower facilities in their homes and thus still use the hamam on a weekly basis for bathing. The hamams of Fes today are well-hidden and, to those who do not read Arabic, can be almost impossible to discern.

Hamams are well-designed, often as a four-tier network. There is a welcoming room where the fee is paid, goods are stored, and one changes their clothes, followed by a series of increasingly humid and warm steam rooms. Buckets of both cold and warm water are collected to be used for bathing. People are usually expected to bring their own supplies, and massages are usually available for a negotiated fee. Most hamams cater for both men and women, providing separate spaces or hours of operation for each gender. Morocco still has a strong hamam culture, and it is a place where gossip, news, scandal, and even business transactions are exchanged.

Quranic Madrasa

Quranic madrasas are places where children go to learn Quran and obtain a very basic, elementary education. In traditional Moroccan society, educated children would often begin by memorising the Quran. While this took several years, it was ingrained in the society and was facilitated by the community and family. Today, traditional Islamic centres of education still try to encourage children to memorise the Quran by an early age.

Hanut

The hanut is the lifeline of the local community. Hanuts are spread throughout the medina and provide a variety of basic goods such as bread, water, nuts, grains, flour, oil, and coffees. Some hanuts specialise in certain goods, whereas others carry more general items. Since supermarkets, which are becoming quite popular in the Ville Nouvelle, cannot spread to the medina, the hanut takes their place as the source of most daily goods.

Fountain

Fountains are an important element and fixture of the medina. They are a prominent feature of Islamic architecture and there is a fountain at the centre of most important Moroccan homes or gathering spaces. While most of the fountains were traditionally supplied by natural springs, today most are fed by municipal water sources. Despite this, several locations, such as Moulay Idriss Zerhoun and several fountains throughout the medina, are still supplied by natural underground springs. Fountains served a variety of purposes, as they were the only sources of running water for most households—for laundry, for cleaning, for wudhu, for drinking, and for bathing. Today, the fountains of Fes are scattered throughout the medina as a memory and are in a variety of states. Some have fallen into complete disuse and disrepair. Others still maintain functions as vital water sources for homes that do not have running water. Others have been masterfully restored for touristic and preservation purposes. These are a pleasure to encounter throughout the medina.

Bakery

Bakery furnaces are an important and enduring fixture of medina neighbourhoods. Bread is an enduring staple of the Moroccan diet and many Moroccans will take their home-kneaded goods to be baked at the local furnaces. The furnace owner also sells bread, and there are deals with local hanuts to supply bread. These are dotted around the medina and are a pleasure to explore.

Places of Interest in Fes Bali

Bāb Bujlud (A4)

Bāb Bujlud is one of the main entrances of the medina and is the most popular and widely used entrance for tourists and visitors. This leads to one of the most accessible, tourist-friendly districts of the city. Despite the popularity of Bāb Bujlud, it is actually not a traditional structure. It was built by the French authorities at the beginning of the 20th century with the assistance of the master mason Abū Zubaʿ. It is composed of a central arch with two smaller lateral arches, and decorated with blue zillij on the exterior façade and green zillij on the interior. Because of this, it is affectionately called the "Blue Gate". Most tour groups and individual itineraries begin from Bāb Bujlud.

Tala'a Saghira (C4)

Tala'a Saghira, which means "little slope", is the twin artery of Tala'a Kabira. They run nearly parallel to each other and form the major arteries of the Qarawiyyin quarter of Fes Bali. It links Bāb Bujlud to the Qarawiyyin quarter. The entire road serves as a major shopping thoroughfare, and smaller streets lead in each direction to residential areas. A variety of traditional and modern goods can be found along the street though Tala'a Saghira, along with Tala'a Kabira, often tend to the large numbers of tourists visiting throughout the year.

To get an authentic taste of shopping culture, try one of the traditional suqs located throughout the city. Along the way, the essential urban elements of the Fes medina are encountered—masājid, fountains, Quranic schools, and public baths. Tala'a Saghira offers an excellent taste of traditional urban planning and culture in Fes.

Tala'a Kabira (C3)

Tala'a Kabira is the widest and longest street in the old medina, connecting Bāb Mahruq to the centre of the medina. Along Tala'a Kabira, which means the big slope, one will encounter all of the essential elements of life in the medina—masājid, fountains, hamams, public bakeries, and shops. There are also a variety of restaurants, cafés, and historically important sites—noteworthy madrasas and the homes of luminous figures in Fes' history. Along the way, a variety of goods and services can be found, ranging from blacksmiths and locksmiths to cobblers and carpet sellers. This is a versatile street and pleasant to explore.

Funduq Tazi (C3)

The Funduq Tazi is an excellent example of the architecture and style of the classical funduqs of Fes. A funduq was traditionally a place for travellers, particularly merchants, to spend the night with their animals and goods. They were active centres in Fes and across the Islamic world, and developed along bustling trade routes. Many of the funduqs of Fes have been turned into marketplaces. Some of them have become tanneries; others bookshops and clothing markets. They are still important centres of business activity, infused with the spirit of a rapidly changing Fes.

The date of the original Funduq Tazi is unknown, but the building has undergone many transformations over the years. Today, a wide variety of goods are sold here—leather, ceramics, belghas and cherbils (traditional shoes for men and women), and there is also a drum workshop. The second floor maintains its original function as an inn for travelling merchants. The Funduq Tazi is frequented by both Moroccans and foreign visitors and is a good window into traditional funduq culture, ancient and contemporary.

Batha Museum (B5)

Installed in 1915 in a remarkable 19th century Moroccan-Andalusian style palace, the Batha Museum is dedicated to the traditional arts of Morocco. The exhibited collections include embroidery, pottery, jewellery and traditional clothing, among other things. One of the masterpieces of the collection is a 14th century Merinid minbar, a preacher's chair made of West African ebony and ivory taken from the Madrasa Bu Inaniya. This palace was originally built by Sultan Ḥassan I and completed at the beginning of the 20th century. It was designed to host royal audiences and distinguished guests, and the palace is centred around beautiful garden spaces. It was in this palace that the 1912 Treaty of Fes, establishing Morocco as a French Protectorate, was signed.

The Batha Museum is traditionally the venue for the annual Fes Festival of Sufi Culture. The festival, which is organised under the royal patronage of King Mohammad VI and implemented by the Association du Festival de Fes de la Culture Soufie, aims to rediscover and promote the spiritual, intellectual, and artistic wealth of Moroccan culture that is Sufism. It is usually a week-long event, focused on exhibitions, various discussions and speakers, and nightly performances. It draws a very international crowd. More information about the festival can be found here: http://www.festivalculturesoufie.com.

The Center for Training and Qualification in Craftsmanship, Fes (C5)

The Center for Training and Qualification in Craftsmanship in Fes was inaugurated by King Mohammad VI in 2009. The Center ensures the continuation of traditional handicraft and artisan professions as economically viable fields, and seeks high impact economic development. The mission of the centre is to provide young people with professional qualifications in various crafts through apprenticeships, to preserve endangered handicrafts, organise training sessions for the benefit of artisans, and to encourage young and emerging artisans to develop their own businesses. The centre also provides its students with modern skills necessary for engaging both traditional and contemporary craft methods. The centre seeks to preserve traditional ways of life while staying competitive in a changing economy. This is an excellent place to learn more about traditional craftsmanship culture in Fes.

Bāb al-Gheesa (D1)

Bāb al-Gheesa was the traditional northern gate of the city. The old door was originally built in the 11th century by Prince Agheesa, the namesake of this gate. After the urban expansion of Fes under the Almohads, a new door was fitted to the gate. It kept the name of its founder, and became known as Bāb al-Gheesa. The present gate, which is no longer in service, maintains the traditional Moroccan style of indirect entrance architecture, which forced people to turn corners to enter homes, baths, and public spaces. This was a way of preserving the privacy and intimacy of spaces. Its exterior façade is dominated by a semi-circular arch topped with a multi-foiled arch. Bāb al-Gheesa is famous for the nearby weekend bird suq. It is a traditional setting for many Moroccan folktales. Today, a side entrance is used instead of the gate.

Bāb Mahruq and Suq (A4)

Bāb Mahruq, which literally means "the burned gate", is also known as Bāb al-Sharia. The gate was built by the Almohad Caliph al-Nassir in the early 13th century. The gate was constructed while al-Nassir was repairing the city ramparts damaged by his grandfather. It has a unique hemispherical vault and is built with traditional brick materials. Bāb Mahruq was recently restored through a grant from Banque Populaire.

The Bāb Mahruq suq is a vital source of fresh fruits and vegetables for the local medina populace. It is an active daily market. There is also a used clothing suq closer to Bāb Mahruq.

Suq Ayn Alu

Suq Ayn Alu (or Alu's spring) took its name, according to legend, from a local criminal who lived in the area. He was arrested and condemned to death by Mūlay Idrīs. The spring still flows in the local Saniyya masjid, at the heart of the district. Ayn Alu is a bustling communal centre at the end of Tala'a Kabira which focuses on leather goods. Historically, metal and leather goods were auctioned here every day following the 'asr prayer.

Henna Suq (E3)

The Henna Suq is one of the oldest market places in the medina, set in a beautiful square centred around a massive, leafy tree. The traditional focus of this market was on pharmaceutical and cosmetic goods, with a special focus on items such as soap, rosewater and henna. It is tradition for women to decorate themselves with henna before going to the hamam. Today, mostly pottery is sold in the Henna Suq. On the far side of the suq is a mental asylum built under the Merinids which operated until the 20th century.

Suq al-Atarayn (E3)

This suq stretches along a wide street that connects the Madrasa al-Atarayn to Bāb al-Faraj and the Suq Ayn Alu. This is one of the most famous—and crowded—suqs of Fes. It is about 600 metres long and it is only open in the day; at night, the two wooden gates at both ends of the suq are closed.

The ancient suq has been a part of Fes' memory for centuries. The suq has over 150 shops and a variety of other adjacent suqs. The medicinal products of the suq were traditionally used in the mental asylum of Sidi Farj. The shops of this suq were defined by their masterful wooden furniture, which Leo Africanus said was beyond compare. While the area traditionally specialised in the sale of spices, perfumes, and medicinal products, the goods are diversified today—ranging from tasbīh shops to bookstores. Few traditional shops survive. The entire suq is covered by wooden lattices which shade shoppers during the hot summer months. Despite this, it is an easily accessible suq for visitors.

Suq al-Hayk, which is attached to Suq al-Atarayn, specialises in traditional Moroccan clothing.

Leo Africanus was a 16th century voyager known for his extensive travel logs, most notably his well-known text *Description of Africa*. He was born in Granada at the end of the 15th century and his family soon moved to Fes, where Leo Africanus studied at al-Qarawiyyin University. He journeyed to the Islamic east and upon his return to Morocco was captured by Spanish corsairs. He was imprisoned in Rome but was soon noted for his intelligence. He was presented to Pope Leo X, who freed him and gave him a position of employment. Leo Africanus was shortly thereafter baptized as a Christian. Under papal patronage, he continued to produce many scholarly works and served as a vital source of information on North Africa. His later life remains shrouded in mystery, though it is known that he wanted to return home to his native country.

Suq al-Ashabayn (E2)

The Suq al-Ashabayn was the traditional herbalists' market, where freshly picked herbs would be sold for culinary, medicinal, or religious purposes. It is located on the street connecting Bāb al-Gheesa to the Qarawiyyin district. The very existence of such a specialised suq reveals the rich botanical heritage of Fes and the area. Throughout history, plants and herbs such as thyme, garlic, and soapwort were sold in about 40 shops around the square. Famous doctors wrote about the richness of Fes' herbs, such as al-Ghassani, who wrote *Summary of a Garden of Flowers*, detailing Fes' medicinal plants.

While the Suq al-Ashabayn retains to some extent the traditional herbs and ingredients of ancient Fes, the suq has diversified today to include butchers, birds, grains, and breads.

Rcif Suq (E4)

The Rcif Suq is an excellent daily suq where a variety of goods—ranging from fish and meat to fruits and vegetables to sweets and breads—are sold. It is a source of daily nourishment for most Moroccans living in the area, and is a good place to both buy goods and experience a traditional local suq.

Jamai Palace (E1)

The Jamai Palace was built at the end of the 19th century. Due to its style and architectural arrangement, the palace is considered a masterpiece of Moroccan art. Transformed into a luxury residence at the beginning of the 1930s, it bears witness to the refinement of local bourgeoisie homes. Its sumptuous living rooms, masterful zillij and plasterwork, and well-tended gardens reveal enduring Andalusian influence. Today, it is a five-star hotel.

Kaysariya al-Kafah (E3)

The Kaysariya al-Kafah is a very important suq in the centre of the medina. Situated between the Suq al-Atarayn, the zāwiyah of Mūlay Idrīs, and the Masjid al-Qarawiyyin, this is a bustling modern suq. Recently renovated, it is an area specialising in traditional Moroccan clothing, hats, embroidery, and jewellery.

Al-Najareen Square (D3)

This is one of the most beautiful urban and architectural complexes in Fes. Organised around a square, a suq, a fountain, and a funduq, this is still a very lively area of the medina. The name is derived from the masterful work of the carpenters, woodworkers, and cabinet makers of the area. This was the heart of the carpentry industries of Fes. The funduq dates back to the 18th century. It hosts a well-preserved gate with remarkably designed and preserved plaster and zillij. The wooden canopy over the gate is covered with masterful friezes, geometric designs, and calligraphy. The fountain, which dates back to the 19th century, is still used as a public fountain today for cleaning and drinking. The Najareen funduq was restored by the Muhammad Lamrani Foundation as a museum of wooden arts. It is a necessary stop for anyone interested in the craftsmanship of Fes, both traditional and modern.

Al-Sefarayn Square (E3)

Metalworking, particularly with copper and brass, is one of the oldest trades of Fes. It is mentioned by Leo Africanus in his Fes travel accounts and the metalworkers' area remains in the same location, scattered around the square and the Wad Bukharareb. Throughout the day, the square rings with the often musical sounds of hammers smoothing out metal or etching pots with detailed designs. A variety of goods are produced including bowls, cups, cooking pans, tea-pots, tea-trays, stoves, and kettles. This is an area which preserves the traditional craftsmanship of the old local metalworkers. The square is host to an array of interesting sites, most notably the Qarawiyyin library and the Madrasa Sefarayn. The al-Sefarayn square is one of the most important squares of the medina, connecting the Rcif neighbourhood to the Qarawiyyin neighbourhood.

Dar al-Muwaqit (E3)

The Dar al-Muwaqit is a medium-sized house composed of a central patio and a ground floor dwelling. Attached to the south side of the house is a tower which, while resembling a minaret, is actually an ancient astronomical tower. Known traditionally as Borj Neffara, signifying the place where trumpeters used to blow their horns during festivals and during Ramadan, the tower was designed to keep astronomical observations—essential for delineating prayer times, the lunar months, and the dates of important holidays. The tower was staffed by a learned astronomer, known as the muwaqqit.

The building was renovated under the sponsorship of Her Majesty Margaret II, the Queen of Denmark. There is discussion of turning the space into an astronomy museum, which will highlight the role of science in Islamic history and culture. There has not yet been any development on this proposal.

Mnebhi Palace (D4)

Built at the beginning of the 20th century by a minister of defence for the ʿAlawite sultan Mūlay ʿAbd al-ʿAziz, the Mnebhi Palace was the first official residence of French Marshal Lyautey in 1912. Shortly thereafter, after the signing of the Treaty of Fes in 1912, Morocco became a French protectorate. He was the first Resident-General in Morocco during the French occupation and the palace was one of the first to be used as a restaurant in Morocco.

The palace has been renovated and today serves as a reservation-only restaurant. It is located on Talaʿa Saghira halfway between Bāb Bujlud and Masjid al-Qarawiyyin. The palace is magnificently designed and decorated. The high ceilings, large domes, plasterwork, carved work, and zillij mosaics offer a glimpse into the high-quality material industries of the old local craftsmen. The terrace has a spectacular view onto the medina.

Tanneries (F2)

The tanneries of Fes are one of the major historical, artisanal, and cultural attractions of the city. There are four traditional tanneries in the city. The tanneries are currently undergoing renovations and improvements, in part to facilitate expansion of the tourist industry and to address the overwhelming pollution problem caused by waste drainage. Tanning is still a major economic activity of Fes. It has been a prized career for many generations, and was associated with great social importance. Tanners are still honoured in local society for their hard work and skill.

The tanneries are composed of numerous dried-earth pits where raw hides are treated, scraped, and dyed. The vats are filled with various liquid dyes derived from natural sources such as indigo and poppy flower. The skins of sheep, goats, and cows are treated and trimmed into fine leather to be used by the craftsmen of Fes for a variety of products, such as slippers, leather bags, and shoes. The tanners spend hours standing in these pits, soaking the hides. They are then dried around the area or taken to the outskirts of the medina, such as the Merinid tombs, for further drying and processing.

House of Shaykh Aḥmad al-Tijānī (D3)

The house of Shaykh Aḥmad al-Tijānī is a well-preserved oasis in the middle of the medina. Also known as Dar al-Maraya, the house is located between Tala῾a Kabira and Tala῾a Saghira on a small darb called "Zqaq Rwah". This name refers to the entrance of the Moroccan bride on her wedding night, but has also been used to explicate the mystical power of the Shaykh's residence. The house was originally offered to Shaykh Aḥmad al-Tijānī at the end of the 18th century by the ʿAlawite Sultan Mūlay Sulaymān. It was once the home of the famed Moroccan Sufi master Mūlay Tayyib al-Wazzānī. The Sultan purchased the house from Mūlay Tayyib and used it as a place for scholarly and religious discussions. As a gesture of respect for Shaykh Aḥmad al-Tijānī, the Sultan eventually offered the house as a gift to the Shaykh, who was already renowned at that time.

This was the first Tijānī zāwiyah of Fes and where the Shaykh would meet with his students for dhikr, wazīfa and discussions. In this house, the Shaykh is also reported to have had many direct encounters with the Prophet Muḥammad ﷺ in a wake state. He lived in this house for 17 years, where he would receive all guests, religious scholars, and other shuyūkh. It was also in this house that the decision to build the famed Zāwiyah Tijānīyya was made. King Muḥammad VI sponsored the renovation of this house, completed in 2014, which has been interpreted as a sign of the enduring relationship between the ʿAlawite dynasty and the Tijānī Ṭarīqa.

Upon entering the house one encounters a massive courtyard, the location of the early gatherings of the Tijānī Ṭarīqa. The first room on the left was the Shaykh's bedroom, and the larger opposite rooms were sitting rooms where the guests would be entertained. There are also several khalwa rooms on the first and second floors. The house is staffed by a guard who is willing to show visitors around. A donation is not usually expected. There are no regular Tijānī gatherings in the house, though there is occasionally a gathering, particularly during Ramadan. It is best to ask for more information at the Tijānī zāwiyah.

Shop of the Prophet ﷺ (D3)

One of the pilgrimage sites of this district (al-Zaqaq) is a shop which is popularly referred to as the hanut (shop) of the Prophet ﷺ. According to legend, some people once saw the Prophet ﷺ inside of it, and thereafter it became a very popular site for tabarruk.

One of the scholars at the time of Jaʿfar al-Kattānī complained to him about the name of this mazār, saying that it had confused the ignorant masses of people into believing that the Prophet ﷺ had actually come to Fes in person during his lifetime and sat in that very shop. For this reason he would have preferred that it be called "the vision of the Prophet" or "the place in which the Prophet appeared" or something to that effect.

House of Ibn Khaldūn (B4)

This small passageway, located on Talaʿa Kabira near the Madrasa Bu Inaniya, leads to the old home of the Islamic scholar Abū Zayd ʿAbd al-Raḥmān ibn Muḥammad ibn Khaldūn al-Ḥaramī, known famously as Ibn Khaldūn.

Ibn Khaldūn lived during the 8th century AH and was a skilled historiographer. Best known for his work, the *Muqaddimah*, Ibn Khaldūn is often cited as the original source for many ideas in fields such as economics, sociology, and history. Born in Tunis, Ibn Khaldūn was raised in an upper-class Andalusian family of Arab descent. He had a very thorough Islamic education and after memorising the Quran at an early age, he went on to study in fields such as linguistics, hadith and fiqh. Under Shaykh al-Abilī of Tlemcen, Ibn Khaldūn pursued advanced studies in mathematics and philosophy.

Because of his social status, Ibn Khaldūn pursued a political and scholarly career as a young adult. Caught between the need to establish a stable political career and the exceedingly tumultuous political and social terrain of this region, he often found himself rapidly moving between locations and political allegiances. He began his career in Tunis under Ibn Tafrakīn, but in 755 AH/1354 CE, Ibn Khaldūn accepted an invitation to join the council of ʿulama of Fes and soon moved to pursue higher positions under the Merinid sultans. Ibn Khaldūn furthered his studies and writing career while in Fes. Ibn Khaldūn, in the tough and bloodthirsty political climate, engaged in court politics and was charged for conspiracy against the Sultan. He was imprisoned for several years, only to be released by the Sultan's successor. Ibn Khaldūn eventually moved to Granada in Andalusia to pursue a position under the Nasirid Sultan, Muḥammad al-Ahmar. His career later took him back to Tunis, Fes, and eventually to Egypt, where he passed away during the reign of the Mamluk dynasty. He died in 808 AH/1406 CE and is buried outside of the Bāb al-Nasr cemetery in Cairo.

Unfortunately, there is no information or signage available for this historic site. The former home of Ibn Khaldūn remains a private home for a Moroccan family, and is not open to visitors.

House of Maimonides (B4)

The House of Maimonides is situated on Darb Mergana, a small street just across from the Madrasa Bu Inaniya, just to the left of the water clock. It is marked by a small, faded, and defaced marble placard set in the wall on the right.

Maimonides is one of the most respected Jewish thinkers in history. Noted for being a brilliant rabbinic scholar, Torah commentator and physician, he contributed many original and enduring works on Jewish law and philosophy, which are renowned to this day. Originally from Cordoba in Andalusia, Maimonides pursued a luminous career from an early age and was known for his saintly personality and intellect. He fled Almohad persecution in the 12th century. Between 1159 and 1165, he lived in this house in the old city of Fes and contributed to the intellectual and cultural life of the medina. Maimonides was known for composing his works while travelling and wrote his famed work, a commentary on the *Mishnah*, while wandering in exile. This is a testament to his keen scholarly abilities. Maimonides eventually continued on to Egypt, where he passed away.

The house is not a museum, but a private residence. There are discussions of erecting a formal dedication to Maimonides and his legacy, but this seems to be a plan for the distant future. This is a common stop while passing on to Café Clock, a popular restaurant among tourists offering everything from banana milkshakes to camel burgers.

▲ The courtyard or *sahn* of Zawiyah of Mūlay Idrīs II looking west towards the mausoleum entrance.

► Al-Qarawiyyin University gate.

▼ The tomb of Mūlay Idrīs II in the mausoleum.

▲ The courtyard and minaret of Bu Inaniya Madrasa.

► The Bab Bujlud, also known as The Blue Gate, leads into Fes' old medina.

▼ On the left, Ain al-Kheil, also known as Al-Azhar Mosque in Fes el-Bali's Ain Allou neighbourhood. On the right, the Western side of the Al-Atarine Madrasa courtyard, looking towards the entrance.

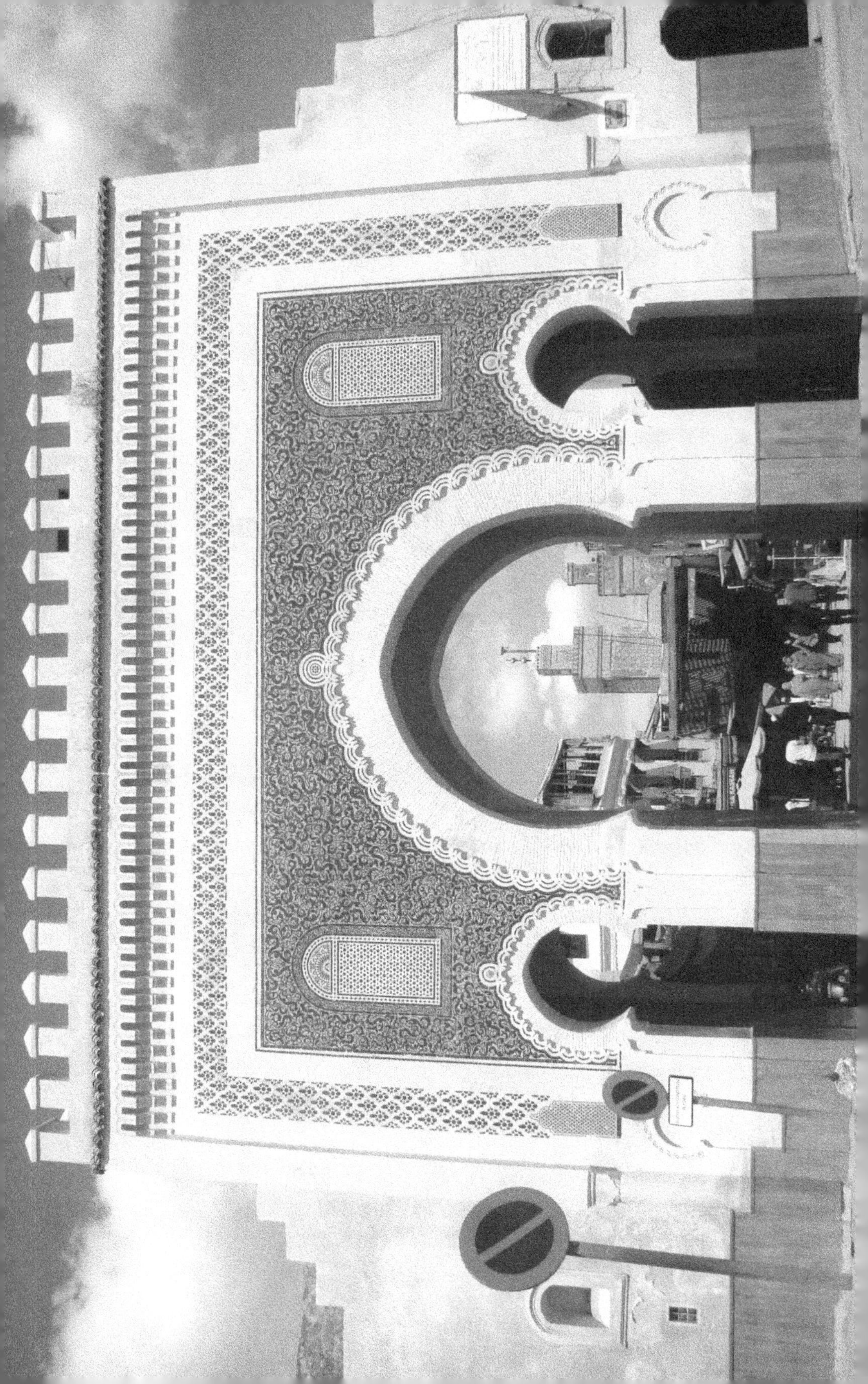

▲ The tomb of Shaykh Aḥmad al-Tijānī.

◀ The famous coloured baths of Fes' tanneries, in which leather skins are softened or given a new tan.

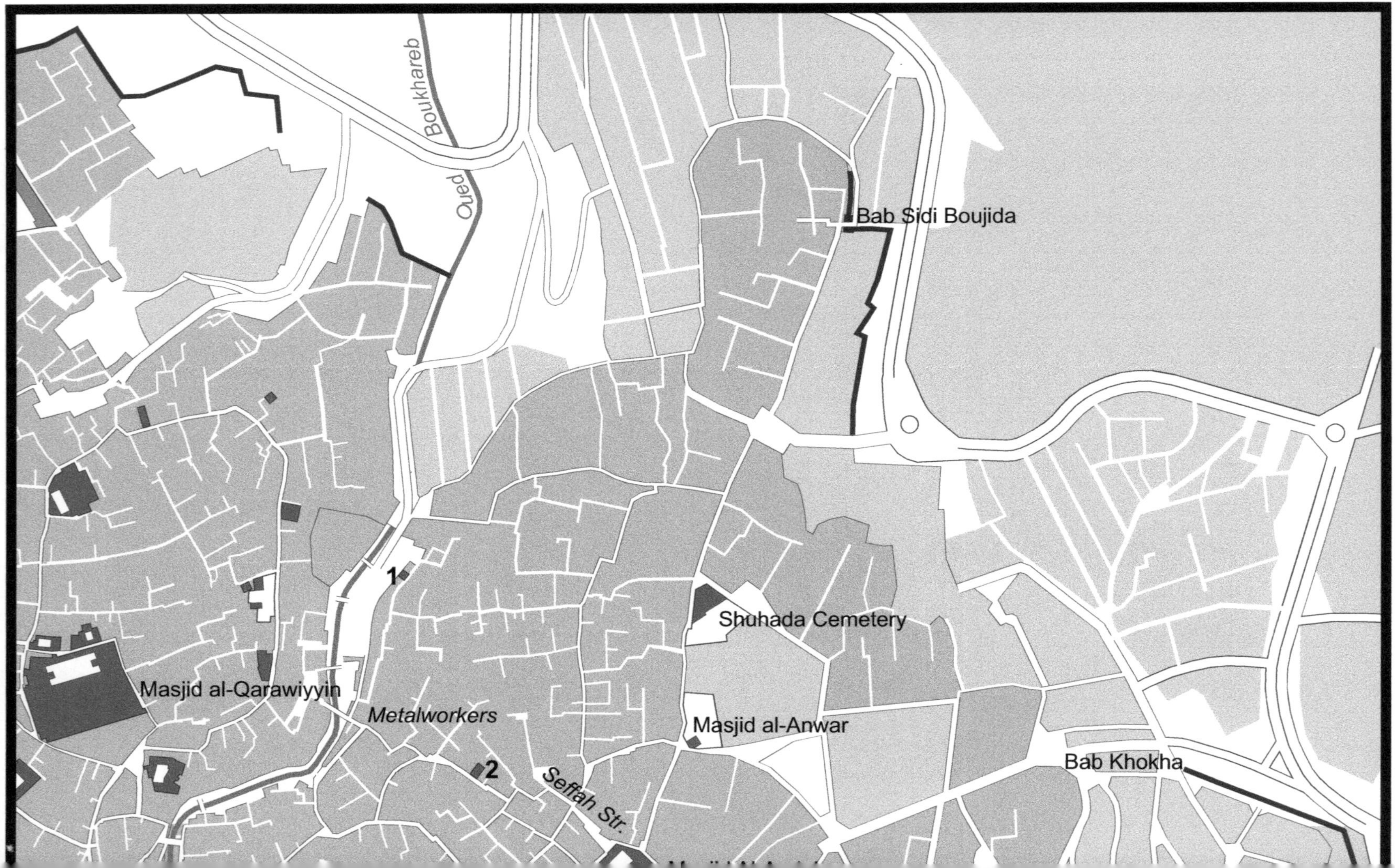
Bab Sidi Boujida
Oued Boukhareb
Shuhada Cemetery
Masjid al-Qarawiyyin
Metalworkers
Masjid al-Anwar
Bab Khokha
Seffah Str.
1
2

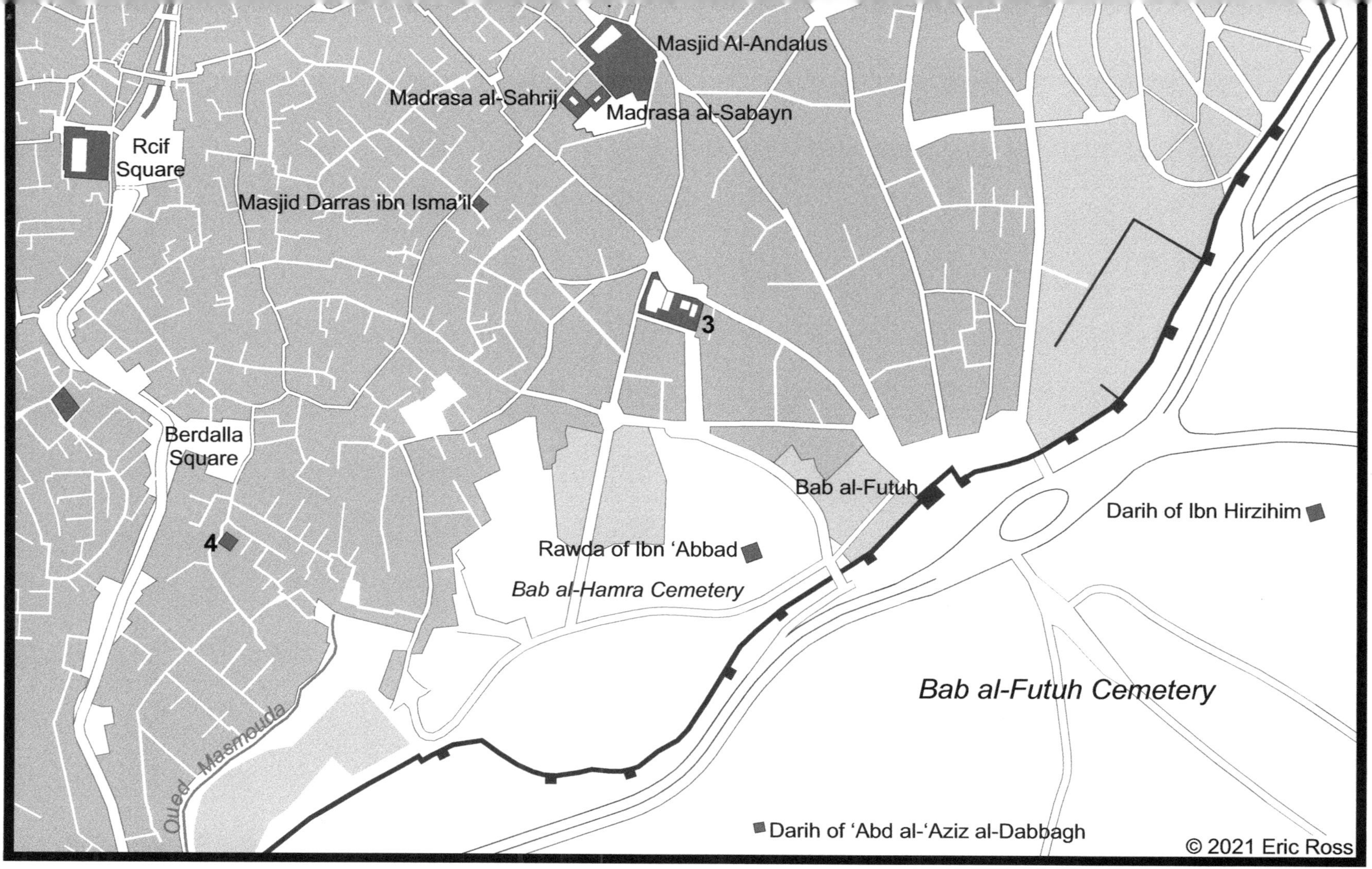
Masjid Al-Andalus
Madrasa al-Sahrij
Madrasa al-Sabayn
Rcif Square
Masjid Darras ibn Isma'il
3
Berdalla Square
Bab al-Futuh
Darih of Ibn Hirzihim
4
Rawda of Ibn 'Abbad
Bab al-Hamra Cemetery
Oued Masmouda
Bab al-Futuh Cemetery
Darih of 'Abd al-'Aziz al-Dabbagh
© 2021 Eric Ross

MAP LEGEND

1. Zāwiyah of Sidi ʿAlī al-ʿImrāni al-Jamal
2. Zāwiyah of Muḥammad ibn Jaʿfar al-Kattānī
3. Dārih of Sidi ʿAlī ibn Abū Ghālib al-Sārīwī
4. Makhfiyya Zāwiyah (Zāwiyah of Abī Maḥasan Yūsuf al-Fāsī)

3 The Andalusian Quarter

The Andalusian Quarter is the other, eastern quarter of the Fes medina. It was here that the first migrant communities from Islamic Spain settled in the 9th century. Hundreds of Andalusian families, both of Arab and Amazigh descent, were expelled from southern Spain after a rebellion against the Umayyad dynasty in 817 and 818 CE. With the relocation of Tunisian Arab families to the other side of the river in the same century, the city of Fes developed a uniquely Arab flavour, which was set in contrast to the surrounding rural areas. The arrival of Spanish Muslims in the Andalusian Quarter in the 9th century deeply influenced local and wider Moroccan culture, particularly its architectural style. The historic centre is set around the Masjid al-Andalus, where visitors can explore the various markets and streets that sprawl out from the beating heart of the quarter.

Zawaya and Awliya

Sidi ʿAlī al-ʿImrānī al-Jamal (the Camel) (d. 1194 AH)

The shaykh and gnostic, the imam of the people of ḥaqīqah, treasure trove of the Lordly Graces, spring source of the divine knowledge: Abū Ḥassan ʿAlī ibn ʿAbd al-Raḥmān ibn Muḥammad ibn ʿAlī ibn Ibrāhīm ibn ʿImrān al-Sharīf al-Ḥassanī al-Idrīssī al-ʿImrānī of the shurufā of Bani ʿImrān, of the tribe of Bani Ḥassan. He is nicknamed "al-Jamal" (the camel) because one day he found a camel resting on one of the roads of Fes and lifted it and put it on the side of the road. Some people saw him and said, "This is indeed the (real) camel!" Thus he became famous for that. As for the angels of the Raḥmān, he is known by them as *al-Jamāl* (The Divine Beauty).

He at first worked for the government in Fes before fleeing to Tunis after the ascension to the throne of Sultan Abū ʿAbdullāh Muḥammad, fearing he would be among those upon whom harm befell from the new Sultan. In Tunis he met numerous shaykhs whom he benefitted from, then they (the shuyūkh) sent him to Wazzān (in Morocco) to Shaykh Mūlay Ṭayyib al-Wazzānī. Mūlay al-Ṭayyib sent him to Fes, where he accompanied the great gnostic Aḥmad ibn ʿAbdullāh Maʿin al-Andalūsī for sixteen years. When his Shaykh died, he built a zāwiyah for himself in Ramila where his tomb is now. Before long, his following and the number of those in his service greatly increased, including eventually the famous saint Mūlay al-ʿArabī al-Darqāwī.

He was versed in the sharīʿah in all of its aḥkām and did not overstep any of its orders. Sometimes he wore the best of clothes and at other times would wear clothes that were ragged and old. Sometimes he would cover his feet with expensive sandals known as the sharbil and at other times he would go completely barefoot and extend his hand in begging.

He reached the greatest station of the quṭbāniyya, and in fact lived in it for the greater portion of his life according to the letters of his student Mūlay al-ʿArabī al-Darqāwī. I quote, "And our teacher—may Allah be pleased with him—used to beg in the Quwarit in Fes Bali, may God prosper him, from shop to shop like Mudhtār al-Kabīr, except that he indeed lived most of his life as a ghawth, and his lifespan passed to be more than eighty years." He knew 24 methods of ḥikma, each one of which was used as the standard to determine the sāʿi for the royal house, and in spite of this he would still beg in the Quwarit from the people in the marketplaces, even as his hands shook from old age.

Most of the time, he could be seen sitting in the Qarawiyyin at the shaded door from the side of the Bāb al-Funduq. Sidi ʿAbd al-Majīd was continuously in contemplation, abundant in tears and admonition. Those who spoke to him found a sea of knowledge and gnosis. He was, as regards shuyūkh of the way, of the people who Divested the Outer and the Inner together: ascetic, oft remembering of his Lord, obedient, humble, empty of pretensions and avoiding of its people, aglow in passion for the unity and its books and the laws of its people. He had the longest hand in its root principles and branches and reality, upon the Ṭarīqah of Abū Ḥassan al-Shushtārī, and the like of him among the greatest of the saints.

Of his miracles, it is said he would exit from a gate of the city and take from the lords of the merchant caravans a dirham for every camel amongst them, and then they would go and profit from their merchandise and return to their homeland safe and sound, laden with spoils. One day, some of the lords of the caravan decided amongst themselves that they would haggle with him over the price of one of the camels, and in the end they paid him nothing for it. So they departed for the region of the Sūs and on the way, that camel was stolen from them, and only that camel—none other than it. News of this spread in the land, and after that not one disputed with him over the price of a camel.

He died in Fes in the year 1193 or 1194 AH according to the biography of al-Kowhen. He was buried in his zāwiyah which is in Ramila, in the Andalusian Quarter. Buried in it as well are a number of his companions and their companions—may Allah be pleased with all of them.

> The small mosque that lies by the side of the zāwiyah was the zāwiyah of Sidi Abū Madyan when he was in Fes. In front of the mosque is the maqām of Abū Yaʿzā al-Mahhājī, the student of Mūlay al-ʿArabi. It is only a door though, and not possible to enter.

Located in the Ramila neighbourhood near the "Bayn al-Mudun" city entrance, the zāwiyah of Sidi ʿAlī al-Jamal is considered one of the most important zawāya in Fes. The zāwiyah was established by ʿAlī al-Jamal, and it was here that Shaykh al-ʿArabi al-Darqāwī first encountered his shaykh, seeking his guidance. For some years, Shaykh al-Darqāwī would have studied here under his shaykh.

There are two entrances to the zāwiyah—one from a small street connected to the metalworkers' area, and one from the Bayn al-Mudun parking lot. The family living in the zāwiyah complex is usually there and open the doors for visitors during reasonable hours. A small donation is expected (though not required) for visits outside of the Thursday evening gatherings.

The zāwiyah once housed the sole original copy of the Shaykh's classical Sufi text, *The Meaning of Man* (*Maʿanā al-Insān*), which has been re-published in Arabic and translated into English. The text today has been moved to a private family collection.

Gatherings: Every Thursday between maghrib and ʿisha, a gathering is held in the zāwiyah. The samāʿ usually lasts beyond the ʿisha adhan. The gathering focuses on a collection of letters by Shaykh Muḥammad ibn al-Ḥarrāq, a renowned student of Shaykh al-Darqāwī who is buried in Tetouan. Several qaṣāʾid are recited before a selection of text is read and commented upon by a local shaykh. There is usually a discussion following the reading and commentary. Occasionally, a ḥaḍra is performed. Tea and bread are usually served.

Zāwiyah Muḥammad ibn Jaʿfar al-Kattānī (1274–1345)

His full name was ʿAbdullāh Sidi Muḥammad ibn Jaʿfar al-Ḥassanī al-Idrīssī al-Kattānī al-Fāsī. He was born approximately in the year 1274 AH and was raised under the care of his father, through whose hands he studied grammar, fiqh, hadith, usūl, tawhīd, and the other sciences, as well over twenty repetitions of the *Sahīh*.

He performed his first Hajj pilgrimage in the year 1321 during which he visited Yemen and Egypt, then in the year 1325 he emigrated with his family to Madina wherein they took up residence until the year 1336. Throughout that time, he performed the Hajj four times and studied in the Ḥaram al-Nabawī. He was then forcefully expelled from Madina on account of the First World War and took up residence in Damascus, where he lived until his return to Morocco in the year 1345. In Yemen he studied the two *Sahīh*, the *Sunan* of Nīsāʿī, the *Shamāʾil* of Tirmidhī and the totality of the *Musnad* of Imam Ḥanbal. In Damascus he was very well-known and everyone, from the scholars to the masses, would attend his lectures in the Jāmʿia al-Ummawiyya.

He was a knowledgeable Imam, an ascetic gnostic, pious, humble and filled with love towards knowledge and the people of knowledge. He took great care in upholding the Sunnah in himself, those around him, and all his works on his madhhab. He was kind and amenable to the young and the old alike, deeply humble and beautiful in his character. He always held to the best opinion (*ḥusn al-ẓann*) regarding everyone, never criticised anybody in their claim to have reached a spiritual station, and was constantly paying visits to both the living and deceased from among the saints, sometimes travelling great distances to see them. He had a luminous face and would hold to a beautiful silence filled with contemplation, interrupted only by wailing and sighing (in longing for the Divine).

He authored numerous works on history, Sufism, hadith and other subjects. He died, may God be pleased with him, in 1345 AH and was buried at first in a qubbah outside of the Bāb al-Futūḥ. Then, twenty years after this burial, he was moved to a zāwiyah which was built especially for him inside the city of Fes. Upon opening his tomb they found his body to be uncorrupted as it was on the day he died, and there wafted from it the scent of musk.

One of the miraculous accounts narrated from him by his student al-Ṣiddīqī is that once, the Shaykh was on the road between Madina and Makka with a tasbīh in his hands, remembering God, when the road suddenly opened up before him all the way to Fes so that he could see the city, and there, standing in front of him, was a beautiful shaykh saying, "Here is the sound road in which there is no hardship, so return to Fes!" He then turned and saw that to his right was another person whom he imagined to be the Prophet ﷺ and so he said to him, "O Messenger of God! I desire from you that we should go!" He then fell quiet, and immediately what had befallen him departed, the rosary still in his hands and the remembrance of God still on his tongue, uninterrupted.

Gatherings: Today, the zāwiyah of al-Kattānī is usually open for maghrib and ʿisha prayers and hosts an annual mawlid gathering in the month of Rabīʿ al-Awwal. Locals at zāwiyahs and masājid can guide visitors to particular gatherings happening in the month, as special mawlid and dhikr gatherings are not fixed.

Ḍarīḥ Sidi ʿAlī ibn Abū Ghālib al-Sārīwī (850s?)

His full name was Abū al-Ḥassan Sidi ʿAlī, though he was known as Abū Ghālib. He is buried on the Qalʿiah, or what was once known as Sārīwa, inside of the Bāb al-Futūḥ. His grave there is famously attributed to numerous miracles, such that they say his miracles in death outnumbered those in life. His burial place is next to such famous names as Ibn Mashīsh and Abū Silhām due to the large crowds of people that performed pilgrimage there each year, and he was renowned both in life and in death for curing the ill.

In spite of this, the exact occupant of the grave or when he died is not known for certain, and rumours such as that it is one of the companions of ʿĪsā عليه السلام or some unknown prophet who is buried there developed in the absence of certainty (though these are clearly fabricated). What can be ascertained is that he most likely lived and died before the year 914 AH, up to as early as the mid 8th century AH.

Some of what has been recorded of Sidi Abū Ghālib was that his family were Idrīssī Shurufāʾ who fled from the governor Mūsā ibn Abū al-ʿĀfiyya al-Maknāsī during his reign of Fes and settled in the land of Sārīwa in the Banī Yāzigha. A number of them returned and settled in the district, which came to be called al-Sārīwī on account of them, and Sidi Abū Ghālib was born to a family among these.

It has also been said that his shaykh in the Sufi way was Shaykh al-Kūmī or ʿAlī al-Hawārī, but both of these speculations are historically impossible, as both of them lived more than two hundred years after the best estimated time and place of his death.

It has become the norm for pilgrims seeking healing at the tomb to take water from a miḥbas[4] which has been placed near the tomb, and rub it over whoever is sick, then drink from it. This has its origins in a story related of Shaykh Sidi Yūsuf al-Tawdī, which Muhammad ibn Jaʿfar al-Kattānī found written in a notebook of one of the many poets extolling the healing virtues of Abū Ghālib's tomb, which goes as follows:

> One day he (the owner of the notebook) went to visit the tomb of Sidi Abū Ghālib al-Sarīwī and when he arrived there he found the shaykhs Yūsuf al-Tawdī, Ibn Razūq, Muḥammad ibn Ḥussayn, the Murābit ʿAbdullāh al-Darāʿwī, and Sidi ʿAbd al-Salām ibn al-Hajj. When Sidi Yūsuf desired to leave, he approached the miḥbas near the tomb and drank a mouthful of water from it. The faqīh Muḥammad ibn Hussayn then said to him, "O Sidi! It is your example the people follow and by whom they seek guidance, and you are drinking from this miḥbas which is the collecting point of filth and mud?!" Sidi al-Tawdī said to ʿAbdullāh al-Darāʿwī, "Answer him." So al-Darāʿwī responded by reciting the verse, "And He Creates what you do not know" (Surat al-Naḥal: 8), and then said, "And this is among those things you do not know!"
>
> Shaykh al-Tawdī then commented, "And add to that one other thing, which is that, I encountered in the Bāb al-Kashf (Chapter on Unveilings) of the Shaykh and Gnostic Sidi ʿAbd al-Raḥmān al-Fāsī—may God be pleased with him—that every day seventy thousand saints come to this miḥbas and place

4 In this case, a duct or basin of some sort near the tomb where water congregates.

their hands in it seeking divine grace (baraka). We merely wish to obtain something of the blessings of those blessed hands. May God include us to be among their ranks, and make us to be among the lovers... Āmin."

Sometime in the centuries since, one of the leaders of Fes, Bujīda al-Majdūlī, constructed a water fountain outside of the rawḍa of the tomb. Sultan Mūlay Sulaymān al-ʿAlawī refurbished this tomb during his reign and added to it a mosque wherein they conduct the prayer, a place for the sick who come to visit seeking healing, and another fountain on the side of the mausoleum.

It is important to note that this tomb is not that of the similarly famous Abū Ghālib al-Qasrī al-Anṣārī buried in Kasr al-Kabīr, who is considered one of the Awtād.

Gatherings: The ḍarīḥ of Sidi Abū Ghalib is one of the most important awliyāʾ of the Andalusian Quarter. The darīḥ is often open in the morning until maghrib, and it is a popular ziyārah destination for local women. The walī is known for his healing baraka, and locals visit seeking alleviation from a variety of illnesses.

Blessed oil hangs near the tomb of Sidi Abū Ghālib. It has absorbed the baraka of the shaykh and is used for healing. The oil is rubbed on the skin to cure both internal and external illnesses.

Zāwiyah Makhfiyya Abī Maḥāsin Yūsuf al-Fāsī

The Zāwiyah Makhfiyya is nestled in a small alley behind the Cinema Amal in the Makhfiyya neighbourhood. It is primarily an active masjid. For a biography of the shaykh, please see the entry in the chapter entitled "Bāb al-Futuh Cemetery".

Gatherings: On Friday afternoons after ʿasr prayer, a small dhikr is held in the Zāwiyah Makhfiyya with members of the Zarrūqiyya branch of the Shādhiliyya Ṭarīqa. Usually, a ḥizb of the Quran is recited communally, followed by the Wazīfa Zarrūqiyya and several Qaṣāʾid. A dars is usually offered by a shaykh following the dhikr. The gathering finishes before maghrib prayer. Occasionally, the gathering is cancelled if the shaykh is travelling or busy.

Masajid

Masjid al-Anwar

Built by Mūlay Idrīs, Masjid al-Anwar (or "mosque of lights") is the oldest masjid in the Andalusian Quarter. It was also called jamaʿ al-ashiakh, referencing the local influential tribal leaders who allied with Mūlay Idrīs. While this is an important architectural and archaeological gem of Fes, it is oft neglected. A bustling suq has been built up around the old masjid foundations.

Masjid al-Andalus

Masjid al-Andalus was built in the 9th century by the pious Maryam al-Fiḥrī, the sister of the famed founder of Masjid al-Qarawiyyin, Fāṭima al-Fiḥrī. At the time, both masjids were founded as small, simple community mosques. Masjid al-Andalus, along with the rest of the Andalusian Quarter, takes its name from the waves of

Andalusian immigrants who settled in this area and contributed to the construction of the Fes medina.

Since its foundation, the mosque has vastly expanded, undergoing a series of repairs, decorations, and extensions. The Almohads, who ruled Fes from 1145 to 1248 CE, were credited with the most influential expansion of the masjid. Employing an architect from Toledo, the huge monumental gate dominating the northern face of the masjid offers a glimpse of the great artistic and architectural care taken in expansion. It is one of the few examples of Almohad architecture available to visitors.

Over the centuries, the masjid served as an important madrasa and hundreds of religious scholars studied within its walls, including the famed Imam al-Jazūlī. Today, Masjid al-Andalus is the religious centre of the Andalusian Quarter. It is a good place to pray jumaʿ, tarawīh during Ramadan, and to listen to communal recitations of the Quran.

Mosque of Sidi Darrās

This mosque is located in a long street known as Maṣmūdah. Sidi Darrās, who is buried outside the walls of the Futūḥ, was the teacher of the famous Bin Abī Zayd al-Qayrawānī who composed the *Risālah,* a key text in Mālikī law which is still taught today. His mosque was believed to have the most accurate prayer niche directed towards Makka in the city.

Madaris

Madrasa Sabaʿyn

This madrasa was also named al-Saghir, to distinguish it from Madrasa Sahrij. Along with Madrasa Sahrij, it was constructed between 1321 and 1323 CE under the Merinid sultan, Abū Ḥassan. The name of the madrasa references the seven styles of reading the Quran, all of which were studied in the madrasa. Students from this madrasa also studied at Masjid al-Andalus, along with students of Madrasa Sahrij and several other madrasas. These madāris also trained future civil servants and government officials. Students across the country were based in different madāris. Madrasa Sabaʿyn has a rectangular design with a central patio, surrounded by galleries and rooms on the first and second floors. It is characterised by a beautiful marble fountain and central pool. The spectacular work of the fountain offers a glimpse of the once-famous work of the local marble masons.

Madrasa Sahrij

This madrasa, which takes its name from the pool in the central courtyard, was built between 1321 and 1323 CE by the Merinid sultan Abū Ḥassan. It is located adjacent to Masjid al-Andalus, and it was one of the main dormitories for students studying there. The zillij here is some of the earliest to be found in the madāris of Morocco. It is noted for its stunning architectural unity and rich geometrical, floral, and epigraphic embellishment on the walls. It was styled as a traditional madrasa, with the rooms of the students circling an open courtyard. Advanced students were given rooms facing the courtyard, which afforded more light and space, and younger students were given smaller and darker rooms in the interior.

The madrasa has been recently renovated as a functioning dormitory for local students.

Places of Interest in the Andalusian Quarter

Zinqa Seffah

Zinqa Seffah, or Seffah street, is the major commercial thoroughfare connecting Bāb al-Futūḥ with the Bayn al-Mudun and Rcif areas in the centre of the city. Flanked entirely by old shops and funduqs, this has been an important economic hub for centuries. A variety of different traditional and modern goods are to be found here—including clothing, embroidery, olives and sweets. There are also specialised areas for glassmakers, designers, and carpenters. The funduqs are dedicated to leather goods and shoe production. It is a major shopping artery of the al-Andalus quarter.

Metalworkers' Area

The ringing of hammers pounding copper sheets echoes throughout this section of the city, drowning out the din of the busy streets. The areas surrounding the tanneries and across the Ramila neighbourhood on the other side of the river, is a traditional area for metalworkers, or sudūr. Along with the al-Sefarayn Square, it is an excellent place to sample the traditional copperware craftsmanship of Fes. Common goods, which can be purchased directly, are pots, cauldrons, plates, and buckets.

Gazīrah Street: Sandal of the Prophet ﷺ

Just across the mosque of Sidi Darrās on a street called Gazīrah is a house that belonged to the Ṭahrī Ṣaqallī family, who were in possession of what was believed to be a pair of the sandals of the Prophet ﷺ. Every year, just before the month of Rabīʿ al-Awwal, the family would display the sandals in their home to the public so that they could take blessing from it. This practice continued until the family sold the home.

In the book *Nashr al-Mathānī* by Muḥammad b. Ṭayyib (d. 1187 AH), it is mentioned that the sandal was placed in an ornamented wooden box and kept in a high place in the house in one of the upper rooms. The sandal has a certificate in which a number of prestigious scholars attested to its authenticity. In the year 1067 AH, ʿAbd al-Qādir al-Fāsī and a number of other prestigious scholars visited the sandals and measured them according to its descriptions mentioned in the religious sources.

In the year 1114, Sultan Mūlay Ismāʿīl demanded the inhabitants of Fes repay their debts so the people of the city went to the Ṭahrī family, who possessed the sandal, and begged them to take it before the Sultan and ask him for the sake of the sandal to forgo the debt. The family agreed and took it before the Sultan and gave it to him, which he subsequently placed in his palace in Meknes to take blessing from. He built a dome over it which is today called the Dome of the Sandal. It remained in his possession until he passed away, but the people do not know of its whereabouts after that.

Authenticity of the Sandal

Some of the scholars have questioned the authenticity of the sandal as they believed time would have eroded the sandal and contemporaneous scholars never made mention of the sandal being in the possession of the Ṭahrī Ṣaqallī family. However, Muḥammad ibn Jaʿfar al-Kattānī argues:

- Many respectable scholars attested to its authenticity and such luminaries would not do so if they were not certain. Just because certain scholars did not make mention of it does not disqualify it because many scholars present at the time who were just as well-respected testified to its authenticity.

• Allah forbade the bodies of the Prophets from decomposing and thus it is not far-fetched that He could have honoured certain artefacts of the Prophet ﷺ by preventing them from decomposing too.

• As long as leather is protected from water and sunlight, it will not completely deteriorate. There are many examples of papers which are over seven hundred years old yet are still intact. If this is the case with paper, then what of leather, which is far more durable?

Benefits of possessing the image of the sandal: In the year 1144 AH, one of the scholars described his visit and how he took the blessed sandal and rubbed it over his upper half and asked Allah Almighty to fulfil his needs through the blessings of the sandal and he remarked how his prayer was answered soon after. Muḥammad ibn Jaʿfar al-Kattānī also mentions some of the benefits of possessing the image of the sandal:

• Whoever places it on an area of pain with a sincere intention will be healed immediately.

• Whoever holds onto it seeking its blessing will be safe from oppressors and guarded against evil spirits as well as the evil eye of those who harbour jealousy.

• If a woman in labour holds it in her right hand she will find ease.

• Whoever frequently has it with him will receive acceptance from the people and will be blessed with a visit to the Prophet ﷺ, or see him in a dream.

• Whoever travels with it by land or sea and is confronted by fear or possible destruction will be delivered.

▶ The main entrance of the al-Andalus Mosque, or Mosque of the Andalusians.

◄ A town square that is home to Fes' copper and brass workers.

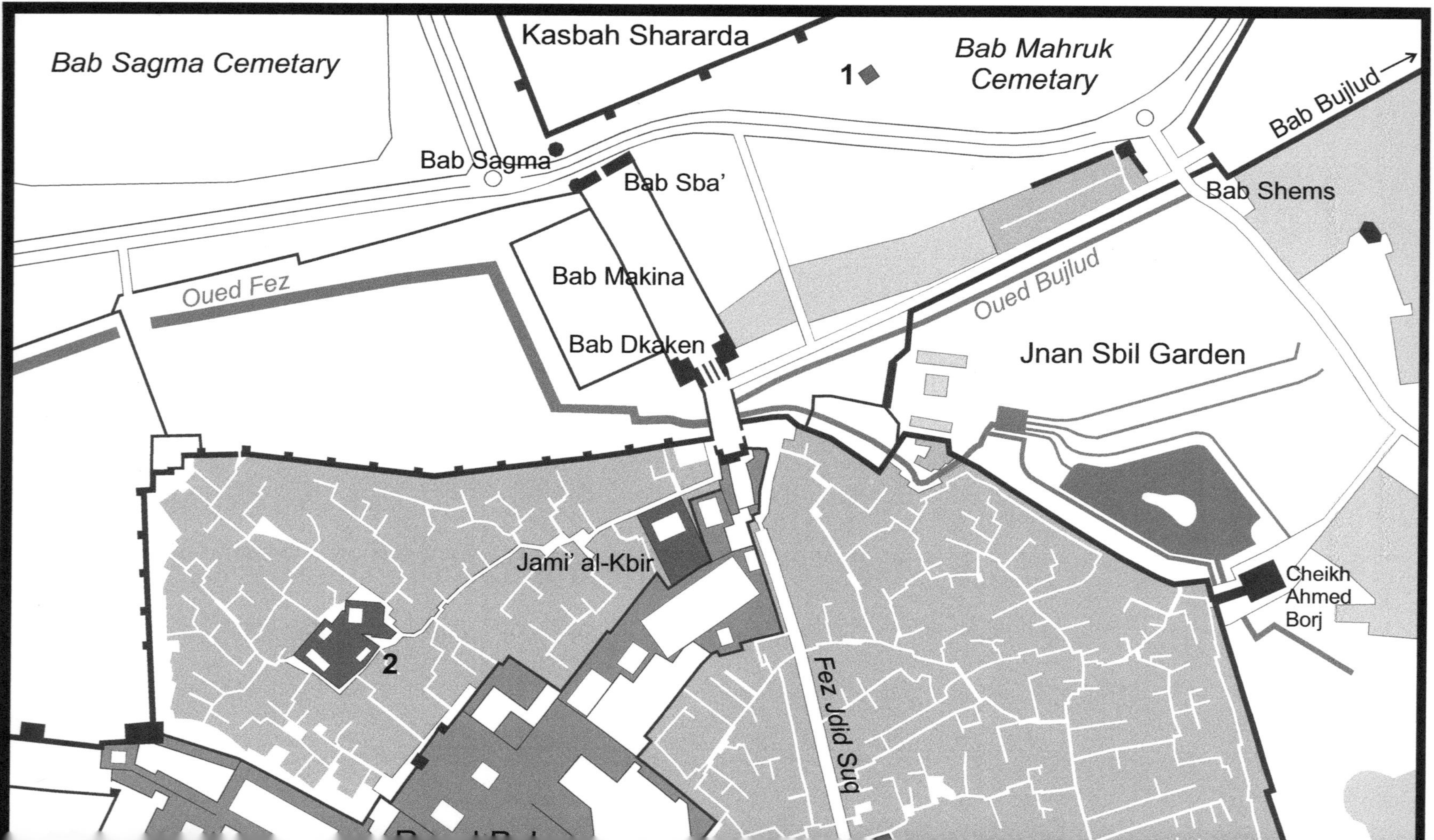
Bab Sagma Cemetery
Kasbah Shararda
Bab Mahruk
Cemetary
1
Bab Bujlud
Bab Sagma
Bab Sba'
Bab Shems
Bab Makina
Oued Fez
Oued Bujlud
Bab Dkaken
Jnan Sbil Garden
Jami' al-Kbir
2
Fez Jdid Suq
Cheikh
Ahmed
Borj

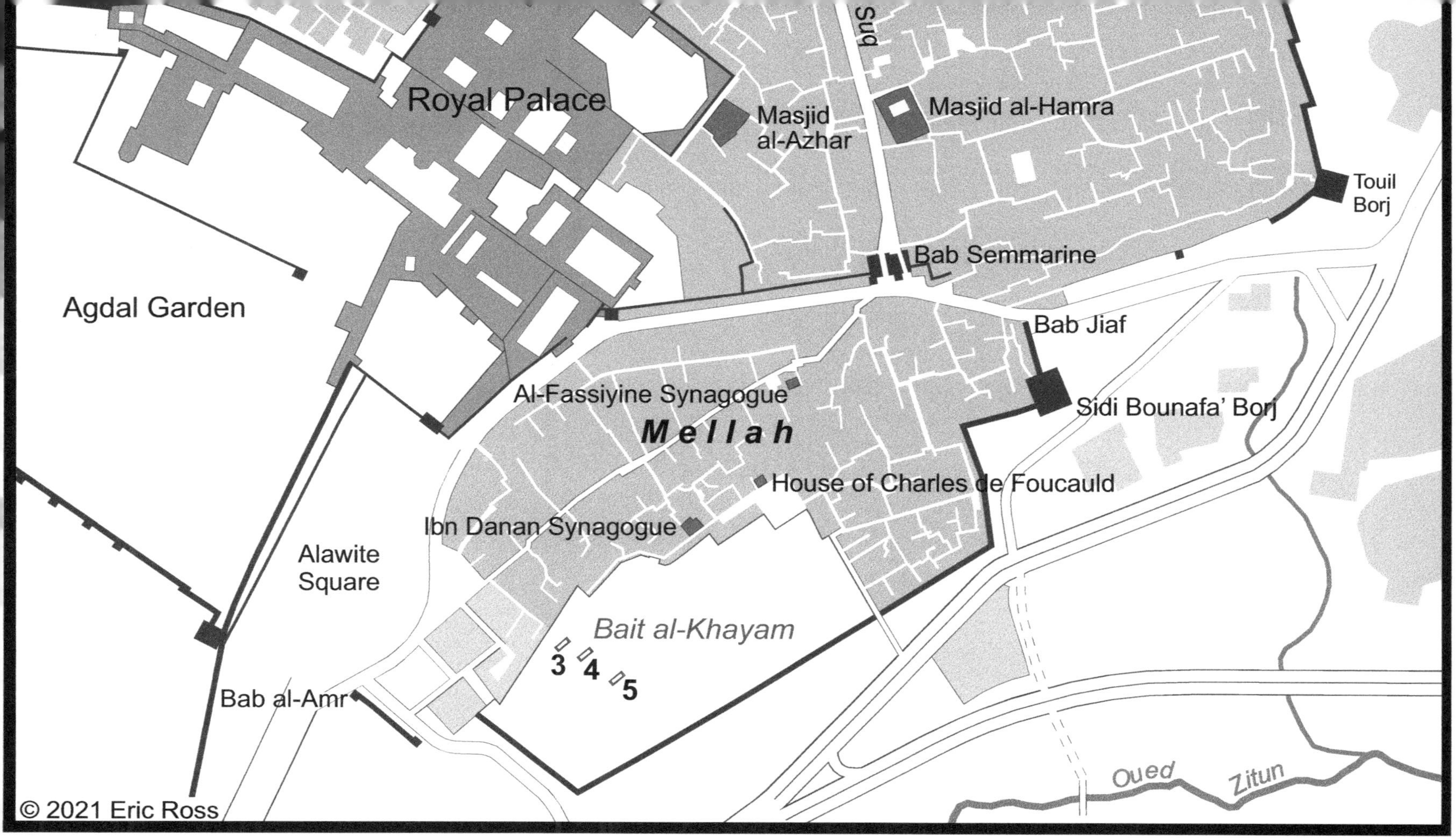
Royal Palace
Masjid al-Azhar
Masjid al-Hamra
Suq
Touil Borj
Bab Semmarine
Agdal Garden
Bab Jiaf
Al-Fassiyine Synagogue
Sidi Bounafa' Borj
Mellah
House of Charles de Foucauld
Ibn Danan Synagogue
Alawite Square
Bait al-Khayam
3
4
5
Bab al-Amr
Oued Zitun
© 2021 Eric Ross

MAP LEGEND

1. Ḍarīḥ of Mūlay Abu Bakr ibn ʿArabī
2. Ḍarīḥ of Mūlay ʿAbdallah
3. Grave of Rabbi Abner Ha-Tsarfati
4. Grave of Lalla Sol Ha-Tseddiqa
5. Grave of Rabbi Yehuda Ben-Attar

4 Fes Jdid and the Mellah

Fes Jdid: The Medieval New City of the Merinids

After their conquest of Fes in the 13th century, the new Merinid dynasty decided to create a second, new city of Fes to serve as an administrative and residential centre, separate from Fes al-Bali, the old medina. Constructed by Sultan Abū Yūsuf Yaʿqūb, it was an elite centre housing royals, court officials, bureaucrats, and soldiers (most notably, Syrian mercenaries). It was built with two perimeter walls surrounding the area to better protect the ruling class and to display the power and glory of the Merinids.

Today, Fes Jdid is primarily a residential area and lies between the medina and the Ville Nouvelle in both location and character. One can still get lost in the winding, twisting lanes, but the vastness of the palace looms over everyone in Fes Jdid, fulfilling its purpose as a bulwark of regal glory. Outside of the Jewish Mellah, this area is not as touristic as the medina. One is more likely to have authentic human and suq encounters here, including unavoidable Arabic language practice!

The Mellah and the Jewish Community of Fes

The Jewish community of Fes has a long history, tracing back to the founding of the city under Mūlay Idrīs II. Over the centuries, the Jewish community has contributed significantly to the intellectual, cultural, and economic production of the city. Fes was home to many great Jewish scholars, teachers, and saints, many of whom were renowned internationally and remain significant figures in Jewish thought.

Fes' tumultuous history—rising and falling as a political and intellectual centre over the course of many dynasties—was also felt by the Jews, whose experience ranged from relative freedom and integration to ghettoization and persecution. This history is in danger of being lost. Today, less than a hundred Moroccan Jews live in Fes. The Jewish history of Fes is an integral aspect of the spiritual and religious history of city, and should not be forgotten.

Important Sights of the Mellah

The cultural and religious sights of the Mellah speak of the importance of this community. Two restored synagogues—the Synagogue al-Fasiyine and the Synagogue ibn Danan—offer a glimpse into the once-flourishing religious activity of the Mellah. While there were once 18 active synagogues in the Mellah, only two remain for visitation. The others have been turned into private homes, stores, or have fallen into disrepair. The expansive and well-maintained Jewish cemetery, known in Hebrew as Bayt al-Khayam, or "House of the Living," is home to three important tzidiqim, Jewish saints who are still visited to this day by Muslims, Jews, and pilgrims from abroad. The narrow streets of the medina also reveal unique architectural elements and hidden stories, such as the home of Charles de Foucauld, where the French explorer stayed for several weeks.

Awliya and Tzidiqim

Rabbi Abner Ha-Tsarfati

Rabbi Abner Ha-Tsarfati was born in Fes in 1827 and died in 1883. He is buried on the northern wall of the cemetery, and is often visited by those seeking healing for illnesses. Below is an account about the healing power of the tzidiq.

> In the name of God and the precious saints, they grant the request of everyone. We go to these saints to plead for things. They are better than the doctors... I had a child who was dying, so I said, "I'll go to the grave of Rabbi Abner Ha-Sarfati..." Then I went close to the grave and took a handful of earth. I mixed it with water and strained it through a strainer and gave it to him [the child] to drink until his belly was full, and I rubbed him all over with this water... I gave him food and since then he has improved.
>
> You see, this shows that the saint is better than the doctor. If you believe in God, He will help you. Look, just the dust of the saint cured him, and the doctor gave him many medicines and they didn't help.

His annual hilloula (death anniversary) takes place on 8 *Tishri* in the Jewish calendar.

Lalla Sol Ha-Tseddiqa

Lalla Sol Ha-Tseddiqa, also known as Sol Hachuel or Lalla Suleika, was born in Tangier in 1817 and martyred in 1834 at the age of 17. She is one of the most famous female saints among both Jews and Muslims in Morocco. She was born to a very religious family, and her father was a merchant and scholar of the Talmud. She was known for her striking beauty and her firm religiosity.

The details of her martyrdom vary. Some say she was cleaning in her neighbourhood one day, where she caught the attention of one of her Muslim neighbours. The neighbour took her to his home and commanded her to marry him, or he would lie and say that she converted and subsequently renounced Islam—a punishable crime. Others say that Lalla Suleika was approached by the governor of Tangier, but she refused his advances and he claimed that she falsely converted to Islam. The most popular legend recounts that she was accused by her female Muslim neighbour of converting to Islam, which she subsequently denied due to her strong faith.

The story spread, and the governor of Tangier had Lalla Suleika arrested. She was forced to kneel before the governor, and he offered her safety and wealth if she affirmed her conversion to Islam. She refused, boldly testifying to her Jewish faith. The governor sent Lalla Suleika to the Sultan in Fes. The Sultan summoned the Jewish sages of Fes and warned that if the young girl did not convert, she would be executed and the Jewish community punished. The rabbis tried to convince her to convert for the sake of the community but she remained steadfast in testifying her Jewish faith. She was condemned to death and beheaded in a public square in Fes. It is said that her last words were the *shema*, the testification of faith in God. The Jewish community had to pay for her body, head, and the bloodstained earth where she was killed.

She was instantly declared a martyr. Her tombstone bears Hebrew and Jewish descriptions. The French text reads:

> Here rests Mademoiselle Solica Hachuel born in Tangier in 1817, refusing to enter into the Islamic religion. The Arabs murdered her in 1834 in Fes, while she was torn away from her family. The entire world mourns this saintly child.

Lalla Suleika is primarily visited by women, both Jewish and Muslim, who have issues in conceiving or bearing a child. She is also known to be visited by those seeking healing. Like the tombs of the other two tzidiqim of Fes, her grave is known to be illuminated by a divine light during the night.

> If you are interested in the story of Lalla Suleika, the novel *The Road to Fes* by Ruth Knaffo Setton is worth reading. The story revolves around the journey of 18-year-old Brit Lek, an American woman—born to Sephardic-Jewish parents—who makes a pilgrimage to Fes to visit the tomb of Lalla Suleika, the dying wish of her late mother.

Rabbi Yehuda Ben-Attar

Rabbi Yehuda Ben-Attar was born in 1655 and died in 1733. He was already named and considered a saint during his lifetime. While Mūlay Idrīs II is considered the Muslim patron saint of Fes, Rabbi Yehuda Ben-Attar is considered the Jewish patron saint of Fes. Muslims visit his tomb as well. He is also known as Rabbi Yehuda al-Kabir (Rabbi Yehuda the Great) and Rabbi el-Kabir (the Great Rabbi). Visitors would often go to the tomb of the rabbi weekly, and noticed a brilliant light illuminating the tombs of all three Jewish saints of Fes. It was said that a sentence passed by any rabbi without his signature or blessing was invalid. He is famous for settling a case between a Muslim and Jewish merchant in which the Jew cheated the Muslim out of his pay. Rabbi Yehuda ruled in favour of the Muslim merchant according to Jewish law, thus earning the favour of the local Muslim community for his justice and equanimity.

Darih

Ḍarīḥ Mūlay Abū Bakr ibn al-ʿArabi

This ḍarīḥ houses the Imam Abū Bakr ibn al-ʿArabī al-Muʿāfarī (468/469–543 AH). His full name was Abū Bakr and Abū Yaḥyā Muḥammad ibn ʿAbdullāh ibn Muḥammad ibn ʿAbdullāh ibn Aḥmad al-Muʿāfarī, though he was famous as Ibn al-ʿArabī. He was born in the city of Ishbiliyah in al-Andalus in the year 468 or 469 AH. He was the last great imam of the scholarly tradition of al-Andalusia and its seal (*khatm*).

When he turned seventeen he travelled with his father to the East and they first went to Syria, where he met and studied fiqh with Shaykh Abū Bakr Muḥammad ibn Walīd al-Tartūshī. Then, in the year 489, he travelled to the Hijaz where he met and studied with numerous shaykhs, and travelled twice to Baghdad where he accompanied Abū Bakr al-Shāshī and Abū Ḥāmid al-Ghazālī. He also met a number of the scholars of Damascus, such as Abū Fatḥ Naṣr al-Muqaddasī, and in Egypt he met with Abū al-Ḥassan al-Khalʿī.

He then moved for a time to Iskander in Egypt. It is there that his father passed away in the year 493, prompting Imam Abū Bakr to finally make his return to Andalusia, with a vast collection of knowledge from his travels as had never been seen before in the West (Morocco).

On account of this, when he settled back in his country he swiftly became very famous, and the local people would travel to visit and learn from him, or to receive his counsel regarding their affairs. His fame eventually became so great that he garnered the nickname Khizānat al-ʿIlm (the storehouse of knowledge), as well as the nickname "the Quṭb of the West".

He was also recorded as being a very pious and generous man who would spend a great deal of his own wealth in the way of God. One of the best recorded examples of this is that he paid for the walls which surround the city of Ishbiliyah from his own pocket.

He authored numerous books, among them *Aḥkām al-Quran* in two versions, the lesser and the greater; *al-ʿAwāsim min al-Qawāsim*, a book that discusses the different sects of Islam and Islamic history; a commentary on the *Muwatta* of Imam Mālik; *al-Nāsikh wa al-Mansūkh min al-Quran*, which discusses verses of abrogation in the Quran; *Anwār al-Fajr Fī Tafsīr al-Quran*, a book of Quranic exegesis which reportedly took him twenty years to compile, and many, many more.

In the year 528 he was made the judge of Ishbiliyah. However, he also gained a certain degree of notoriety for the severity of his rulings. One famous story related about him is that he once passed by a man carrying a glass of wine, and when he asked about this man he was told that he owned a Christian slave girl and he had purchased the wine for her. Imam Abū Bakr then contemplated the affair for a moment, before raising his head and declaring, "The Prophet ﷺ cursed wine ten times...!"[5] He then cursed the man and ordered that all those under his jurisdiction in Ishbiliyah should curse him, which they did and continued to do throughout the country. Eventually, the severity of his rulings

5 Unto the end of the hadith.

inspired such contempt from the people of Ishbiliyah that they ransacked his house and stole all his possessions and books. Imam Abū Bakr later commented that if he hadn't hidden himself in the women's quarter of his home he would have certainly been martyred that day.

Among those who studied with him were Shaykh Qāḍī ʿĪyād, Shaykh ʿAlī ibn Ḥirzihim, Abū Qāsim al-Suhaylī, Abū Bakr ibn Khayr, and other figures of similar magnitude in the realm of scholarship. Sidi Abū Bakr ibn al-ʿArabī was famous for his mastery of the outward sciences but not as much for his mastery of the inward, though Shaykh Mūlay al-ʿArabī al-Darqāwī did in fact count Abū Bakr as among the important people of the Sufi way.

He was poisoned during a journey from Murrākesh near the outskirts of Fes, and so he was carried into the city to be buried, where eventually he was laid to rest in the Bāb al-Mahrūq.

Today, the ḍarīḥ is open throughout the week for visitors. It is popular among locals who seek the baraka of Mūlay Abū Bakr ibn al-ʿArabi. There are often several beggars outside the complex, and it is adab to offer them something before proceeding to greet the walī. There is an old woman living as caretaker inside the complex, and she is happy to answer any questions, provided the visitor can speak Arabic.

Masajid

Masjid al-Ḥamrāʾ

The origin of the name "al-Ḥamrāʾ" is a mystery. There are no decorative or architectural elements which highlight the significance of this name. Legend has it that it comes from the supposed founder of the masjid, a red (*ḥamrāʾ*) woman from the south of Morocco. However, historical evidence suggests that this masjid was established by the Merinid Sultan Abū Inan in the 14th century. It is a plainly decorated mosque with a rich and ornate mihrāb.

This is the main masjid of Fes Jdid. All five prayers are offered here daily, including juma' prayer on Fridays. A reading of a hizb of Quran is offered daily after the fajr and maghrib prayers.

Synagogues

Synagogue al-Fasiyinem, "Salat al-Fasiyine"

This synagogue, also known as "Salat al-Fasiyine", was used by the native *toshavim* Jews of Fes, those Jews who lived in Fes before the arrival of the expelled Jews, *megorashim*, from Spain in the 15th century. The synagogue was built in the 17th century. A small entrance leads to the prayer hall, and two separate staircases lead to separate seating for women above. Over the years, it fell out of use as a synagogue and was used as a workshop for carpets and inhabited by a family. The family eventually sold the property, and the new owner used the space as a private gym, using the four central pillars as the support for a boxing ring. It is said that the owner of the gym, in honouring the sacred memory of the synagogue, would light candles on the Sabbath despite not being Jewish.

This synagogue was restored thanks to the initiative of Mr. Simon Levy, the former general secretary of the Judeo-Moroccan Heritage Foundation, the Jewish community of Fes, the Jacques Toledano Foundation and the Foreign Affairs Ministry of Germany. The restoration was carried out in 2010–2011. The synagogue was reopened and inaugurated in 2013 with the blessing of King Mohammad VI.

In the back of the synagogue is a small collection of items and pictures displaying the history and restoration of the building.

Synagogue Ibn Danan

This synagogue dates from the 17th century and was built by Mimoun ben Sidan, a wealthy Moroccan merchant. It is heavily influenced by Islamic and Moroccan patterns and designs; the seating was painted with geometric patterns common in Islamic architecture. The synagogue is named after a rabbinical family that goes back 50 generations. The *bimah*, or raised platform where the Torah was read, sits opposite the Torah Ark, known as *Aron Kodesh*, where the 17th century Torah scroll is still kept. In the basement, there is a *mikvah*, a pool used for ritual bathing in Judaism.

While the Salat al-Fasiyine was attended by the toshavim, the attendants of the Ibn Danan synagogue were megorashim. There was a difference in language, liturgy, and custom between these two synagogues.

The synagogue underwent an initial renovation in the 19th century. It was closed for services during World War II, and severely deteriorated in the succeeding decades. The plaster was peeling, the waterlogged beams were rotting, and the walls and windows were broken and vandalised. The World Monument Fund, in partnership with Morocco's Ministry of Culture, the Jewish community of Fes, the Judeo-Moroccan Cultural Heritage Foundation, American Express, and private donors, worked to restore the building. A major restoration project began in the 1980s and the synagogue was reopened in 1999 and visited by King Charles III in 2011 on a visit to Fes.

Places of Interest in Fes Jdid and the Mellah

The House of Charles de Foucauld

The famous French explorer and Catholic priest Charles de Foucauld lived in Fes for several weeks in the summer of 1883. De Foucauld served as an officer in the French military in Algeria. After leaving the army, he decided to travel independently in North Africa. Due to restrictions on Europeans travelling in Morocco, de Foucauld disguised himself as a Jewish rabbi, calling himself "Rabbi Joseph." This was a very risky expedition, but de Foucauld was committed to exploring Morocco. Travelling with a Jewish companion named Mordecai, he was greeted by a representative of the Jewish community of Fes. He travelled across Morocco pretending to be a Jewish rabbi, eventually reaching the Algerian border and crossing into Algeria successfully.

"Rabbi Joseph" was certainly an oddity among the Jews of Fes, as he did not know certain basic prayers, recite the Torah, or understand the manners of synagogue worship. De Foucauld later went on to become a Catholic priest, living in Algeria among the Taureg and composing an essential dictionary of the local language. He was killed in 1916 by a band of thieves attempting to rob him.

The Jewish Cemetery of Fes: Bayt al-Khayam

The Jewish cemetery is a cornerstone of the Mellah. The original Jewish cemetery was located under the nearby square of the royal palace. During the expansion of the royal palace in the 17th century, the cemetery was moved to its current location. The cemetery is known in Hebrew as Bayt al-Khayam, the "House of the Living." This is rooted in the central notion in Jewish thought of life after death.

The cemetery, besides the graves, contains an active museum, housed in the former Habarim synagogue, which is opened upon request and prior arrangement with the groundskeeper. The museum features a unique collection of items left by or donated to the Jewish community. It serves as a unique and eclectic record of the Jewish community of Fes—those who remain and those who have left.

Around the grounds, you will also encounter a *genizah*, a storehouse for keeping worn out sacred texts that can no longer be used, and a *bayt mekhitza*, where the bodies are cleaned and prepared for burial.

The cemetery is still in use today, and many people visit to pay their respects to the three patron tzidiqim, the rabbis of Fes, or their ancestors. It is common for people to leave stones, olive pits, or water at Muslim and Jewish graves, which has roots in Amazigh culture and visitation practice. Placing candles at graves, which symbolises the continuing life of the deceased, is particularly common in Jewish grave visitation. Judaism generally discourages excessive grave visitation. Being a strictly monotheistic faith, there is a concern that the mourners would pray to the dead, rather than God. Despite this, occasional grave visitation is encouraged, particularly to keep the memory of ancestors alive.

There are various opinions among Jewish scholars as to when graves may or may not be visited. Grave visitation is often encouraged on certain holidays, such as Erev Rosh Chodesh, but is discouraged at other times, such as the middle days of Passover, or Purim, as these are holy days of joy. If one has not visited a cemetery in 30 days, the following blessing should be addressed to the deceased:

> Praised be the Eternal, our God, the Ruler of the Universe who created you in judgement, who maintained and sustained you in judgement, and brought death upon you in judgement; who knows the deeds of every one of you in judgement, and who will hereafter restore you to life in judgement. Praised be the Eternal who will restore life to the dead.

It is encouraged to study or read a Jewish text, such as the *Mishnah*, at a grave for several minutes. Several chapters from the Psalms are often read at a grave, particularly Psalms 23 or 119. There are also specific prayers for mourning and for the deceased, such as the Mourner's Kaddish and the Kel Maleh Rachamim, the Prayer for the Soul of the Departed.

The Tzidiqim

Including the three Jewish patron tzidiqim, there are nineteen Jewish tzidiqim of Fes scattered throughout the cemetery in total. They are often visited on Mondays or Thursdays. They are also visited during the hilloula, usually held on the anniversary of his or her death. Tradition says that these tombs are always mysteriously illuminated with pillars of light by the Divine Presence.

Aside from Rabbi Abner Ha-Tsarfati, Rabbi Yehuda Ben-Attar, and Lalla Sol Ha-Tseddiqa, the other 16 Jewish saints buried here are:

- Aharon Monsonego
- David Haqadmon
- Hayyim Cohen
- Iza Cohen
- Lalla Cohen
- Mattityahu Serero
- Menashe ibn-Danan
- Moshe Ha-Cohen

- Raphael Aben-Tsur
- Sepher Zabaro
- Shaul Serero
- Shelomoh ibn-Danan
- Vidal Ha-Tsarfati
- Yaʿqob Qadosh
- Yaʿqob Qanizel
- Yehonathan Serero

Old City Walls

The ancient city ramparts were an essential defensive element of the medina and Fes Jdid and served to protect the people of the city. They are an integral sampling of important Moroccan military architecture, and the skills of the local craftsmen passed down through the generations ensured strong ramparts. While the royal palace, Fes Jdid, and the medina are self-contained areas, the building styles of the ramparts are similar. They are marked by the *tabiya* technique, which consists of using different materials—a combination of earth, lime, and stone—with a detachable wooden framework. This is a very common Moroccan building style. Beyond defending the city, these ramparts served to delimit the city boundaries, revealing the traditional urban local mindset. The city ended at the ramparts, and one immediately entered the countryside. The city ramparts are dotted with a variety of important central gates, highlighted elsewhere in this text.

Bāb Sammarine

This gate was formerly known as "ʿUyun Sanhaja," or, "The Springs of the Sanhaja tribe." This magnificent gate dates back to the founding of Fes Jdid in the 13th century. In the 20th century, the gate was modified to accommodate vehicle and pedestrian traffic. Before this, there was an indirect entrance and the gate was adorned with domes. The outer façade presents a solid semi-circular arch, reinforced by a decorative multi-foiled arch. A band of intertwining geometrical shapes surrounds the gate. These elements reveal the grace and attention to detail of the traditional local craftsmen.

Royal Palace Gates

These gates offer a glimpse of the hidden splendour of the royal palace. It was constructed in the 1960s under the reign of King Ḥassan II. The greatest local craftsmen were employed in the construction of this façade. It is an excellent example of the essential elements of Moroccan art—smoothness, symmetry, repetition, and Moroccan-Andalusian infusion. The decorative arches, the white marble columns with stylised capitals, bronze gilded frames, and masterfully set zillij are not to be glanced over quickly. The majority of the royal palace complex is off-limits and well-guarded. The beauty of the massive complex can only be tasted at its gates.

Suq Fes Jdid

The Grand Rue de Fes Jdid is the main artery of Fes Jdid and the main suq and economic hub of this section of the city. Suq Fes Jdid offers a vast array of traditional clothing for both men and women alongside many modern clothing and shoe stores. Besides this, there are also a variety of cafés, sandwich shops, and hanuts lining the suq. This is a good place to shop for traditional clothing and to experience a non-touristic market at an interesting intersection between traditional and modern suq offerings.

Garden Jnan Sabil

Garden Jnan Sabil is a relaxing oasis of greenery nestled between the medina and Fes Jdid. It covers an area of about seven hectares and is split in two parts by the river. This area, which was formerly an Almohad fortress, was transformed into an imperial park in the 19th century. At the beginning of the 20th century, it was turned into a public space and remains a very popular relaxation spot for locals to this day. It is an attractive weekend and afternoon destination for locals. There is a variety of greenery, including orange, lemon, pomegranate, and myrtle trees. The park occasionally hosts music festivals.

Kasbah Shararda

The Kasbah Shararda lies just north of the ancient ramparts of Fes Jdid. This is a massive enclosure (14 hectares) adorned with massive walls and looming guard towers. It was built by the ʿAlawite Sultan Mūlay Rashīd in the 17th century, and was designed for house members of the tribe of "Sharaga" who were tasked with maintaining peace and order in the Fes medina. The kasbah also housed other tribes such as the Udayas and the Sharardas, the namesake of the kasbah. Today, the kasbah hosts a hospital complex. This location offers a glimpse of traditional kasbah architecture and fortifications, which were important to military culture across Morocco.

Borj Nord

There are two fortresses which flank the medina—Borj Nord and Borj Sud. Both fortresses were built in the 16th century by Sultan Aḥmad al-Mansūr. Rather than being built to defend the city from invasion, they were built to keep the potential dangerous and disloyal people of Fes from revolting. The fortress was inspired by the Portuguese fortresses of the era, and was also used as a cannon factory. Borj Nord served as a barracks and prison during the French Protectorate. Today, it houses a weaponry museum which is open to the public.

During Ramadan, false shots fired from the cannons of Borj Nord signal the end of suhūr and the beginning of iftār. During this time, rather than wait for the adhān, the people of the medina wait for the cannon shot, which can be heard throughout the medina.

The Merinid Tombs

These tombs were once constructed to house the graves of important personages dating from the Merinid period. Though they were once magnificently adorned and decorated, these 14th century tombs are now mere shells of their former glory. There is no ziyārah activity associated with them. The main attraction of this area is the views. This is one of the best spots to catch a panorama of the medina and beautiful sunset shots. If you are lucky, you will also catch tanners laying out their hides to dry in the morning sun. Unfortunately, the area has become something of a garbage dump. There is both an easily discernible walking path and paved road that leads up to the Merinid Tombs.

Moroccan Judaism

Early History: "The Golden Age"

The Jews of Fes were once a thriving, productive, and well-connected community, and one of the most significant Jewish communities in Morocco and wider North Africa. The Jews of Fes were present at the founding of the city. Mūlay Idrīs II, the founder of Fes, opened his new capital to Jewish settlers in exchange for normal taxation on *dhimmi* populations protected under Islamic law. The Jews were allowed a great deal of economic freedom and many became prosperous. Fes soon became a great intellectual and cultural centre and was home to many early and important Jewish scholars such as Dunash ben Labarat and David ben Abraham al-Fāsī. During the 12th century, Fes was also home to the distinguished Jewish philosopher Moses ben Maimon, or Maimonides, who settled in Fes from 1159 to 1165 after fleeing Almohad persecution of non-Muslims in southern Spain. The Jews of Fes were able to flourish alongside their Muslim neighbours.

In 1244, with the establishment of the Merinid dynasty, the Jews were able to flourish once more. Under the Merinids, Fes was reinstated as the capital of the dynasty and expanded to become one of the largest cities in the world at the time. The rulers supported education and cultural activities, establishing many of Fes' great madāris. While the Merinids supported Islamic scholarship and cultural development, the Jews also flourished in economic and religious affairs. The Jews continued to live largely integrated with their Muslim neighbours in the old city. However, towards the end of Merinid rule, the Jews were forced to live in a separate, allocated Jewish quarter, the Mellah.

Despite the early golden age of Judaism in Fes, there were several disasters and setbacks. In 1033, following the conquest of the city by the Banu Ifrane Amazigh tribe after the fall of the Idrīssīd dynasty, there was a massacre of Jews. Over six thousand Jews were killed, their properties ransacked and stolen, and their women and daughters captured. In the following century, large parts of the city were destroyed by the Almoravids, which proved disastrous for the entire city. In 1276, there was another massacre of Jews in reaction to the preferential treatment afforded the Jewish community by the Merinid sultan.

The Jews of Morocco: A History of a People

The history of Judaism in North Africa is long and rich, a history of which many are unaware. The Jews of Morocco were largely well-integrated and essential in Moroccan society, often playing important roles in trade, finance, and governance. At other times, the community faced severe persecution. While the Jewish population of Morocco has severely declined in recent decades due to emigration to Israel, Europe, and North America, Morocco was home to the largest Jewish community in the Muslim world before the founding of the State of Israel.

There are many legends among both Moroccan Jews and Muslims which seek to explain Jewish origins in Morocco. One legend suggests that in ancient times, groups of rabbis came to North Africa from the Holy Land to spread Judaism. Another legend states that Joab, a Jewish hero, was sent to Morocco to fight the Philistines who had been driven out of Canaan. The early history remains shrouded in speculation. While the exact origin of Jewish communities in northwest Africa remains unclear, oral traditions place the arrival of early Jews with Phoenician traders to North Africa and after the destruction of Solomon's Temple in Jerusalem in 587 BC. The majority of Jews most likely arrived after the Roman conquest of Judea in present day Israel/Palestine and the first failed Jewish revolt of 66 CE. Jews dispersed throughout the Roman Empire, even settling in the Roman provinces of northwest Africa.

The Jewish communities of North Africa were generally allowed to flourish under Roman rule. They were integrated into the Roman cities of North Africa, and remnants of Hebrew tombstones have even been found at Volubilis (Walīli) near Meknes, a once-bustling Roman city. Eventually, Jewish communities mixed among the native Amazigh population. The presence of both

Jewish and Christian communities and Amazigh tribes is often traced back to the era of Roman rule in Morocco. A number of tribes purportedly converted to Judaism over time. While the "Judaization" of Amazigh tribes is a contested theory, it remains popular among locals. Whether indigenous Amazigh converted to Judaism, or whether Jewish migrants adopted Amazigh language and culture is still debated. Others attribute the development of Amazigh Jewish communities to the persecution and migration of Jews to the Atlas Mountains under the Byzantines in the 6th century and the Almohads in the 12th century. These communities spoke Judeo-Amazigh, a dialect of Amazigh which was heavily influenced by Hebrew loan words. Across the Arabic-speaking world, Jewish communities in each region developed their own unique mixed dialects, due to the variety of rich linguistic confluences. In Morocco, both Judeo-Moroccan Arabic and Judeo-Amazigh developed as dialects.

After the Umayyad conquests of North Africa in the seventh and eighth centuries, and after the development of the Idrīssīd dynasty in the eighth century, the process of Islamization spread rapidly across Morocco and North Africa. While several Jewish communities were hostile to and actively resisted Arab invasion, several Jewish tribes participated in the Idrīssīd conquest of Morocco, thus taking an active role in early Moroccan political history. Under Idrīs II, Jews were subject to a special tax and were thus allowed to settle in the capital of Fes and other cities. With relative economic freedom, these communities were allowed to prosper and contribute to the social life of these important and developing urban centres, particularly Fes.

The fate of the Jewish community of Morocco was subject to the great volatility of Moroccan dynastic history. After the fall of the Idrīssīd dynasty, there was a period of social and political instability as various tribes vied for power. In 1033, a massacre of

Fes' Jews occurred as several Amazigh tribes sought control of the city. A Sanhaja Amazigh confederation, later known as the Almoravid dynasty, soon rose to power. They spread rapidly across the region, choosing Murrākesh as their capital. While the Jews were allowed to prosper under Almoravid rule, there was increasing hostility towards Jewish communities. Although Jews were allowed to trade in the capital, they were not allowed to establish residence there. Despite this, many important religious texts were written under the Almoravids, inspiring some to label this as a "Golden Age" of Jewish thought.

Under the Almohad dynasty, successors to the Almoravids, the Jewish community of Morocco fared much worse. Led by Ibn Tumart in the 12th and 13th century, many Jews in Morocco and Andalusia were forced to convert or flee to avoid persecution and execution. Maimonides, for example, fled Almohad persecution in Andalusia, stopping in Fes and eventually travelling to Egypt. Jews were often forced to wear special clothing to set them apart, for easy identification. Several scholars, however, challenge this narrative of systemic Jewish persecution under the Almohads, saying it is an exaggeration based on few historical sources.

The Almohads were succeeded by the Merinids. The Merinids ruled Morocco from the 13th to the 15th century and Moroccan Jews fared well under their control. The Merinid sultan Abū Yūsuf Yaʿqub ibn ʿAbd al-Ḥaqq often intervened on behalf of the Jews, providing them protection and immunity in times of conflict. Jewish ambassadors from Spain were entertained by the royal court, and Jews were welcomed as royal advisors. While the Merinids were actively concerned with promoting Islamic scholarship, Jewish scholarship also flourished, particularly in the fields of mysticism and philosophy. However, the implementation of the Mellah, which segmented Jewish communities and eventually led to a process of ghettoization, also began under the Merinids, starting in the capital of Fes. The Jewish community was attacked in 1465, when the Merinids were overthrown after attempting to appoint a Jewish wazir in Fes.

The Merinid dynasty was soon replaced by the politically unstable Wattisid dynasty, which ruled for under a century. During this time there was extensive Portuguese expansion along the Moroccan coastline. Following Queen Isabella's Edict of Expulsion in 1492, waves of tens of thousands of Sephardic Jewish fled to Morocco. While this exodus of Jews to North Africa began several centuries earlier, it accelerated in the late 15th century. The Wattisid dynasty did little to assist or prevent this influx. While many of these Jews continued eastward, particularly to parts of the Ottoman Empire, a new Jewish community settled across Morocco's urban centres.

Under the later Saadian and ʿAlawite dynasties, Moroccan Jews faced periods of harassment and success. At times, Jews took a greater role in royal affairs as diplomats, emissaries, physicians, and translators. At other times, particularly under the ʿAlawite sultans Mūlay Yazīd and Mūlay Ismaʿīl, there were open attacks upon Moroccan Jews across the country. Despite this, the Moroccan Jews continued to flourish and led very active lives in religious scholarship, trade, and diplomatic work.

Origins of the Mellah: Persecution and Survival

The story of the Mellah is central to the history the Jewish community of Fes. Established in 1438 by order of the sultan, the Mellah was established to concentrate the Jews of Fes in a single area in close proximity to the royal palace. Before this, the Jewish community was clustered in the north of the old city, near Bāb al-Gheesa in a neighbourhood known as Funduq al-yuhud, which means "the Hostel of the Jews." Today, no significant remnants of

Jewish heritage exist in the Funduq al-yuhud neighbourhood of the old city.

The term Mellah is etymologically connected to the Arabic word for salt. The origins of how this term came to be associated with the Jewish community are varied and disputed. Some say that it arose from the practice of forcing Jews to salt the heads of executed prisoners. Others say it originated from unique food preservation practices of the Jewish community or Jewish involvement in the local salt trade. The site was also known to be built on a salt mine, and the name remained after the relocation of the Jews. Despite the origins of the name, the Mellah of Fes was the first Mellah of Morocco and set a precedent for the creation of similar communities across Morocco. Many Moroccan cities that once hosted a significant Jewish community developed a Mellah (though not all). This process of relocating Moroccan Jews to specific quarters was accelerated across Morocco in the 19th century under Sultan Mūlay Sulaymān.

The Mellah was established to concentrate the Jewish community near the centre of power, the royal palace. This occurred for a number of reasons. Originally, life in the Mellah was seen as a protection and honour, given the fortified protection from Arab attacks. Proximity to the palace made it possible for Jews to take refuge within the royal compound. Additionally, many Jews were involved in political life as ambassadors and translators, and their proximity to the centre of power was essential.

Despite this, relocation to the Mellah became a process of ghettoization. In time, the Mellah became a miserable place due to an expanding population, rising poverty, and the loss of certain freedoms. There was also a lack of adequate housing, leading to the development of a unique style of architecture in the Mellah that was not traditionally found in the old city. While the traditional houses of the old city usually centred on an open-air courtyard, the housing in the Mellah did not follow this design. Alternatively, balconies were developed to allow fresh air and sunlight into the house.

The Mellah was not always successfully defended from attacks or riots. In 1465, the sultan attempted to appoint a Jew, Harūn, as wazir. The inhabitants revolted, overthrowing the Merinid dynasty and massacring a large portion of the Jewish community of Fes. This sparked a wave of violence against Jews across Morocco during a time of great political ferment.

In the 15th century, waves of Sephardic Jews fled to Morocco from the Reconquista occurring in the Iberian Peninsula. While Jews expelled from Visigothic Spain in the 7th century also settled in Morocco, the influx of Jews in the 15th century produced massive social and cultural shifts in the Moroccan Jewish community. The Jewish community of Fes was divided into two separate communities; the toshavim, or the native Jews who, according to oral tradition, arrived in Morocco after the destruction of the First Temple in Israel and lived among the Amazigh tribes, and the megorashim, the Jews expelled from Spain in the 15th century. This wave in the 15th century brought a large influx to the Jewish population of Morocco. Fes became a centre for Jewish immigration and settlement. Immediately, there were many tensions between the toshavim and the megorashim. The megorashim, who were often very well-educated and wealthy, included scholars, painters, and artisans whose work transformed local Jewish culture. The toshavim spoke Arabic while the megorashim spoke Castilian Spanish. Intermarriage was often discouraged, and different religious rites were accentuated by the development of separate synagogues for the communities.

Despite the differences, this influx assisted the Jewish community of Fes. The megorashim brought intellectual, cultural, and economic revival, and established several yeshivot, or Jewish religious schools. Many famous and significant rabbis came out of Fes between the 16th and 18th centuries. With increasing European presence in Morocco, the linguistic expertise of these Jews was often sought by political leaders, advancing the status of many members of the Jewish community. The megorashim came to redefine the Jewish community of Fes, giving it a new, Iberian-influenced flavour. Fes began to decline in economic and political importance towards the end of the 16th century. During this time, many wealthy Jews left Fes and its Spanish character was lost. Jews developed different economic outlets, becoming involved in the manufacturing of thread and embroidery, tailoring, and metalworking.

After the rise of the ʿAlawite dynasty in the 17th century, the Jewish community continued to face harassment. Under Mūlay Ismaʿīl, Jews were largely protected, though heavily taxed. Under one of Mūlay Ismaʿīl's successors, Mūlay Yazīd, attacks on the Mellahs of Morocco, especially Fes, were encouraged. He ordered the Jews to leave the Mellah of Fes for two years; an effective exile that was disastrous for the community. The Jews were eventually allowed to return and rebuild their lives in the Mellah. After this, the life of the community improved and scholarly activity in Fes was reawakened through the establishment of several yeshivot.

The Present Day: Emigration and Memory

With the expansion of European influence and presence in Morocco in the 19th century, many Jews took advantage of the cultural and economic opportunities available. With European encouragement, in 1864 Sultan Mūlay Muḥammad issued a decree affirming the equality of Jews under the law. The Alliance Israelite Universelle, a Paris-based organisation which aimed to preserve and develop the Jewish people globally, established a school in

Fes. This school encouraged the assimilation of Moroccan Jews into French culture and language well before the establishment of the French Protectorate in Morocco in 1912. Because of this, many Jews were in a good economic position, though they were also seen as conspirators with the French, earning further scorn and persecution. Under French rule, the situation of the Jews did not drastically change. In 1912, a Moroccan military rebellion against French occupation resulted in a three-day assault on the Fes Mellah, resulting in the loss of many homes and shops, the death of at least 50 Jews, and the injury of dozens more. This event is often referred to as the Fes Pogrom of 1912. After this, many Jews began to leave the Mellah for the newly established Ville Nouvelle, the French-built, French-styled new city of Fes.

After World War II, Moroccan Jews faced further difficulties. This was exacerbated by a wave of attacks on the Jewish community of Morocco in 1948. During these difficult times, Sultan Muḥammad V warned against anti-Jewish violence, citing the rich and long Jewish history of Morocco. With the growing struggle for Moroccan independence in the 1950s, Jews were often suspected of collaboration with the French. After the foundation of the state of Israel in 1948 and growing anti-Jewish sentiments in the Arab world in the wake of the Arab-Israeli war, many Moroccan Jews emigrated out of Morocco—to Israel, France, or Canada. Today, the Jewish community of Fes, and Morocco at large, has severely dwindled. While the Jewish population of Morocco was over 250,000 before the founding of the state of Israel, the Jewish community is now under 3,000. Most contemporary Moroccan Jews are based in Casablanca and Rabāt, though small communities still exist elsewhere. In Fes, there are less than 100 Jews left from a community that once numbered around 20,000. All of the Jews live in the Ville Nouvelle, and there are no Jews remaining in the Mellah.

Today, the Mellah is a museum and a testament to the long memory of the Jewish community of Fes and Morocco. Their stories and activities are interwoven with the spiritual history of the city, and reveal a unique and diverse element of Fes; one of the most historically important cities of the Islamic world.

◀ Tombstone of Sol Hachuel with inscriptions in Hebrew and French.

◀ Bab Semmarine, the main southern gate of Fes Jdid. From here a street goes south towards the entrance of the Mellah, which was oriented towards this gate.

▶ Next page on the left, the tombs of Jews buried in the Jewish Cemetery of the Mellah. On the right, the main gates of the Royal Palace.

▼ Interior of the Al-Fassiyine Synagogue or Slat Al-Fassiyine.

▲ The Merinid tombs of Fes overlook the main medina.

◀ The main avenue of the gardens at Jnan Sbil.

▼ The Merinid tombs of Fes.

5 La Ville Nouvelle: The French New City

Ville Nouvelle

The Ville Nouvelle is the newest addition to the expansive metropolis of Fes. This city was built under French rule beginning in the early twentieth century and was meant to mirror French urban planning with wide open boulevards, tree-lined lanes, and long avenues. French-designed "ville nouvelles" are found in most major Moroccan cities such as Murrākesh, Rabāt, and Tangier. In most Moroccan cities, the French chose to preserve rather than destroy or expand the traditional medinas. This led to a policy of creating new urban centres adjacent to the old cities, which was a great blessing for historical and cultural preservation. The French built these cities and the rest of the remarkably modern infrastructural projects such as roads, railways and dams, with the intention of keeping Morocco under French dominion indefinitely. Post-independence, Morocco was left to manage both indigenous and foreign inheritances.

The Ville Nouvelle is a radically different face of Fes. One leaves the crowded, winding alleys of the cobble-stoned medina and arrives in a concrete jungle of high rises. Instead of dodging donkeys, one must avoid speeding mopeds. Instead of traditional riads, spacious apartments and glittering villas line the streets. The Ville Nouvelle is where most of the local upper-class lives—an inversion of the traditional order of the sacred city, where the elite lived in the centre of the medina, and the poorest lived on the outskirts.

For those interested in cultural and spiritual history, there is not much to see here. For those who are interested in Fes as a living city with two faces—one turned towards tradition and the other towards Europe and modernity—the Ville Nouvelle offers the latter. It is a good place to meet locals, particularly students, and to visit a posh café or restaurant while catching a glimpse of some of the contemporary local elite.

Lafayette

Lafayette is a bustling hub of the Ville Nouvelle and offers an excellent introduction to a different side of Fes. This is the gateway from the medina and Fes Jdid to the Ville Nouvelle, and offers many modern attractions, such as cafés, restaurants, bookstores, and shopping, if one is looking for a break from the medina. The biggest attraction is Borj Fes, a recently-built shopping mall offering many American and European products and chain restaurants. On weekends, the mall is booming with young Moroccans.

It is worth visiting Lafayette in the early evenings and on weekends, where families, friends, and young couples stroll along the extensive Avenue Hassan II, enjoying the open space. It is a good place to visit with children. From here, one can usually catch a red taxi to any other part of the city.

Zawaya and Awliya

Zāwiyah Shādhiliyya Darqāwiyya ʿAlawiyya

The Zāwiyah Shādhiliyya Darqāwiyya ʿAlawiyya is located in Hayy Ben Suda on the outskirts of the Ville Nouvelle. Once a separate village, Ben Suda has now become incorporated into the ever-expanding city of Fes. The zāwiyah is so far outside of town that there is a grand taxi route to Ben Suda. This zāwiyah is home to Shaykh ʿAbdullāh al-Ḥaddād, inheritor of Shaykh Budaylemī, who was the student of Shaykh Aḥmad al-ʿAlawī, the saint of Algeria made famous by Martin Lings' classic text, *A Sufi Saint of the Twentieth Century*. The zāwiyah is located in a modern building with new facilities, an open seating area, and a separate gathering area for women upstairs.

Getting there: Take a red taxi and ask for "Hayy Ben Suda." Once on the way, clarify that you would like to visit "Zāwiyah Ben Suda." The zāwiyah was once an obscure destination, but is becoming more well-known. If the driver does not know, instruct him to ask someone for further guidance at Hayy Ben Suda. Alternatively, it is possible to take a white grand taxi from outside Bāb Mahruq to Hayy Ben Suda. At your final destination, ask anyone for directions to "Zāwiyah Ben Suda."

Getting back: The Thursday night dhikr often goes on late into the night. It can be very difficult to find a taxi back to the medina. It is best to arrange a red or white taxi to wait for you, which will be slightly more expensive. Otherwise, the fuqarā of the zāwiyah can help you find the best spot to wait for a red taxi at the main road.

Outside of the formal gatherings at the zāwiyah, Shaykh ʿAbdullah al-Ḥaddād often welcomes visitors for private audiences after ʿasr. It is best to visit beforehand and arrange a private meeting with one of the caretakers and servants of the zāwiyah.

After the Thursday night dhikr, the Shaykh gives particular attention to the questions and concerns of foreign visitors. Shaykh ʿAbdullah al-Ḥaddād speaks in clear, well-paced Fusha, which is of benefit to beginner students of Arabic. There are often several foreign visitors at the zāwiyah for the weekly Thursday night dhikr.

Gatherings: On Thursday nights after ʿisha there is a dhikr gathering at the zāwiyah, which consists of the wazīfa of the ṭarīqa, recitation of several qaṣāʾid of Shaykh Aḥmad al-ʿAlawī, a ḥaḍra, Quranic recitations, and a lesson (in Arabic) offered by the Shaykh. There is a meal served after the lesson. On Friday afternoons after ʿasr, the *Dalāʾil al-Khayrāt* is read at the zāwiyah.

Masajid

Masjid Hayy Fadila

This masjid is located in the Ville Nouvelle, just off of the main road Tariq Ayn Chikaf. The masjid is rather new, and is open for all five daily prayers.

Gatherings: Every Monday–Thursday, after ʿasr and until ʿisha, there is a full reading of the *Dalāʾil al-Khayrāt* in this masjid.

Masjid Imam Mālik

This is one of the biggest and most beautiful masjids in the Ville Nouvelle. It was financed by a wealthy local businessman and opened in 1994. Situated near the train station, it is a very active hub of the Ville Nouvelle. There is a busy suq and many shops lining the street. This masjid is a good place to catch jumʿa prayer if arriving by train on Friday.

Gatherings: On Friday mornings, directly before jumʿa prayer, there is a communal recitation of Imam al-Busīrī's *Burda*. This is followed by a reading of a hizb of Quran.

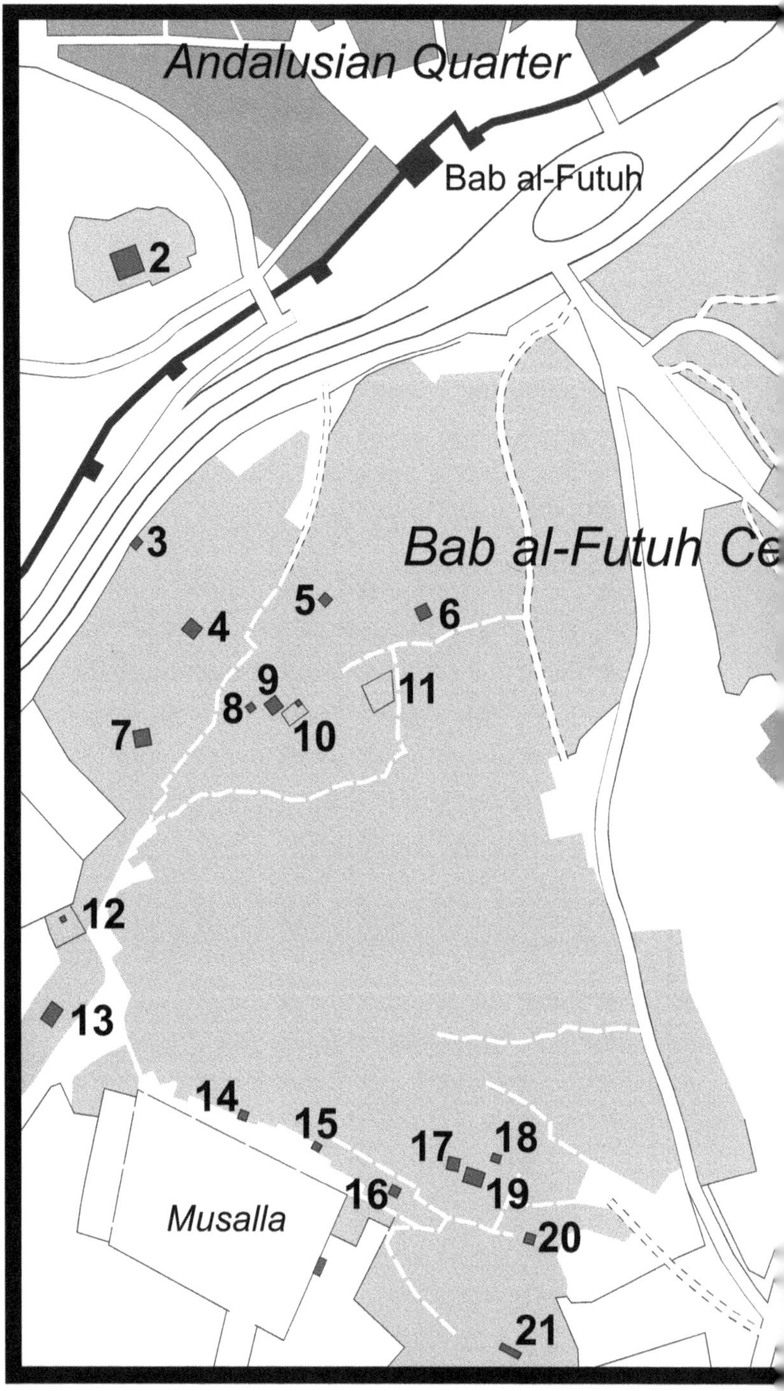
Andalusian Quarter
Bab al-Futuh
2
Bab al-Futuh Ce
3
4
5
6
7
8
9
10
11
12
13
14
15
16
17
18
19
20
21
Musalla

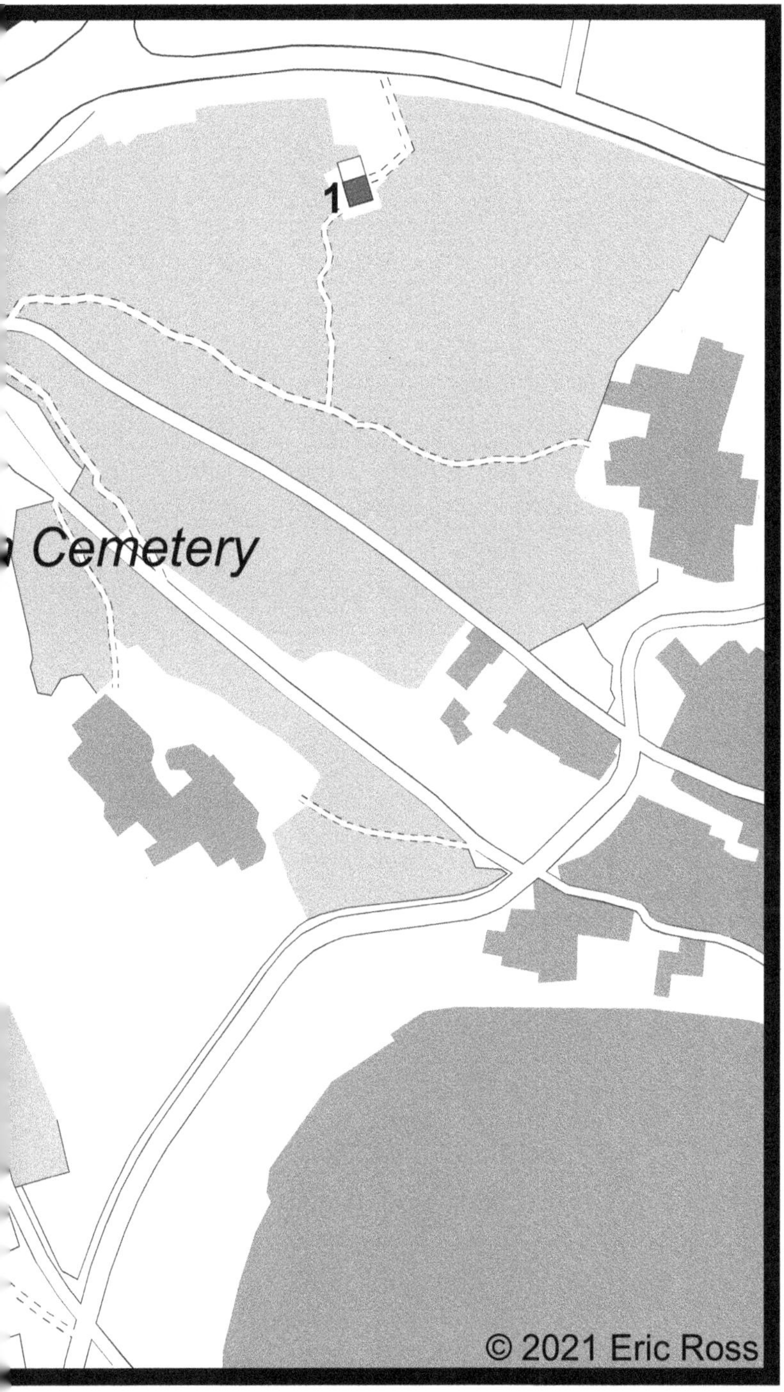

1
Cemetery
© 2021 Eric Ross

MAP LEGEND

1. Sidi ʿAlī ibn Ismāʿīl ibn Ḥirzihim
2. Rawḍa of Sidi Maḥmed ibn Ibrāhīm ibn ʿAbbād al-Nafzī (al-Rondī); Muḥammad ibn Muḥammad ibn Dāwūd ibn Ājurrūm
3. Sidi Aḥmed bel Khader
4. Sidi Darrās ibn Ismāʿīl
5. Sidi Yūnus
6. Sidi al-Ghayātī
7. ʿAbd al-ʿAzīz ibn Masʿūd al-Dabbāgh
8. Sidi ʿAydi al-Saghīr
9. Sidi ʿAbd al-Wahhāb al-Tāzī
10. Sidi ʿAydi al-Kabīr
11. Shaykh Ḥasan al-ʿIraqi
12. Sidi ʿAlī ibn Aḥmed al-Dawwār al-Ṣinhājī; Sayyidah Āminah bint Aḥmed ibn ʿAlī ibn al-Qāḍī
13. ʿAlī ibn Muḥammad Humāmūsh; Sidi al-ʿArabī ibn Aḥmed al-Fashtālī
14. ʿAbd al-Wāḥid ibn Aḥmed ibn ʿĀshir al-Anṣārī
15. Sidi ʿAbd al-Raḥmān ibn Idrīs al-Manjarah
16. Sidi Ḥusayn al-Jazūlī
17. Qāsim ibn Qāsim al-Khaṣāṣī
18. Qubbah of the Seven Shuhadā
19. Sidi Yusuf Abu al-Maḥāsin al-Fāsī al-Fihrī; ʿAbd al-Raḥmān ibn Muḥammad al-Fāsī Maḥmed ibn Maḥmed ibn ʿAbd Allāh Maʿan Aḥmed ibn Maḥmed ibn ʿAbd Allāh Maʿan Al-ʿArabī ibn Aḥmed ibn ʿAbd Allāh
20. Sidi Aḥmed al-Yamanī
21. Sidi al-ʿAttār

6
Bab al-Futuh Cemetery

Bāb al-Futūḥ literally means "the gate of victory." It is the south-eastern portal of the medina and connects the city of Fes with the great cities of the east: Taza, Tlemcen, and the road to Egypt. The gate was originally constructed in the 11th century and was expanded in the 18th century by Sultan Mūlay Sulaymān. The gate is one of the largest of the medina and is unusual in that it was designed as a direct entrance, rather than the traditional indirect entrance of Moroccan architecture. Its unadorned façade has a central arch flanked by two smaller symmetrical arches.

The Bāb al-Futūḥ cemetery, with its many domed qubbahs rising from the earth, is affectionately referred to as the garden of saints. Nestled at the south-eastern corner of the medina, it springs up just beyond the medina gate of Bāb al-Futūḥ. This cemetery has endured the test of time. Its rolling hills are studded with thousands of graves—some well-maintained while others lie buried under trash; some graves are home to world-renowned scholars while others have faded, nameless, into the earth. It is a vast, whitewashed hill that can be spotted as far away as Jebl Zalagh, the mountain looming over Fes. Of the hundreds of awliyāʾ of Fes, there are many who now call the Bāb al-Futūḥ cemetery home. It is one of the largest and most important cemeteries of Fes.

It is best to visit the cemetery with a group and during the day. The cemetery has a very negative reputation among locals, and there are many vagrants lingering around the tombs. While people are generally safe in the daylight, it is discouraged to be in the cemetery at night and to visit during the twilight hours, such as fajr and maghrib. There are no designated walking paths, and visitors must unfortunately walk over graves to visit most of the awliyāʾ buried here. It is common to visit graves on Friday mornings. At this time, there are many visitors in Bāb al-Futūḥ cemetery visiting the awliyāʾ, family members, and deceased friends, so it is recommended to go at this time, though not necessary. This guide attempts to provide the visitor with a rough walking path and proposed sequence of awliyāʾ visitation. Bāb al-Futūḥ cemetery is one of the treasures of Fes, and there are many wells of baraka for those who would make the journey to drink.

Those interested in entering the tombs should arrange a visit with representatives of the International Academic Centre for Sufi and Aesthetic Studies (IACSAS), who have access to all of the important keys. IACSAS is based in an office in the Ville Nouvelle near the Triq Ayn Shqaf. More information can be found at http://www.iacsas.org

Zawaya and Awliya

Maḥmad ibn Ibrāhīm ibn ʿAbbād al-Nafzī al-Rondī (733–792 AH)

His full name was ʿAbdullāh Maḥmad ibn Abū Isḥāq Ibrāhīm ibn Abū Bakr ʿAbdullāh ibn Mālik ibn Ibrāhīm ibn Muḥammad ibn Mālik ibn Ibrāhīm ibn Yaḥyā ibn ʿAbbād al-Nafzī al-Hamīrī. He is known simply as Ibn ʿAbbād.

Ibn ʿAbbād was born in Ronda, Spain in the year 733 AH. By seven years old he had memorised the Quran, and he then travelled to Fes and Tilimsan in pursuit of knowledge. He studied there for a time and learned Arabic, the uṣūl and fiqh, and then left for the city of Salé outside Rabāt, where he took the Sufi way from the famous Shaykh Aḥmad ibn ʿĀshir. Upon the Shaykh's death he travelled again to Fes where he attained a position as a lecturer *(khaṭīb)* at the mosque. He remained in this post for fifteen years before passing away, after which he was buried in the Bāb al-Ḥamrāʾ.

It says in *Uns al-Faqīr* (Intimacy of the Mendicant), "And among the righteous men I saw in Fes was the famous *khaṭīb* and great gnostic, Abū ʿAbdullāh Muḥammad ibn Ibrāhīm al-Rondī. His father was an eloquent *khaṭīb* (speaker), and Abū ʿAbdullāh himself was an intellectual and tranquil man, who combined asceticism with righteousness... among his marvellous sayings about the Sufi way was, 'Whoever sticks excessively to the creation, remains with it, reduces his passion on account of it, and there does not open to him the path of the unseen (mysteries) of the *Malakūt* (Angelic Realm), nor does he arrive with his secret to the space wherein is witnessed the Divine Oneness, then he is imprisoned by his surroundings, and encompassed by the altar of his essence.'

He used to attend the samāʿ celebrations on the Prophet's ﷺ birthday at the Sultan's palace, though he didn't want to, and I never saw him sitting next to somebody except at a teaching circle. It was the good fortune and fate of those who saw him to be standing exclusively with him (due to his aversion to people). If ever I sought him out to supplicate for me, his face would turn red and he would become very shy, and then supplicate for me. He took most of his pleasure in the lower world from perfumes and incenses, took care of his own self, never married and did not possess a female slave. In his home he wore nothing more then patched rags, which he would cover with a white or green djellaba upon leaving."

Ibn ʿAbbād is known internationally for his commentary on the *Ḥikam* of Ibn ʿAṭā Allāh, which is widely considered to be the best commentary on the *Ḥikam* next to that of Aḥmad Zarrūq's. Aḥmad Zarrūq in fact mentions Ibn ʿAbbād in his own commentary, saying, "He was the master of the gnostics in his time, the crème of his age, one of a kind."

Shaykh Abū Masʿūd al-Ḥarās wrote, "One night I was sitting in the courtyard of the Qarawiyyin reciting the Quran as the muʿadhins were sounding the adhān when Abū ʿAbdullāh (Ibn ʿAbbād) exited from his house and began to fly through the courtyard as if he was sitting cross-legged, until he entered the tiled area (*balāṭ*) which is near the minaret. I then went after him, and found him praying near the mihrāb."

Upon his death he willed that a bundle of wealth that he kept near his head should be given in charity to the Qarawiyyin. After his passing, when they inspected the bundle they found it to contain the entirety of what he had earned from his fifteen years of lecturing in the Qarawiyyin.

Muḥammad ibn Muḥammad ibn Dāwūd ibn Ājurrūm (672–723 AH)

His full name was Abū ʿAbdullāh Muḥammad ibn Muḥammad ibn Dāwūd al-Ṣinhājī (from Ṣanhāja in the provinces of Sefrou) al-Fāsī, though he was known as Ibn Ājurrūm. Imam al-Suyūṭī wrote a biography about him, in which he wrote:

> ... he was famous by the name Ibn Ājurrūm, which means, in the language of the Amazighs: the Sufi Faqīr. He is the author of the famous *Muqaddama* known as the *Ājurrūmiyya*, and those who wrote commentaries on his *Muqaddama* such as al-Rāʿī and al-Makūdī... described him as holding a position of imāma (authority) in grammar, as well as divine grace and righteousness. And those who bear witness to his righteousness are the great multitude who have benefitted beginners of grammar by use of his *Muqaddama*...
>
> And another thing is, I personally understood from reading his *Muqaddama* that he was a follower of the Kufan school. For, he expressed himself by use of Khafdh (خفض), which is how they did, and he wrote that the ʿamr is majrūm. The apparent of the matter is that it is muʿarab, and this was the Kufans' opinion...

It is recorded that Ibn Ājurrūm travelled to the East and performed the Hajj pilgrimage and visited the men of the East. He met and studied with Shaykh Abū Hayān, who gave him ijāza, and wrote his famous *Muqaddama* while directly facing the Kaʿba in Makka. According to legend, after returning home he then threw it into the sea, saying, "If it was written purely for the sake of Allah, then it won't be lost!" And when he retrieved it he found that not even a word of it had been lost. He also wrote a commentary called *Sharḥ al-Amānī fī al-Qirāʾāt*, and was in addition to being a grammarian a famous Faqīh, an imam and ʿārif.

He was born in the year 672, which is the same year that Ibn Mālik, the author of the famous grammatical text *al-ʿAlīfiyya* passed away, and it is said he died in the year 723 in the month of Safar. It is said that he was buried in the Bāb al-Ḥadīd, yet it is the opinion of al-Kattānī, upon reviewing numerous texts that he was in fact buried in the Bāb al-Jiziyyīn, which today is known as the Bāb al-Ḥamrāʾ and lies to the right (from the perspective of one exiting it) of the Bāb al-Futūḥ. However, the answer to this dispute may be found in one of the commentaries of Abū al-ʿAbbās al-Sudānī of the Ājurrūmiyya, wherein he writes "... and he was buried in the Bāb al-Ḥadīd, which is today known as the Bāb al-Ḥamrāʾ." So, it is possible that originally the Bāb al-Ḥamrāʾ was known as the Bāb al-Ḥadīd, and then the vernacular changed so that the Bāb al-Ḥamrāʾ became the Bāb al-Jiziyyīn, and then finally as it is known today (al-Ḥamrāʾ), whereas Bāb al-Ḥadīd came to refer to another Bāb altogether. And Allah knows best.

Gatherings: There is a family living inside the Ḍarīḥ of Shaykh Ibn ʿAbbad al-Rondī, and they are often willing to allow visitors in. A small donation is expected by the family. Sometimes, the tomb is locked and inaccessible.

ʿAbd al-ʿAzīz ibn Masʿūd al-Dabbāgh (d. 1131 AH)

Among those buried in the Bāb al-Futūḥ is Shaykh Abū Fāris ʿAbd al-ʿAzīz ibn Masʿūd, son of the famous faqīh and grammarian Masʿūd and a descendant of the Ḥassanī-Idrīssī Shurufāʾ, popularly known as al-Dabbāgh. He belonged to the famous Dabbāgh family of Fes, who were from the progeny of ʿĪsā ibn Idrīs, may Allah be pleased with him.

He was born on Saturday evening on the 11th of Safar in the year 1095 AH to his mother Fārīḥa. She was the niece of the famous walī al-ʿArabī al-Fishtālī, who used to say to her husband Masʿūd, "Allah will increase you with a son whose name is ʿAbd al-ʿAzīz. He will have a great station in wilāya (sainthood)."

His wird at the beginning of his life was to recite 7,000 times each day:

اللَّهُمَّ يَا رَبِّ بِجَاهِ سَيِّدِنَا مُحَمَّدِ ابْنِ عَبْدِاللَّهِ صَلَّى اللَّهُ عَلَيْهِ وَسَلَّمَ، اجْمَعْ بَيْنِي وَبَيْنَ سَيِّدِنَا مُحَمَّدٍ فِي الدُّنْيَا قَبْلَ الآخِرَةِ

Allāhuma yā rabbī bijāhī sayyidina Muḥammad ibn ʿAbdullāh ṣallallāhu ʿalayhī wasallam, ijmaʿ baynī wa bayna sayyidina Muḥammad fī al-dunyā qabla al-ākhirah

O Allah, O Lord, I beseech you by the rank of our master Muḥammad ibn ʿAbdullah, your peace and blessings be upon him, to gather together myself and our master Muḥammad in this world before the next.

This wird was given to him directly by al-Khiḍr ﵇ upon their meeting one night near the door of the rawḍa of ʿAlī ibn Harzihim. Al-Khiḍr also directed him to the caretaker of the aforementioned rawḍa, ʿUmar ibn Muḥammad al-Hawārī. He continued reciting this wird until his master al-Hawārī's death, and three days after al-Hawārī's passing he achieved his spiritual opening. That same month he then attached himself to Sidi ʿAbdullāh al-Barnāwī, who was a Quṭb.

He inherited from a total of ten of the greats of his time. These included, in addition to the two already thus far mentioned: Sidi Yaḥyā (author of *al-Jarīd*), Manṣūr ibn Aḥmad, Muḥammad al-Sirāj, ʿAlī ibn ʿĪsā al-Maghribī, and Aḥmad ibn ʿAbdullāh al-Miṣrī. All of these, but for the last, were among the Aqṭāb of their time.

As for Sidi Aḥmad ibn ʿAbdullāh, he was the Ghawth, and it is from him that ʿAbd al-ʿAzīz learned Siriyyaniyya. It says in *al-Ibrīz* that this was, "A secret language known only to the Ghawth and the seven Aqṭāb under him..."

It also says in *al-Ibrīz*, "And he was not to his students—may Allah have mercy on him—anything but overflowing mercy. He interceded for them in their mistakes, provided for them in times of disaster, bore the burdens of matters whose outcomes they feared, and took greater concern with their affairs than his own... He said to me, 'Anyone who does not share in the evils of his companion, then he is not truly his companion.' Altogether, he was to his companions nothing short of a mercy sent from Allah; it is by the likes of him that the weepers weep. He used to—may Allah have mercy on him—joke with us, laugh with us, and dispel our shyness from us. He would approach us on matters before we could even ask him about them, and say to us, 'Do not put me in the station of a shaykh. I am between you but as in the rank of a brother. Don't burden yourselves with the etiquette of the station of the shaykh. I pardon you from that, and make you all absolved from that, so make me but as in the rank of a brother so long as our companionship lasts.'

He died in the year 1131 or 1132. He is buried in Bāb al-Futūḥ near the Rawḍa al-Anwār and a small qubbah was constructed over his grave.

Gatherings: The tomb is always locked except for Friday morning ziyārah and occasional gatherings. The representatives of the International Center for Sufi and Aesthetic Studies can provide the key and arrange a visit.

Darrās ibn Isma'īl (d. 357 AH)

His full name was Abū Maymūnah Darrās ibn Isma'īl al-Fāsī. They called him Darrās (the one who studies much) because of his constant pursuit and wide breadth of knowledge. He was one of the first scholars to introduce the Mālikī madhhab to Morocco (which today is the dominant madhhab in the country). Before that, people primarily followed the madhhab of the people of Kufa.

In addition to his well-respected reputation as a scholar he was also considered to be one of the Awtād of his time and a venerated saint. It is narrated that when the Shaykh Jawhar first arrived in Fes he stood at its gates for a while but it would not open its doors to him, which grieved him. Then, he saw a man in his dream saying, "You will not be able to enter this country ever even if you stood here for years, for there are already four of the Awtād of the Earth herein." The speaker then listed their names, among whom was Darrās."[6]

During his travels to the East he spent time in Qayrawan with Abū Zayd al-Qayrawānī. Later, Abū Zayd came to Fes to visit him only to find that he had passed away, so instead he spent three nights at his tomb before leaving Fes. It is said that this is the reason that the people of Fes began and continued to visit the graves.

Shaykh of the Shaykhs, Sidi Yūsuf Abū al-Maḥāsin al-Fāsī al-Fihrī (938/939–1013 AH)

Shaykh Abū al-Maḥāsin was born in the year 938 or 939 AH on the 17th of Rabi' al-Awwal in the city of Qasr al-Kabīr. It is there

6 This is a reference to Sufi cosmology, mainly, that a certain region should only contain so many of the men of a certain rank of wilāya so that other regions of the Earth do not become deprived due to all the world's baraka (divine grace) accumulating in one place.

that he grew up though it is in Fes that he was ultimately laid to rest, and it is in Qasr al-Kabīr that his father and his grandfather lived before him.

Abū al-Maḥāsin initially did not know anything about the Sufi way—even what it was—and so God put in his path Shaykh ʿAbd al-Raḥmān al-Majdhūb. Abū al-Maḥāsin studied the Quran under Abū al-Ḥassan ʿAlī al-ʿArabī in his mosque and Shaykh ʿAbd al-Raḥmān would hover around and keep watch over him as he studied. At times he would visit him in his study and mention to him some of the great things God had in store for him, how he would one day move to Fes and what would become of him there. He would say to those around, "I came to him first before someone might beat me to him!"

His companionship with the Shaykh exceeded twenty years, and throughout all that time the Shaykh constantly sung his praises and prided himself on his student. He used to say, "I have the son of al-Fāsī! By him we are instructing the West." He would also frequently say, "He is the Ghazālī of his age," and, near his passing, "Sidi Yūsuf, at first I was his shaykh, but today he is my shaykh." By the end of Abū al-Maḥāsin's Quranic studies with Abū al-Ḥassan his teacher performed a recitation of tabarruk of the Quran at his hands on account of all the good things he used to hear Shaykh al-Majdhūb say about him.

At that time Abū al-Maḥāsin had reached the age of maturity yet while he was still a student, he received the spiritual state from his Shaykh and his chest illumined with the light of unity. All other than God vanished from his heart and he plunged headlong into the spiritual way of the Shaykh, constantly adhering to his side and entrusting all his affairs to him. In spite of this he remained intent on learning and studied under the people of his country such books as they prescribed for him in fiqh, the Quran, and otherwise.

He consequently travelled to Fes to study. When he returned to Qasr al-Kabīr after that he carried with him a vast knowledge of the religion and his fame quickly spread. After the death of Shaykh al-Majdhūb, Yūsuf al-Fāsī also inherited his following and became the new guide of the Tarīqa. He remained in Qasr for another eleven years in this way, until he eventually decided to move to Fes in the year 988 AH. There he became very famous and was visited by everyone from kings to ascetics, thereby vindicating the saying of his Shaykh that, "He is like salt: no one is without need of him."

Shaykh Maḥmad ibn ʿAbdullāh, his son Abū al-ʿAbbās Aḥmad al-Fāsī and others attributed to him the station of the Quṭbaniyya. A great many biographies of the Shaykh have also been written, in particular the *Mirʿat al-Maḥāsin* by his son Muḥammad al-ʿArabī. Even the ʿAlawite sultan Mūlay Sulaymān ibn Ismaʿīl wrote a small booklet in praise of him and the Fāsī family as a whole.

His brother and inheritor ʿAbd al-Raḥmān al-Fāsī also said of him that he was the mujaddid (renewer) of the tenth century. Shaykh Aḥmad Bāba al-Sūdānī said regarding him that, "It is not far-fetched to me [to say] that he was the mujaddid sent for the beginning of the tenth century in consideration of the knowledge he possessed."

Shaykh Yūsuf al-Fāsī died in Fes in the year 1013, during the first third of a Sunday night on the 18th of Rabiʿ al-Awwal, at the age of 75 or 76. Upon his death a white light radiated from him which was witnessed by all those present.

ʿAbd al-Raḥmān ibn Muḥammad al-Fāsī (972–1036)

His full name was Abū Zayd ʿAbd al-Raḥmān ibn Yūsuf ibn ʿAbd al-Raḥmān ibn Abū Bakr Muḥammad ibn ʿAbd al-Mālik ibn Abū Bakr Muḥammad ibn ʿAbdullāh ibn Yaḥyā ibn Farāj ibn al-Jadd al-Fihrī, who was al-Kanānī in lineage and Andalusian in origin. He was born and raised in Qasr al-Kabīr, yet was known in relation to the city of Fes (al-Fāsī), where he died.

He was born in Qasr al-Kabīr in the year 972 AH on Sunday the 19th of Muharram. His father died while he was still a baby or small child and so he grew up primarily in the care of his brother Yūsuf Abū al-Maḥāsin al-Fāsī. He and the son of his brother, Abū al-ʿAbbās Aḥmad, were of the same age and so grew up together, nursing from the same milk, attending the same school, and taking the same courses in education like recitation and fiqh.

Then in the year 986 Abū al-Maḥāsin sent them both to Fes to study. At that time there was an abundance of scholars in Fes. So, the young Fāsīs attached themselves to these scholars and studied a wide variety of sciences under them. In particular, ʿAbd al-Raḥmān studied a great deal with Shaykh al-Qassār, with whom he reviewed many texts and was eventually given the *ijāza ʿāmm* (general permission to teach). Al-Qassār would often praise his student ʿAbd al-Raḥmān and bear witness to his merit.

After Abdur Raḥmān completed his studies of the outward sciences, he focused his time primarily upon attending the circles of his brother Abū al-Maḥāsin for a great many years. From him, he studied tafsīr, hadīth, and other such sciences, in addition to the wayfaring of the Sufi path. In time he became established as a teacher of hadīth and tafsīr himself. Eventually he achieved his spiritual opening at his brother's hands and went on to devote himself primarily to the Sufi way.

When his brother Abū al-Maḥāsin passed away it was he who inherited his station and his secret. He took on the role of shaykh and became one who called people to God. He thereafter became a great figure in the eyes of the people, next to whose name they would not mention anybody as an equal, neither in knowledge of the shariʿah nor the ḥaqīqah. Numerous and great miracles manifested from him. His fame spread so far and wide that many people came to attend the recitation in his zāwiyah, and many of them attested to seeing a couch floating in the sky above his gatherings upon which would sit al-Khiḍr ﷺ.

Sidi ʿAbd al-Raḥmān remarked once that he and Shaykh Abū al-Maḥāsin had been created from a single ball of light which was then divided between the two of them. Yet, he remarked as well that, "My Shaykh is better established than myself; as for myself, I am overcome by the ḥaqīqah." By this he meant that he was more often than not overcome by the state of absence and immersed in witnessing the Divine Unity. Shaykh Abū al-Maḥāsin said about him that, "If it were not the case that he found a shaykh [to guide him] he would have been one of the people that urinated on his own legs [due to the strength of that which descended upon him]."

His student Maḥmad ibn ʿAbdullāh said about him, "Whenever ʿAbd al-Raḥmān saw his brother Abū al-Maḥāsin while he was in a state of absence, it would suddenly occur to him who he was and he would return from his state. Conversely, if Sidi Yūsuf saw his brother ʿAbd al-Raḥmān while in his own state of absence, he too would return to his senses. For the two of them were as if one."

Sidi ʿAbd al-Raḥmān died late on a Wednesday night on the 27th of Rabiʿ al-Awwal in the year 1036, at the age of 64. He was buried in the rawḍa of his brother Abū al-Maḥāsin, near to him.

The Seven Shuhadāʾ: The Qubbah of the "Seven Men"

In front of the Qubbah of Sidi Yūsuf Abū Mahāsin al-Fāsī stands a Qubbah known popularly in Fes as the Qubbah of the "Sebʿatu Rijāl" (the Seven Men). Their names are not recorded in any books nor mentioned in any of the long poems written about the saints of Fes, and some say that there are ten men buried there rather than seven. All that is known about these men is that they are martyrs who returned wounded from the famous battle of Wādī Makhāzin alongside Shaykh Abū al-Maḥāsin al-Fāsī.

The battle of Wādī Makhāzin occurred in the year 982 AH, when a great Christian fleet the likes of which had never been seen before attacked Morocco. However, Allah provided for the Muslims during this battle and the invading forces were nearly annihilated, the King of Portugal was slain, and the Muslims obtained a tremendous booty. Only a few of the invading army escaped.

This is the story associated with this Qubbah. However, some say that if this was really true then earlier biographers of the saints of Fes would not have neglected to mention these seven men in their books, as they have. And God knows best.

Qāsim ibn Qāsim al-Khaṣāṣī (d. 1083)

His full name was Abū Faḍl Qāsim ibn Qāsim al-Khaṣāṣī. His family originated from Andalusia, but it was in the city of Fes that he was born, lived, died and was buried. As for his name, it comes from Khaṣāṣa, a town on the beach near Mount Qalʿiah with brackish waters.

He was born in the first or second year of the second millennia AH (1001 or 1002), and he was raised an orphan in the care of his mother. His father died when he was not yet born.

He was known to have a mischievous personality. Then, he began to feel regret for the life he was living and he came by chance one day upon the grave of Sidi Yūsuf Abū al-Maḥāsin al-Fāṣī without intending it, nor knowing who was buried there or even his name. He called out to him, saying, "O you in this grave! If you are truly a walī of God, then I beseech God in your name that he gathers me together with a shaykh whom I may serve for the sake of God, and whom no one other than myself serves alongside me." After that, God brought him together with his first shaykh, Shaykh Mubārak ibn ʿAbābūl Kowsh, who is buried outside the Bāb Gheesa. He served him for a time until his death, after which he took to following al-Fāsī. Under him he achieved his goal and had his great spiritual opening. His master used to say to him, "You are *gharīb* (peculiar)—you have no brother," indicating that he was unique in his spiritual way, his gnostic knowledge and in what he had realised. And God knows best.

After his Shaykh's passing, he accompanied his inheritor Maḥmad ibn ʿAbd Allah Maʿin al-Andalūsī and remained in his service for twenty-six years. These were the three shuyūkh upon whom he relied and through whom he achieved his goal.

He would often be overcome by the state of ghayba (absence), and it was usual for his state of ghayba to intensify once every month for about five days. During this time he would be unable to differentiate the ground from the sky, nor would he eat or drink. He would only come to his senses once every hour to ask about the prayer times—except that even then, he would ask about the daytime prayers when it was already evening. When this period came he would stay indoors and not leave his house.

His spiritual way was the way of love, and the *fanā* (annihilation) in *tawhīd* (the unity of God). He would not mention anything but this way in his speech, and it is by these things that he encouraged people towards the path to God. He did not pay any heed to the way of fear nor indicate anything about it in any of his teachings. He also was greatly moved by the samāʿ and would seek out its practitioners and their circles, only to stand amongst them in ecstasy, not dancing himself.

He died in the middle of a Sunday night on the 19th of Ramadan in the year 1083. He was buried in the rawḍa of his shuyūkh, on the side of the garden, in front of the Qubbah of Shaykh Sidi Maḥmad ibn ʿAbdullāh.

Maḥmad ibn Maḥmad ibn ʿAbdullāh Maʿan

His full name was Abū ʿAbdullāh, and Abū Nasāʿiḥ, Sidi Maḥmad ibn Maḥmad ibn ʿAbdullāh ibn Maʿan al-Andalūsī, and he was born approximately in the year 978 AH. Previously he was known as Maʿan but now he is referred to as Ibn ʿAbdullāh and he is a descendant of the Almohad King Yaʿqūb al-Manṣūr. The prominent historian Abū Qāsim al-Suhaylī wrote that he was a sharīf of Ḥassanī-Idrīssī lineage from the descendants of Muḥammad ibn Qāsim ibn Idrīs, but that he used to advise his children not to mention their noble lineage to anyone. It is recorded that once, when his son asked him about his lineage, the Shaykh simply replied "Arab; and God knows best."

He grew up in peace and security, studying the sciences with the people of his time until he was versed in the Islamic sciences. He learned how to recite the Quran in both the Warsh and Qālūn style, and among his teachers in the outward sciences was also his shaykh on the spiritual path, ʿAbd al-Raḥmān al-Fāsī. He then occupied himself with spiritual striving and acts of worship grew beloved to him, so that he used to perform them to the utmost of his capacity.

He attached himself at first to visiting Shaykh ʿAbdullāh al-Tawdī, buried outside Bāb Gheesa, until when he reached about thirty God brought him together with Shaykh Abū al-Maḥāsin al-Fāsī. He then served him for three years until his death, in which time he achieved his spiritual opening and benefitted greatly. Upon the Shaykh's passing he fell into the service of his inheritor Sidi ʿAbd al-Raḥmān al-Fāsī, with whom he remained for another twenty-three years and under whom he reached his perfection on the path.

When Shaykh ʿAbd al-Raḥmān died Sidi Maḥmad inherited from him but he was not yet given permission to teach. He remained in his house for six months in this state, until finally he went one day to visit his spiritual predecessor and master on the Sufi way, ʿAbd al-Salām ibn Mashīsh. It is there at Mashīsh's tomb that he finally received the permission to guide others on the path to God, and upon returning to Fes he established himself in the zāwiyah of Shaykh Abū al-Maḥāsin Yūsuf al-Fāsī and began calling the people to the path. People then came to him from all over, and he said to them with tears pouring from his eyes, "Ride this neck for I have been threatened to have my spiritual rank stripped from me if I don't come out to [guide] you."

From then he committed himself to guiding the faithful and raising them to spiritual maturity on the path. He even indicated to having a following among the djinn and that they used to attend his gatherings, saying, "The first of those who commit to the service of the *makhṣūṣ* (elite) are the djinn, for they are more subtle [beings] than the Adamic [humans]."

Sidi Maḥmad used to particularly emphasise to his students not to interact with the people of that time, due to the lack of honest and sincere men in their age. He also emphasised the remembrance of God, in particular the saying of "There is no God but God", seeking forgiveness, and sending blessings upon the Prophet ﷺ. If his students needed anything, he told them to merely sit in his presence with their need in their heart and that it would be taken care of, without them needing to even mention anything to him.

He died an hour after sunrise on Sunday the 3rd of Jumādī al-Thāniyya in the year 1062, and was buried near his shaykh, Yūsuf Abū al-Maḥāsin al-Fāsī. His grave lies near and to the right of Abū al-Maḥāsin, and a qubbah was built over it similar to his qubbah.

Aḥmad ibn Maḥmad ibn ʿAbdullāh Maʿan (1042–1120)

Buried next to Sidi Maḥmad is his son ʿAbū al-ʿAbbās Aḥmad ibn ʿAbdullāh Maʿan, who was born in the year 1042 and raised in the Makhfiyyah district of Fes wherein operated his father's zāwiyah. He was a student of both the outer and inner sciences, and achieved recognition in his time for both. The learned scholars of the time used to come to him with their questions and seek his advice in matters of both the inward and outward.

It says in *Al-Ṣafwah* that, "He did not instruct his students to recite awrād, nor would he greet those who instructed their students to do so. He hated to be called a shaykh, and was of the view that those acts of negligence that the Sufis of his day used to perform were matters far from the Divine Law. Like his father he was very strict in following the Sunnah, and did not allow anything that did not conform to the practice of the Prophet ﷺ into his house, from dress to social norms. That being the case, and being that the practices common in his time were not something found in the Sunnah of the Prophet ﷺ, he considered them to be of no value and no benefit. He and Shaykh Muḥammad ibn Saʿīd al-Tarāblisī had a long and ongoing dispute over this issue, yet anyone who came to him seeking a shaykh he would merely send to his zāwiyah and instruct him to help out and perform the aḥzāb with his brothers there, and not do anything else in addition to that."

Sidi Aḥmad took from his father in the spiritual path by way of baraka during his lifetime, and after his death he completed his spiritual wayfaring under the guidance of his father's inheritor Sidi Qāsim al-Khaṣāṣī. Yet, after the passing of Sidi Qāsim Aḥmad he had not yet completed on the path and thus he took to following Sidi Aḥmad al-Yamanī (a Qādirī shaykh) with whom he became extremely close. Shaykh Aḥmad al-Yamanī said regarding

Sidi Aḥmad that he reached a station greater than that of both his shaykh, Qāsim al-Khaṣāṣī, and his father Maḥmad ibn ʿAbdullāh. He even humbled himself before Sidi Aḥmad, saying when asked about him that "his feet are upon my neck" and "he is [as] Yazīd al-Bisṭāmī."

On one occasion, upon Sidi Aḥmad's passing through the city of al-Ṭarābulus, he came across a holy man. He was amazed upon seeing him and considered him to be among the highest rank of the saints. The man exclaimed, "There is no God but God! What great righteous men there are in this ummah!" He commented afterwards, "When I first beheld him, I saw him as if he was the sun rising." This holy man bore witness that Sidi Aḥmad was among the highest rank of saints, and mentioned the name of the station he possessed which was specific to him and which none in Morocco had heard of before: a station in the mould of the Prophet ʿĪsā عليه السلام, a wise man who put everything in its right place.

Aḥmad ibn ʿAbdullāh passed away in the year 1120. He was buried in the Qubbah of his father, his head laid to rest at his father's legs.

Al-ʿArabī ibn Aḥmad ibn ʿAbdullāh (1079–1166)

Among those buried in the rawḍa of Sidi ʿAbū al-Maḥāsin al-Fāsī is the son of Sidi Aḥmad ibn ʿAbdullāh and his student, Sidi al-ʿArabī ibn Aḥmad ibn ʿAbd Allāh. Sidi al-ʿArabī was born in Dhul-Qaʿdah in the year 1079 and grew up in the blessed care of his father, immersed in the recitation of the Quran and the pursuit of the Islamic sciences. Aḥmad al-Yamanī predicted what would become of him from the time of his youth, prophesying that there was much goodness in him and that one day he would be among the righteous.

At first he took the spiritual path of the Shādhiliyya from his father, then after his father's passing he completed his affair under the guidance of his father's dear companion Aḥmad al-Yamanī. Thus, he was instructed in both the Ṭarīqa of Imam Shādhilī and ʿAbd al-Qādir al-Jīlānī, and in him the ocean of the Shādhiliyya and the Qādiriyya met, as was mentioned by Aḥmad ibn ʿAjība in his autobiography.

Sidi al-ʿArabī had only a few yet prominent students, among whom was Sidi ʿAlī al-Jamal. Both Shaykh al-Tawdī ibn Sūda al-Murī and Shaykh Aḥmad al-Tijānī also sought blessings from Sidi al-ʿArabī and mentioned him among the lists of saints they had met.

Many precious sayings about the Path are attributed to Sidi al-ʿArabī, among which is his advice, "Do not neglect to glorify and honour the one at whose hands you achieved some of your spiritual opening, because in glorification and honouring his sanctity is a mighty key to an increase in spiritual provisions, lights, secrets and blessings. Do not neglect this door [to spiritual progress]. It is a necessity, so beware!" He also said, "We did not reach the arrival (*al-Wiṣāl*) except by the edge of a blade (*al-Niṣāl*)," and, "Do not yearn for anyone, be only one who is yearned for, and if you find yourself with no other choice then do not yearn for anyone except he whom yearns for you."

His death came in the year 1166, and his burial was attended by the most prominent scholars, Sufis and leaders of Fes. He was buried just outside the Qubbah of his father in the open courtyard beyond from the direction of ʿAbū al-Maḥāsin's Qubbah, with his grave plot attached to the Qubbah [of Sidi Aḥmad ibn ʿAbdullāh].

Sidi ʿAlī ibn Ismaʿīl ibn Ḥirzihim (d. 560)

His full name was ʿAbū Ḥassan Sidi ʿAlī ibn Muḥammad ibn ʿAbd al-Allāh ibn Ismaʿīl ibn Ḥirzihim. He was born and grew up in Fes, and was considered one of the foremost faqīhs of that time. He was also a follower of the Malāmatī branch of Sufism, which in those days was uncommon in Morocco and so the people of the land used to disapprove of some of the [ecstatic] states that occasionally manifested in him. In spite of this, his honesty and good character inclined people toward him.

Sidi ʿAlī was well-known for his mastery of tafsīr, fiqh and the other external sciences and emphasised their importance. Yet, his true inclination was to the internal [spiritual] sciences, and so he travelled the lands in search of someone who might teach them to him. He had numerous teachers, among them the famous mujāhid Sidi ʿAbū Bakr ibn al-ʿArabī, though he only took the outward sciences from him. He also studied with ʿAbū ʿAbdullāh al-Khayyāṭ, buried on the Talaʿa of Fes, and Shaykh ʿAbū Bakr ibn Uthmān ibn Mālik, and his father Ismaʿīl ibn Ḥirzihim.

In tasawwuf, his true shaykh was his uncle ʿAbū Muḥammad Sāliḥ ibn Ḥirzihim. A great many biographers also record that he took the way from Muḥyuddīn ibn al-ʿArabī. There are inconsistencies in this account, however, and a more likely conclusion is that he was given the Khirqah by Ibn al-ʿArabī, who was given it by Imam Ghazālī, from al-Makkī, and so forth until Junayd, and that this is merely a sanad of tabarruk.[7]

He travelled to Murrākesh, where under his leadership a great many people repented and turned to God. He garnered a large following of students who took the Sufi way from him and achieved their spiritual opening at his hands, including Shaykh

7 Meaning, they did not inherit each other's secret nor perhaps even study Sufism with one another, but rather passed on the Sufi robes to one another and gave from one to the other their blessings – so that it is a chain of blessing.

ʿAbū Madyan al-Ghawth and Sidi Yūsuf al-Tawdī (buried outside the Bāb Gheesa), who travelled the path as brothers under the same shaykh. Shaykh ʿAbū Yaʿzā took from him as well, along with Sidi ʿAbū ʿAbbās al-Fāsī and others. He was a very humble and noble man, who loved and was loved by everyone, the young and the old. He did not harbour envy nor hatred towards anyone, nor did he consider himself above anyone.

Shaykh al-Subkī, in his biography of Imam al-Ghazālī, relates the following story: "When Sidi Ḥirzihim obtained a copy of the *Iḥyāʾ* he looked into it, and then remarked, 'This is an innovation that contradicts the sunnah!' He was a well-respected shaykh whose opinions were followed by the people of Morocco, and so he ordered that every copy of the *Iḥyāʾ* in the country be gathered and brought to him and he requested the Sultan to enforce his order. He wrote to every region of Morocco and emphasised this demand, threatening anyone who might conceal a copy. They gathered together all the copies of the *Iḥyāʾ*, then the faqīhs gathered and looked into the matter, and decided to burn the books the following day (Friday).

That night, Sidi ʿAlī had a dream in which he entered the mosque from the door it was his habit to enter from, when he saw a light by one of its pillars. He then realised it was none other than the Prophet ﷺ sitting alongside ʿAbū Bakr and ʿUmar. In front of them was Imam al-Ghazālī, in whose hands was a copy of the *Iḥyāʾ*, and he was saying to the Prophet, 'O Messenger of God! This is my antagonist!' He then knelt down and crawled forward until he reached the Prophet and handed him the *Iḥyāʾ* and said, 'O Messenger of God, look into this book. If you find that it is an innovation that contradicts your sunnah as he claims then I repent to God Most High. However, if you find it to be good, then grant me your blessing and deliver justice to my enemy!'

So the Prophet ﷺ looked through it in its entirety, page after page, then exclaimed 'By God! This is an excellent thing!' Then 'Abū Bakr looked into it likewise and commented, 'Yes. By He who sent you in truth, it is indeed excellent!' Then ʿUmar looked into it as well, and remarked as 'Abū Bakr had. So the Prophet ﷺ then ordered for 'Abū al-Ḥassan to be stripped of his clothes and lashed for the crime of slander. After five lashings, however, 'Abū Bakr interceded on his behalf and said, 'O Messenger of God! He only did this striving to follow your sunnah, in veneration of it.' Following this, Imam al-Ghazālī pardoned him. When he woke, he informed his companions of what had transpired in his sleep, and for a month afterwards he continued to suffer from the pain of his lashings, though the marks remained on his back until his death."

Sidi 'Alī thereafter became one of the main proponents and propagators of the *Iḥyā'* in Morocco, and had his students 'Abū Madyan and others study it. He died in Shaʿbān in the year 559 or 560, and was buried in a small Qubbah in the Bāb al-Futūḥ which was eventually torn down and reconstructed into the tremendous structure that exists today on the order of Sultan Muḥammad ibn ʿAbdullāh al-ʿAlawī.

Gatherings: The tomb is usually open, and the descendants of the walī maintain the complex. A donation is usually expected. It is common to visit Shaykh ʿAlī ibn Ḥirzihim if you seek to study the classic *Iḥyā' ʿUlūm al-Dīn* of Imam al-Ghazālī. Since the Shaykh was a representative of al-Ghazālī's school of thought in Fes, he is believed to still grant openings for students seeking to study the text.

Sidi Muḥammad ibn ʿAlī Ibn Ḥarāzim (633 AH)

His full name was ʿAbū ʿAbdullāh Sidi Muḥammad ibn Abū al-Ḥassan ʿAlī ibn Ismaʿīl ibn Muḥammad ibn ʿAbdullāh ibn Ḥarāzim al-Andalūsī al-Fāsī. Sidi Muḥammad descended from an Uthmānī Umayyad lineage, and was the son of the famous shaykh ʿAlī ibn Ḥarāzim—and some say Ḥirzihim—buried in the Bāb al-Futūḥ in Fes. He is buried in al-Sakhīnāt, from the provinces outside Fes, though today the whole area is called Sidi Ḥarāzim.

His father passed away while he was still young so he received his training from his father's greatest remaining companion, Shaykh Abū Muḥammad Ṣāliḥ al-Mājirī al-Dakālī (buried in the city of Āsfī, south of Rabāt). Under him he struggled and strove in the pursuit of both inner and outer knowledge, and it was at this Shaykh's hands that he took the Khirqah and the Ṭarīqa. This continued until eventually he reached a great station—some even describing him as attaining the Quṭbaniyya.

His most famous student was the great shaykh and Imam of the Shādhilī Ṭarīqa, Abū al-Ḥassan Shādhilī. It is Sidi Ḥarāzim who inducted him onto the Sufi path and passed on to him the Khirqah, and from whom he first studied the way until he later took the hand of the great Quṭb Sidi ʿAbd al-Salām ibn Mashīsh.

And the Shaykh of Sidi Ḥarāzim, Sidi Muḥammad Abū Ṣalīḥ, took first from Shaykh Muḥammad ʿAbd al-Razzāq al-Jazūlī, who was one of the companions of Sidi Abū Madyan, then after him and by his command directly from Abū Madyan. Abū Madyan then sent him to Shaykh ʿAbd al-Qādir al-Jīlānī, who placed him in khalwa for 120 days before sending him back to Abū Madyan with some writings he had dictated to Abū Ṣalīḥ.

A white Qubbah was constructed over his tomb, and the spring at which he is buried is very famous.

Gatherings: This tomb can be found outside Fes at a site called Sidi Harazim, which is actually today a family-friendly water park, as well as the headquarters of a fresh spring water bottle company that goes by the same name. There are fountains where the water flows all day, and so locals frequent this spot to take advantage of this fresh, free resource. To access the park one takes a grand taxi from a grand taxi stand adjacent, on the left hand side, to the Bāb al-Futūḥ cemetery.

ʿAlī ibn Muḥammad Humāmūsh (933 AH)

Among the Qubbahs outside the Bāb al-Futūḥ is that of ʿAlī ibn Muḥammad Humāmūsh, an ʿĀrif who traces his lineage back to Sultan Yaʿqūb al-Manṣūr. It is also reported that he was a Sharīf from the descendants of Muḥammad ibn Qāsim ibn Idrīs.

ʿAlī ibn Muḥammad was a student of the famous Jazūlī Shaykh al-Ghazwānī and took from him directly. He was buried in his zāwiyah outside the Bāb al-Futūḥ and in front of Shaykh Sidi ʿAlī al-Ṣanhājī at an unknown date, possibly 933 AH. Later, a Qubbah was constructed over his tomb.

Sidi al-ʿArabī ibn Aḥmad al-Fashtālī (1092 AH)

His full name was Abū Muḥammad Sidi Muḥammad al-ʿArabī ibn Aḥmad ibn ʿAbd al-Karīm. He was as famous as al-Fashtālī. He was among the most famous scholar-saints of Fes, greatly venerated by his contemporaries. He foresaw the coming of ʿAbd al-ʿAzīz al-Dabbāgh and the great station he would reach, as is mentioned in al-Dabbāgh's biography, and was also greatly praised by the saint Aḥmad ibn ʿAbdullāh Maʿin. Sidi Aḥmad said, "He was among the greatest of the gnostic saints," and attributed to him a perfect station of sainthood.

He was a knowledgeable scholar who studied from such greats as ʿAbd al-Qādir al-Fāsī and Sidi al-Ḥassan al-Yūssī. As for his Ṭarīqa, he was a student of Sidi Aḥmad ibn Nāṣir al-Darʿī, then later of Muḥammad ibn al-Mubārak, and it is from the second shaykh that he achieved what he did.

He died in the year 1092 and was buried in the mausoleum of Sidi Humāmūsh.

Majdhūb Sidi ʿAlī ibn Aḥmad al-Dawwār al-Ṣinhājī (947 AH)

His full name was Abū Ḥassan Sidi ʿAlī Aḥmad ibn ʿAlī ibn Aḥmad ibn ʿAbd al-Raḥmān al-Ṣinhājī al-Fāsī al-Malāmatī, but the people took to calling him al-Dawwār (the one who constantly circulates). Some say this is because of how he used to circulate (*dawwara*) the gift of the Divine secrets and states. Others say that he was given this name because of his habit of circulating around places and markets, exclaiming: "Allah! Allah!" This is the more likely reason for his being named as such, although it is reported that he hated the nickname.

He was born in the greater region of Sanhāja, which used to be called Sanhāja al-Hajar. Therein lived his ancestors, among whom were a number of saints. He left this land when he was still young, and thereafter took up residence in Fes, wherein he lived until his death. He took the Sufi way from his master Ibrahim Āfaḥām al-Zorhūnī of Mount Zorhūn, who took it from Sidi Aḥmad Zarrūq, and was the inheritor of his shaykh, for upon his shaykh's death only he manifested the overwhelming spiritual states of absence in the unity of God that his shaykh used to experience. Indeed, he was the only one who even knew his shaykh existed at all.

His sainthood was as clear to the people of Fes as the rising sun. He followed the Malāmatī way of blame and intense attraction to the Divine, and was possessed by states of *jadhb* (attraction) in every moment. He had no family nor established place of residence, and did not care about praise or criticism. He would enter the houses of the Merinid kings and the women and children within would come forward to meet him, kissing his hands and feet, and still he would not be fazed by it. They would give him amazing gifts and priceless treasures, and the Sultan would dress him in the finest of robes, yet he would give it all away in charity. Then he would pass by the shops of the oil-sellers and dip the sleeves of the fine robes which had been given to him in oil or fat until their finery was obscured and continue on, wandering around pronouncing the name of God. Nobody knew if he had any home in particular that he returned to.

Among the miracles attributed to him is that one day he passed by a house and threw his hand underneath the threshold. He then called out to the inhabitants, "O people of this house, get out! Get out!" They exited and when there was no one left in the house, he took out his hand from under the threshold and the entire house collapsed instantly, but no one was harmed.

On another occasion, it is recounted that he entered upon the inner chamber of a house without first asking its inhabitants for permission. Inside he found the lady of the house washing her clothing with the sleeves of her robes rolled up [so that she was baring her skin]. She was greatly displeased with his entering upon her in such a state, yet at the very moment he entered a child fell from the ceiling and into the arms of Sidi ʿAlī. He set the child down safely on the ground and remarked to the women, "This is what caused me to enter." He then took off swiftly back the way he came.

On another occasion, he was sitting at the door of the Qarawiyyin mosque eating a cucumber while the people were praying the ṣubh prayer when a man passed him on his way to join in the prayer. When the man saw the Shaykh, he thought to himself, "The people are all praying while Sidi 'Alī eats a cucumber and doesn't pray with them!" Then he joined in the prayer, all the while his thoughts revolving around a donkey he needed to buy later that morning at the Thursday market. When he exited, Sidi 'Alī called out to him, saying, "O stranger! To eat a cucumber (*akl al-khiyār*) is better than to perform a donkey-prayer (*ṣalat al-ḥimār*)!"

No boundaries bound him, and no doors nor walls could prevent him. He was witnessed numerous times at the Ka'ba, and was the master of his time amongst the people of the unseen. Some of his statements allude to his possessing the rank of an abdāl, whereas some described him as having obtained the quṭbāniyya.

Whatever the case, his fame was great amongst the people of Fes, due to the numerous uncountable miracles that they witnessed from him. When he died the people tripped over themselves attending his funeral procession and divided up amongst themselves the wood from his bier as well as his prayer rug and clothing. All attended, from scholars to Sufis to the Sultan himself, and he was buried outside the Bāb al-Futūḥ.

Sayyida Āminah bint Aḥmad ibn 'Alī Ibn al-Qāḍī (960 AH)

Her full name was Sayyida Āminah, daughter of the Qāḍī Abū al-'Abbās Aḥmad ibn 'Alī 'Abd al-Raḥmān ibn Abū 'Āfiyya al-Maknāsī. Along with Sidi 'Abd al-Raḥmān al-Majdhūb she was one of the two inheritors of Shaykh Sidi 'Alī al-Ṣanhājī al-Dawwār, next to whom she was buried, and in her lifetime she never left his side. She performed the role of a servant to her Shaykh, and her brother on the path, Sidi 'Abd al-Raḥmān, attested to her having reached the station of Khuṣūṣiyya (the Elite) and that she was among the highest ranks of the awliyā'. Upon their Shaykh's death he remarked that his secret was split between them, though with himself receiving double the share, and upon her own death he remarked that now he had finally inherited his Shaykh's secret in its entirety.

It is recorded that her family—a very respectable family from Meknes—disapproved of her accompanying the Shaykh. This was to such an extent that one day they locked her in a room and bound her legs with iron shackles merely to prevent her from going to him. Yet, unbeknown to them, Sidi ʿAlī went and stood in the centre of the home, and called out to her, "O Āminah!" To which she replied, "Yes, Sidi?" He said, "Come down here!" Then the shackles fell from her legs and her family watched as she walked out of the room and down to her Shaykh, in spite of the room being completely enclosed.[8] After that, they tolerated her service to him and left them in peace.

ʿĀrif Murrabī Sidi ʿAbd al-Wahhāb al-Tāzī (1099–1206 AH)

His full name was Abū Muḥammad Sidi ʿAbd al-Wahhāb al-Tāzī and he was a companion of the Quṭb Aḥmad al-Ṣaqalī. However, in his youth he met and took from a very large number of shuyūkh, both in Morocco and throughout his numerous pilgrimages to Makka. He was also the foster-son of Shaykh ʿAbd al-ʿAzīz al-Dabbāgh by way of nursing.[9]

Sidi ʿAbd al-Wahhāb became a shaykh of tarbiyya himself and developed a sizeable following in his lifetime. When he passed away he was buried in the Bāb al-Futūḥ graveyard, between Shaykh al-ʿĀidī al-Kabīr and Shaykh al-ʿĀidī al-Ṣaghīr. The Sultan Mūlay Sulaymān al-ʿAlawī then built a Qubbah with a green roof over his grave, much like that of Sidi Darrās ibn Ismaʿīl.

8 It is insinuated here that the door either miraculously unlocked at her approach, or even more amazingly, she simply walked right through it like a specter passing through walls.

9 When he was a baby he nursed from al-Dabbāgh's wife, thus making him a son of sorts according to Islamic custom.

ʿAbd al-Wāḥid ibn Aḥmad ibn ʿĀshir al-Anṣārī (1040 AH)

His full name was Abū Muḥammad Sidi ʿAbd al-Wāḥid ibn Aḥmad ibn ʿAlī ibn ʿĀshir al-Anṣārī. His family were descendants of the Anṣār and immigrants from al-Andalus, though he himself was raised and lived in the city of Fes.

He was among those who achieved a deep grounding in the sciences and arts. In particular, he achieved a mastery of the sciences of qirāʾāt and grammar, in which fields he published some remarkable works, as well as in Sufism, medicine, fiqh, logic, *bayān* (rhetoric), *ḥisāb* (arithmetic), *al-farāʾiḍ* (religious obligations), *tawqīt* (astronomy) and *al-ʿarūḍ* (prosody), to name a few. He was unique in his time for his mastery of recitation of the Quran, and wrote a marvellous commentary on *Mawrid al-Zamʿān* which he called *Fatḥ al-Mannān*.

He studied the Quran under Shaykh Abū al-ʿAbbās Sidi Aḥmad al-ʿUthmānī al-Lamātī[10] and its seven forms of recitation under Shaykh Abū al-ʿAbbās al-Kafīf, then Shaykh Abū ʿAbdullāh al-Sharīf al-Murabbī al-Tilimsānī, and others. His student Miyyāra, in his commentary on his master's book *al-Murshid al-Muʿīn,* commented, "And there is no doubt that he surpassed all his teachers in the arts of tawjīhāt and taʿdīlāt."

In fiqh, he took from a number of teachers including Abū al-ʿAbbās ibn al-Qāḍī, the son of his cousin Abū al-Qāsim, Abū al-Ḥassan ʿAlī ibn ʿImrān, Abū ʿAbdullāh al-Hawārī, and Shaykh al-Qasār. From the East, he took from Sālim al-Sanhūrī, Abū ʿAbdullāh al-Ghazī, and others. Finally, in tasawwuf, he took from Sidi Muḥammad al-Tujībī, popularly known as Ibn ʿAzīz, buried in the Darb al-Ṭawīl in Fes.

He wrote many excellent books, among them his particularly famous guide to the five pillars of Islam and tasawwuf titled

10 As in, of the Malāmatī school of ecstatic Sufism.

al-Murshid al-Muʿīn ʿAlā al-Ḍarūrī min ʿUlūm al-Dīn, which he began writing at the time he entered the ritual state of ihrām for Hajj. The first section he wrote dealt with the rules of Hajj, after which he completed the sections pertaining to the other four pillars. He also wrote a book on the *Sharḥ* of al-Imam al-Tatāʿī al-Ṣaghīr called *Jawāhir al-Darār ʿAla Mukhtaṣar Khalīl*, which became famous and spread throughout the Muslim world.

He became afflicted early one morning on a Thursday with a disease people called al-nutqah[11] when he was fifty years old in the year 1040, and died later that afternoon. He was buried near the Muṣalā outside the Bāb al-Futūḥ to the west of and directly facing the rawḍa of Sidi Yūsuf al-Fāsī, and a Qubbah was constructed over his tomb.

Sidi ʿAbd al-Raḥmān ibn Idrīs al-Manjarah (1179 AH)

His full name was Abū Zayd Sidi ʿAbd al-Raḥmān ibn Sidi Idrīs ibn Maḥmad ibn Aḥmad al-Manjarī al-Ḥassanī al-Tilimsānī al-Fāsī. He was a descendant of one of the Manjarī Shurufāʾ of Tilimsān who emigrated to Fes in the tenth century AH, and in his time he was the khatīb of the Idrīssī Ḥaram in Fes.

Sidi al-Manjarah was born in the Makhfiyya district of Fes and came to be considered the foremost shaykh of recitation (*qirāʾāt*) in all of Morocco in that age, familiar with all ten schools of recitation. He became the Imam of the Idrīssī Ḥaram and remained so for fifteen years until his death, in all that time striving hard to teach and educate the people of Fes. His most famous student was perhaps the great Quṭb Mūlay al-ʿArabī al-Darqāwī, who listed him in his collection of letters as one of his teachers of the Quran. Shaykh Mūlay al-ʿArabī also recounted the miraculous

11 This disease is described by the author as starting with a heaviness of the tongue and limbs, followed by complete paralysis, before the inner organs become paralysed as well, resulting finally in death.

nature of his teacher, and how once when al-Darqāwī fell ill with a disease called al-ḥumm he was advised by his companions to visit his teacher's tomb for he was known to cure this disease. He did so and immediately was cured, and never thereafter contracted the disease again.

Upon his death he was buried near his father and Shaykh Ibn ʿĀshir near the Muṣalā outside the Bāb al-Futūḥ.

Sharīf Sidi Aḥmad al-Yamanī (1113 AH)

His full name was Sidi Abū ʿAbbās, son of the distinguished saint Sidi Abū ʿAbdullāh Muḥammad, himself the son of the very famous saint and gnostic Abū al-ʿAlā Idrīs. His grandfather ʿAlā was of Qādirī-Ḥassanī sharīf lineage.

Their ancestry stemmed from a province in Yemen but Sidi Aḥmad and his family in fact lived in a village called Maʿallaq which was between Egypt and Ethiopia. The tomb of his grandfather Abū ʿAlā was a famous site of pilgrimage in that land and both his father and brother possessed stations of sainthood.

His birth was sometime around the year 1040, and his family were princes and sovereigns of Maʿallaq. When he achieved his spiritual opening he rejected the wealth and prestige of his family and took to wandering the world, much like the famous gnostic Ibrāhīm al-Adham.

His departure from his homeland was in the year 1075, and he left with the intention of making the Hajj pilgrimage, seeking knowledge and meeting various shuyūkh of the Sufi way. To accomplish this he took to traversing all corners of the lands, and throughout his travels he accomplished his pilgrimage to Makka, spent a long time in Sudan, then made his way through the nations along the Sahara desert until he arrived at Sijilmāsa, where he took up residence for a time. Throughout his travels he met a great number of shuyūkh in both the East and the West, though in Morocco the only shaykh he actually took anything from was Sidi Ibn ʿAbbād al-Rondī.

Sidi Dafʿ Allāh, the son of al-Ghazālī, was the shaykh upon whom he truly relied and at whose hands he achieved his spiritual opening. Dafʿ Allāh lived in the city of Arbajī, and had taken the Ṭarīqa from his father who took it from his uncle Habīb al-ʿAjamī, who in turn had a direct sanad to ʿAbd al-Qādir al-Jīlānī. Thus, Sidi Aḥmad al-Yamanī's Ṭarīqa was the Qādirī. He also frequently talked about the great Shaykh Abū Muḥammad Sidi ʿAbdullāh ibn ʿAbd al-Jalīl ibn ʿUmar al-Barnāwī, from the city of Barnū in Sudan.

In the year 1079 or 1084 he left Sijilmāsa and departed for the city of Fes, where he spent his first night taking shelter in the Qarawiyyin mosque. The next day he was granted permanent residence by the Qāḍī Abū ʿAbdullāh Ḥassan al-Majāsī, who set him up in a room in the al-Sirāj mosque. There he stayed for two years, dressing all the while in the style of the country folk.

When Aḥmad ibn ʿAbdullāh came to learn of his existence, he insisted the Shaykh move into a house situated between his own house and his zāwiyah in the Makhfiyyah district of Fes. It is after this that his fame truly spread amongst the people; he gained students and followers, the common people took to visiting him, and even the dignitaries in government recognised him and venerated the house he lived in.

Aḥmad al-Yamanī is mentioned in both the *Risālāt* of Mūlay al-ʿArabī al-Darqāwī and in the autobiography of Sidi Aḥmad ibn ʿAjība, who described him as having reached the station of the quṭbāniyya. He and Aḥmad ibn ʿAbdullāh once travelled together to Sijilmāsa where they met the holy men of that city, who also described Aḥmad al-Yamanī as having reached the maqām of ʿĪsā عليه السلام.[12]

Buried next to him in his Qubbah is Shaykh Abū Bakr ibn Muḥammad al-Dilāʾī, grandson of the famous founder of the Zāwiyah Dilāʾiyya, who was a close and dear student of the Shaykh. He too was described as having reached the station of Quṭb.

Shaykh al-Islam Sidi Riḍwān ibn ʿAbdullāh al-Janawī (d. 991 AH)

His full name was Abū Naʿīm and Abū Riḍā Sidi Riḍwān ibn ʿAbdullāh al-Janawī al-Fāsī. His lineage was from the city of Janwah on the easternmost region of Andalusia, but he was born, raised, and eventually died in Fes. His father was a Christian convert and his mother a Jewish convert, who migrated to Fes somewhere around 890 AH. In his youth he encountered Shaykh al-Ghazwānī who sprinkled him with some water, and later he credited the baraka of this act for helping him to grow into a pious and upright man. Thereafter and throughout his youth he constantly yearned to meet with Shaykh al-Ghazwānī again, who had moved to the city of Murrākesh. When he grew older he finally accomplished his wish and travelled there and he spent four months studying directly from the Shaykh.

He later returned to find that the zāwiyah of al-Ghazwānī in Fes had been taken over by one of his students, Abū ʿAbdullāh Sidi Muḥammad al-Ṭālib, and so he entered into the service of this Shaykh and served him sincerely for a great many years. Later still, he committed himself to the pursuit of knowledge and began

12 This is not to say that he became a prophet. Rather, in Sufi terminology this is a way of saying that he reached a station whose essence flowed from and was in the mould of the Prophet ʿĪsā, carrying the spirit of his way, so that he became something akin to how ʿĪsā was.

studying the outward sciences with Shaykh Abū Muḥammad Abd al-Raḥmān al-Suqayyān (whose own teacher took from Ibn Ḥajar al-ʿAsqālanī), and later still he visited and became the student of the famous Sufi shaykh Al-Hajj Abū ʿAbdullāh Muḥammad ibn ʿAlī al-Andalūsī al-Burjī, of the Banī Zarwāl. He also took from Shaykh Abū ʿAbdullāh Sidi Muḥammad ibn ʿAlī al-Jazūlī al-Tarāblisī, who commented on the *Ṣalat al-Mashīshiyya.*

Thereafter he took up teaching the path and became spectacularly famous, such that he was described by various men as truly one of a kind, the wonder of their age. Some commented that the likes of a shaykh such as himself had not been seen in Fes since the time of Ibn ʿAbbād (al-Rondī). He had a profound humbleness and serenity to him that awed hearts, and used to weep so much that his teacher took to calling him "Riḍwān al-Bakkā" (Riḍwān the Weeper). He did not allow himself to be called a shaykh or considered as such, and in gatherings of knowledge he would sit with such stillness and calm that one would think he was sleeping.

He in fact went on to become one of the most famous saints of Fes, and the only companion of al-Ghazwānī to gain any particular fame in that city. He died in the year 991 AH and was buried in the Bāb al-Futūḥ cemetery. He had no sons but one daughter, and his progeny in Fes through her are known today as the Awlād ibn Mubārak (the sons and daughters of the Blessed One).

▲ Bab Futuh cemetery, with Borj Sud visible in the distance on the right.

◀ Previous page, the Bab Futuh cemetery. On the left of the image, one of the larger mausoleums, the Mausoleum of Sidi Ḥarazim under restoration.

▼ The Mausoleum of Sidi Ḥarazim in the Bab Futuh Cemetery, pictured in 2014, while it was under restoration.

7 Visiting Outside of Fes

Noteworthy saints, scholars and sultans buried in the provinces directly around or near Fes

As the distinct spiritual and intellectual capital of Morocco, Fes was the place of residence, in life and then in death, of countless notable saints and scholars of the Western Islamic world. However, to restrict this guidebook to those saints who are to be found strictly within the city limits would do a great disservice to both the saints of Morocco as well as to the modern spiritual tourist seeking to immerse his or herself in its tradition. Many important saints travelled to Fes to study, drinking from the overflowing fount of baraka and knowledge that sprang from the city, before emigrating to nearby lands to establish themselves. Others lived such a short distance away that their teachings and followers could not help but penetrate the city, to such an extent that the tale of one city cannot be done justice without giving at least a passing glance to the other.

In either case, these saints who established themselves outside of Fes unequivocally belong to the family of Moroccan Sufism that the city is known for today, and deserve equal mention in this guidebook. Many of them were so influential that they have become synonymous with the Sufi tradition of the country, providing examples of saintliness that in so short a list as this are often referenced too briefly to demonstrate their greatness.

In touristic terms, all of the saints mentioned in this section can be visited during a simple day trip from the city of Fes, departing in the morning and returning before sundown. Some of them, like the venerable Ibn Mashīsh, are located in quaint little villages where one can find lodging for the night to extend their visit if they so choose, or are so nearby to other noteworthy cities like Chefchouan that a visit to one can easily extend out of a visit to the other. Visiting the saints in this section can be a great way to see many of the other nearby cities and tourist centres that deserve to be visited, such as Meknes, Chefchouan, Tetouan, and the sacred city of Jabal Zorhūn, which for nearly a thousand years allowed no non-Muslims to step foot in it until the French occupation forced it open.

Individual guides detailing the specific tourist attractions of all of these cities are easily available, and so unlike with the city of Fes, this section will make no effort to delve into the broader history or attractions of the featured regions. Rather, this section will restrict itself to details of the saints' lives, deaths, locations, as well as practical details on how to visit them. Beginning this list is Sidi ʿAbd al-Salām ibn Mashīsh of the Shādhilī Ṭarīqa, often seen as the patron saint of Moroccan Sufism.

Sidi ʿAbd al-Salām ibn Mashīsh al-Ḥassanī al-Idrīssī (559/563–622 AH)

His name was ʿAbd al-Salām, the son of Mashīsh, the son of Abū Bakr, and he was a descendant of the Prophet ﷺ through his noble grandchild Ḥassan and the founder of the Moroccan state Sidi Idrīs. He was the Quṭb of Morocco in his time, a great shaykh who gathered together knowledge of both the ḥaqīqah and the sharīʿah.

It is said that on the day he was born, the great saint ʿAbd al-Qādir al-Jīlānī heard a voice calling to him, "O ʿAbd al-Qādir! Raise your leg from the people of the West, for the Quṭb of the West has been born this day!"[13] So ʿAbd al-Qādir left for the Jabal ʿAlām upon which Sidi Mashīsh was born and approached his father Sidi Mashīsh, saying to him, "Send out to me your son." Sidi Mashīsh sent out one of his sons, to which ʿAbd al-Qādir replied, "This is not the one I want." So Sidi Mashīsh sent out all of his sons, and said that aside from them none remained except for one who had been born just that day. ʿAbd al-Qādir al-Jīlānī replied, "Bring him to me, for he is the one I want." So Sidi Mashīsh brought him out to ʿAbd al-Qādir al-Jīlānī, who stroked the infant and supplicated for him.

It is also said that when Sidi ʿAbd al-Salām was still a nursing babe, he would abstain from nursing during the day in the month of Ramadan, and only approached his mother's breast after the adhān for the sunset prayer.

He was born in a small village slightly below the peak of the Jabal ʿAlām and the house of his birthplace is still preserved today, though it has been transformed into a kutāb wherein young

13 This is a reference to the famous saying attributed to ʿAbd al-Qādir Jilānī, that "his feet are upon the necks" of all other saints, i.e. he is the master of all of them.

children memorise the Quran.[14] The exact date of his birth, however, is not known, with some historians postulating he was born in the year 559 or 563 AH.

Taqī al-Dīn al-Iskandarī mentions that Sidi ʿAbd al-Salām began travelling the Sufi path when he was a child of no more than seven years old, and while he was still barely a youth he experienced unveilings of a mountainous scale. He remained a Quṭb for no less than twenty years. When he prayed, all of the saints from various regions, both male and female, prayed behind him. He possessed a powerful spiritual pull (*jadhb*), such that no sincere seeker who had divested himself of all his previous knowledge reached him but that he raised him up and brought him to arrival at his Lord.

It is sufficient in praise of Sidi ʿAbd al-Salām to say that he was the teacher of the three Quṭbs: Sidi Ibrāhīm al-Dusūqī, Sidi Aḥmad al-Badawī, and Sidi Abū al-Ḥassan al-Shādhilī (though, in other accounts it is said he had only one student in his whole career, and this was al-Shādhilī).

Sidi ʿAbd al-Salām's teacher in the Sufi way was the saint ʿAbd al-Raḥmān al-ʿAttār al-Madanī al-Zayyāt, who has a mausoleum in the city of Targhah on the shore near Tetouan and whom the locals refer to as "Faqīh Mūlay ʿAbd al-Salām". ʿAbd al-Salām is better known by virtue of his own student Shaykh al-Shādhilī and the tale of his legendary search for the Quṭb of his time. As a youth, al-Shādhilī was studying in the Qarawiyyin when his teacher Shaykh al-Ḥarāzim initiated him into the path of spiritual wayfaring. His Shaykh also regaled him with tales of the Quṭbs of the past, such that an insatiable desire to meet and study with the

14 Recently, a great shaykh of the Orient who had travelled a great distance to visit ʿAbd al-Salām happened to pass away right inside the house, and so the locals honoured this event by building him a shrine and burying him inside ʿAbd al-Salām's home.

Quṭb of his time, wherever he was, consumed him and he set out to the East in search of him. As al-Shādhilī himself recounts:

> When I entered the country of Iraq (during my journey East) I met Shaykh Abū al-Fatḥ al-Wāsiṭī and indeed I did not see another shaykh like him in all of Iraq, and there were many shaykhs in Iraq. I was searching for the Quṭb, and Sidi Abū al-Fatḥ said to me, "You are seeking the Quṭb in Iraq while he is in your country?! Return to your country and you will find him." So I returned to Morocco until eventually I met my teacher the saint (*walī*) the gnostic, the *ṣiddīq* (righteously truthful man), the Quṭb and the Ghawth Abū Muḥammad ʿAbd al-Salām ibn Mashīsh al-Sharīf al-Ḥassanī.
>
> When I found him he was living in seclusion (*ribāt*) in a cave at the peak of the mountain. I first washed myself in a spring at the foot of the mountain and emptied myself of all of the knowledge and works I had acquired until that day and climbed up to him as one poor and divest of all things (*faqīran*) when I found him descending to meet me. When he saw me he said, "I bid welcome to ʿAlī ibn ʿAbdullāh ibn ʿAbd al-Jabbār!" He then recited to me my entire lineage all the way back to the Prophet ﷺ. He then said to me, "O ʿAlī, you have come to us divested (*faqīran*) of all of your knowledge and your works, and you have taken from us all the riches of this world and the next." I was amazed by him, and stayed with him a number of days until Allah opened for me my inner sight (*basīrah*). In that time I witnessed numerous miracles and the breaking of norms manifest from him.

A seeker once came to Shaykh ʿAbd al-Salām and asked, "Give me daily practices (*waẓāʾif*) that I may perform." ʿAbd al-Salām replied, "Am I a prophet? The prescribed works (*farāʾiḍ*) of the religion are well known, as are the forbidden actions. So uphold the *farāʾiḍ* and reject that which is forbidden, and protect your heart from yearning for the lower world. Content yourself absolutely with what Allah has prescribed for you. If there comes to you what pleases you, be grateful, and if there comes to you what pains you, be patient."

It is also said that the Shaykh penned the following prayer in verse form:

> O my Lord, verily multitudes have asked you that you grant them the acceptance of people,
>
> And that you subjugate for them your creation, and so you subjugated it for them, and they were pleased with you,
>
> As for myself I ask you for the people's aversion, and that you turn them against me,
>
> Such that I am left with no refuge, but with you.

One of the miracles reported by al-Shādhilī was that once he was sitting in the presence of the Shaykh and thought to himself, "I wonder if the Shaykh knows God's Greatest Name." At that moment ʿAbd al-Salām's son, at that time merely a boy, said, "O Abū al-Ḥassan, the matter is not who knows the name, rather the essence of the matter is who it is that is the source of the Name (*ʿayn al-ʾism*)." On hearing this ʿAbd al-Salām responded, "My boy has explained the matter to you correctly."

In addition to his own, there are two other graves in the rawḍa of Ibn Mashīsh, these being of his oldest son Muḥammad (of the aforementioned anecdote) and his servant. The grave of Ibn Mashīsh was not in fact a well-known pilgrimage site until the famous Jazūlī Shaykh al-Ghazwānī himself popularised it by suggesting pilgrimages to Mashīsh's tomb at a time when all Moroccans had been prohibited from performing the Hajj and were seeking other means of travelling for the sake of God.

The mosque that Sidi Mashīsh used to perform his worship in, and which today is still located near both his tomb and the cave he preferred for seclusion on the Jabal ʿAlām, is called "The Mosque of the Angels" (*Jāmiʿa al-Malāʾika*). The famous fable developed by the local populace regarding this is that it was established by the angels, and it is said when he prayed there thousands of angels in the form of white birds would circle in the sky above.

He died a martyr at the hands of the assassins of Ibn Abū Tawājin, a sorcerer and false-prophet who ʿAbd al-Salām spoke out against. He was buried in his place at the Jabal al-ʿAlām, and thereafter a maqām, a mausoleum, and a small qubbah were built upon his tomb. His tomb is to Morocco as al-Shāfiʿī's tomb is to Egypt, and prayers made there are answered.

The author of *al-Muṭrib* also notes that he found an old document in Spain that claims Abū Tawājin had his followers assassinate the Shaykh because he had a following from among the djinn and that one day they were late coming to him. When he asked them why, they replied that they had passed by a mountain on their way there where a man was engaged in worship, and upon looking at him they had burst into flames from the light he emitted. So, Abū Tawājin then ordered for this man to be killed.

Directions: To reach Sidi ʿAbd al-Salām (as the locals refer to him) is surprisingly easy considering the great saint lived and died on a mountain peak, and that the only roads to reach him stretch along dozens of miles of simple dirt paths with mountains to the left and steep cliffside to the right. While the idea may sound daunting, the roads are actually quite broad and there are some companies in Morocco that even arrange for private buses to the top, when some large group or another requests them. So, unless one has a particularly debilitating fear of heights, or a particularly sensitive stomach averse to swerving and climbing, there is really not much to fear about the trek to the tomb.

The best way to reach the tomb, if one is not part of a large group with a privately hired bus, is to first buy a bus ticket with the company CTM departing from Fes to the city of Chefchouan. The trip takes about four to five hours by bus with stops in between, before depositing its riders securely in the downtown of Chefchouan (about 120–200 dirhams for the fare). The bus conveniently passes through Wazzān for this journey, so if one wishes they can stop there to visit some of the other saints mentioned in this section.

From there, depending on whether one intends to pay a brief or long visit to the tomb, it might be prudent to arrange a hotel for the night in the city of Chefchouan itself. There are many, and the medina of Chefchouan is among the most splendid of any city in Morocco, so the effort is worth it. If, however, one intends to spend the night at the tombside, one can flag down a local taxi and ask to be taken to the grand taxi station at Chefchouan (*Mahatat al-grande taxiyat*), where taxi drivers sit around all day and much of the evening waiting to ferry riders to the city of Tetouan.

The village of Mūlay ʿAbd al-Salām, as it is called, is about halfway between Chefchouan and Tetouan and well-known to the locals there, and it does not take much effort to hire a driver for the trek, though it can take a little more effort settling on a price for the journey. As it is more than a little out of the way the drivers cannot sell other seats for this trip and so you will have to pay for the whole cab, and a reasonable fare to expect is anywhere between 400–600 dirhams ($40–60) roundtrip. Haggling may be necessary.

Once at the little village of the tomb, cheap accommodation can be found for about 100 dirhams a night if you speak to the locals. The rooms are spacious and secure but the beds are thin and hard, so bringing some camping supplies is not a bad idea. Some restaurants can be found near the tomb serving extremely simple fare. If one spends the night there, there are a few small buses that depart every day from the village to the city of Tetouan that can be boarded for 40 dirhams.

Otherwise the best bet is to simply ask your taxi driver to wait for an hour or a few hours—he isn't likely to mind terribly—and then return promptly to Chefchouan (about an hour's drive). If all of these directions seems daunting, however, and one has a poor grasp of Arabic or French making it hard to communicate, then it is quite likely that the front desk of whatever hotel one stays at in Chefchouan would be willing to help arrange the trip for you in exchange for a small commission and a slightly inflated pricetag. Otherwise, it may be possible to convince a grand taxi driver to undergo the whole journey starting from Fes privately for a fee of around 1,000–1,500 dirhams ($100–150), and the grand taxi station of Fes is conveniently located right next to the CTM bus station in the new city. This is not a common request, however.

Sidi Aḥmad Zarrūq (846–899 AH)

His full name was Sidi Aḥmad ibn Aḥmad ibn Muḥammad ibn ʿĪsā al-Barnūsī al-Fāsī, though he was known as al-Zarrūq. He was born in the era of the Merinid kings of Morocco and rose to become one of the greatest figures in tasawwuf, in both his era and beyond. He was famous for not only his knowledge of the path but of the outward sciences of fiqh, sīra, hadith and the like.

Both his mother and father died within a week of his birth so he was raised by his grandmother who was a faqīhah (jurist). She provided for him and enrolled him in a Maktab, and by the age of ten he had memorised the Quran and went on to apply himself to the pursuit of knowledge. He studied under numerous shuyūkh such as ʿAbdullāh al-Fakhār, ʿAlī al-Sebt, ʿAbd al-Raḥmān al-Thuʿālibī, Ibrāhīm al-Tāzī, and the Imam al-Qorwī.

In his time a great many famous shuyūkh also took from him, such as the Quṭb al-Shaʿrānī, al-Qastalānī, al-Hitāb, Nāsir al-Dīn al-Liqānī, and the gnostic Ibn al-Ḥassan al-Bakrī. Upon Aḥmad Zarrūq's visit to Egypt, wherein he gave a lecture at the al-Azhar University, six thousand people flocked to attend; such was his fame in that time.

In tasawwuf, Sidi Aḥmad Zarrūq took first from Shaykh Abū ʿAbdullāh Sidi Muḥammad al-Zaytūnī. Later, there arose something of an alienation between himself and his Shaykh and so Sidi Zarrūq travelled from Fes to Egypt where he became a student of the Shādhilī Shaykh Sidi Aḥmad ibn ʿUqbah al-Ḥaḍramī. Sidi al-Ḥaḍramī informed his companions of Sidi Zarrūq's arrival before he had even arrived, and told them to rise and meet their brother. When Sidi Zarrūq arrived, however, his previous Shaykh al-Zaytūnī in Fes struck him (spiritually) with such a blow that the zāwiyah was brought down around him and he was only saved by the intercession of Shaykh al-Ḥaḍramī. Sidi al-Ḥaḍramī intercepted this strike at the expense of his own hand, which he later showed to Sidi Zarrūq, who saw it had been destroyed.

He then studied under al-Ḥaḍramī until he achieved his spiritual opening and became a profoundly knowledgeable man, a master of both the inward and the outward sciences. He was also described as very severe towards innovations and firm in upholding the boundaries of the Divine Law, to such an extent that it was said about him, "He is indeed the accountant (*muḥtasib*) of the Sufīs" for the way that he held them to account for some of their practices.

One of the miracles attributed to him was narrated by Ibn Ghāzī, who said that he once invited the Shaykh and his companions to dinner at his home. When the time came for dinner, only Shaykh Aḥmad Zarrūq had arrived so Ibn Ghāzī asked him about the others and told him that there was a great deal of food prepared and that it would go to waste. Sidi Zarrūq replied, "It will be used, insha Allah, and will not go to waste." He then instructed Ibn Ghāzī to give him what food he had, and Ibn Ghāzī began passing Sidi Zarrūq the food piece by piece, while Sidi Zarrūq handed the food to people gathered in great throngs in a vast open space, among them men and women and children. Sidi Zarrūq asked if any food remained and Ibn Ghāzī replied in the negation, and then asked about the people they had been feeding. Aḥmad Zarrūq replied that they were the poor and the needy of the city of Tunis and that the open space Ibn Ghāzī had perceived was the courtyard of the Zaytuna mosque.

Directions: It is said Aḥmad Zarrūq passed away in 899 AH in Libya; however, his zāwiyah, which is on the Jabal Zalagh outside Fes, still holds a tomb for him until this day. To access the tomb one takes a grand taxi from the bus and taxi station outside the Bāb al-Gheesa to Mount Zalagh and treks to the top. The mountain is a popular hiking destination, and the zāwiyah is also a fairly well-known tourist destination.

Mūlay Idrīs al-Akbar (177 AH)

His full name was Mūlay Idrīs ibn ʿAbdullāh ibn Ḥassan ibn al-Ḥassan ibn ʿAlī ibn Abū Ṭālib and he was the first of the noble Idrīssīd house as well as the founder of the Moroccan state. The reason for his coming to Fes revolves around the failed uprising of Muḥammad Nafs al-Zakīyah (the Pure Soul), who revolted against the Caliph Abū Jaʿfar Manṣūr al-ʿAbbāsī in the year 145 AH. This revolt was a failure, in which Muḥammad Nafs al-Zakīyah and his six brothers were killed, each of whom had been sent to various countries by their brother Muḥammad to recruit soldiers for the uprising, but were forced to flee to various localities or were in turn killed and their uprisings suppressed. In the aftermath of this devastating event, Mūlay Idrīs fled to Morocco with his servant al-Rashīd.

They departed secretly to the West, deploying all means of subterfuge and advancing slowly, before finally arriving in Morocco in the year 170 AH. Their first stop was in the city of Tilimsān, where they took refuge for a while, and then they advanced to the city of Tangiers which was then the greatest city of Morocco, and indeed the country's oldest, and the mother of all other cities. However, Mūlay Idrīs did not find what he was looking for in Tangiers, so he departed south until he came to the city of Wailīlī at the foot of Mount Zerhoun, which was a city originally established by the Romans and encompassed by a great wall [in that time]. This was the year 172 AH.

The governor of Wailīlī at that time was a man named Isḥāq ibn Muḥammad ibn ʿAbd al-Ḥamīd of the tribe of the ʾŪrubī, which was then the strongest and greatest tribe in Morocco. Isḥaq ibn Muḥammad welcomed Mūlay Idrīs with open arms, venerated his lineage, and accepted him into his own house and care. After a while Isḥāq ibn Muḥammad announced Mūlay Idrīs' presence in the city and his noble lineage, and the whole city of Wailīlī swore fealty to him as their new lord.

After a while the various other tribes of Morocco came to know of Mūlay Idrīs' position and followed the ʾŪrubī tribe in swearing fealty to him. He came to possess in due course a mighty army comprised of the Zanātah, the ʾŪrubī, the Ṣanhāja, the Hawārah and other Amazigh tribes of Morocco. With it, his authority was established and he began to conquer the neighbouring regions, first of Tāmisnā then of Tādla, which were then primarily Christian and Jewish territories. At his hands all of them converted to Islam and became a part of his new kingdom, and thereafter in the year 173 he returned to Wailīlī to rest after his successful conquests. Soon after he set out again and conquered more of the surrounding regions, all the way down to the city of Tilimsān whose governor swore fealty peacefully.

At this time the caliph in Iraq began to take notice of Mūlay Idrīs and his growing prominence. At first Caliph Rashīd was determined to send his army to Morocco to deal with Mūlay Idrīs personally but then retracted his plan, realising that his forces would not be able to withstand the journey all the way to Morocco from Iraq. He then consulted his minister, who advised him that they send instead one capable man to assassinate Mūlay Idrīs and grant themselves relief from him forever, and volunteered a man in his army named Sulaymān ibn Jarīr for the task.

Sulaymān ibn Jarīr eventually made it to Wailīlī where he presented himself to Mūlay Idrīs as one of the slaves of his father and a servant of the family of the Prophet ﷺ who had come all the way from the East out of his love and loyalty to them. Mūlay Idrīs was deeply impressed with Sulaymān's eloquence and fineness of character, as well as starved for equal companionship amongst the uneducated Amazighs of his new kingdom, and so he took Sulaymān into his closest confidence and raised him to a high position in his kingdom.

Sulaymān one day presented Mūlay Idrīs with a vial which he claimed contained a marvellous perfume from the East which in reality was a deadly poison, and after watching Mūlay Idrīs open the vial and inhale its fumes he immediately left. He took a stallion of the finest breeding which he had specially prepared for the occasion and sought refuge in the East, while Mūlay Idrīs collapsed on the ground, sick for reasons none could comprehend.

Mūlay Idrīs died not long thereafter in the year 177 AH, five years after the founding of his kingdom. What followed is as described in the biography of his son, Mūlay Idrīs of Fes.

Directions: To arrive at the mosque and tomb of Mūlay Idrīs requires travelling from either Fes or Meknes to the town named after this saint, Mūlay Idrīs (Moulay Idrīs). The city is almost entirely compromised of the huge mosque Mūlay Idrīs is buried in. Any grand taxi in Meknes will be willing to make the journey for a few hundred dirhams whereas the grand taxi station of Fes, located next to the CTM bus station in the new city, is the best place to hire a taxi from Fes. These taxis perform day trips to all sorts of tourist destinations in the area and have a chart of set prices they follow (though you may still have to haggle). The journey takes at least five hours roundtrip and can cost anywhere between 500–800 dirhams. The taxi will likely offer to stop along the Roman ruins of Volubilis (Wailīlī) along the way.

For those wishing to spend the night, the owner of the popular café in Fes called The Café Clock recently opened a restaurant in Zerhoun called Dar Akrab (The Scorpion House). A British-owned hotel called Dar Zerhoune offers decent accommodation and lots of tourism opportunities.

Mūlay ʿAbdullāh Sharīf al-Wazzānī and The Seven Quṭbs of Wazzān (1089 AH)

His full name was Abū Muḥammad Mūlay ʿAbdullāh ibn Mūlay Ibrāhīm al-Sharīf al-Ḥassanī al-Idrīssī al-ʿIlmī al-Yamlaḥī al-Maṣmūdī al-Wazzānī, and he was the founding shaykh of the Ṭarīqa Wazzānīyah and the quṭb of their noble house. Mūlay ʿAbdullāh Sharīf took from the great saint Abū al-Ḥassan Sidi ʿAlī al-Ṣarṣarī buried in Mount Ṣarṣar, who took from Shaykh Sidi al-Ḥassan ibn ʿĪsā al-Misbāḥī, who it is said took from his father ʿĪsā and so on back to Shaykh al-Jazūlī.

It is also narrated that after Shaykh Mūlay ʿAbdullāh Sharīf's father passed away, his mother remarried a man who desired that Mūlay ʿAbdullāh should give up his studies in order to help perform physical labour for the family. Mūlay ʿAbdullāh's mother assented to this request, and so her son was expelled from his studies and sent out to work.

Then, the first day Mūlay ʿAbdullāh was performing his new work Shaykh Mūlay Muḥammad ibn ʿAlī ibn ʿĪsā, a distant descendant of ʿAbd al-Salām ibn Mashīsh, passed by Mūlay ʿAbdullāh and saw him crying. He asked why the boy was crying and Mūlay ʿAbdullāh explained what had happened. The Shaykh reassured the boy and told him that he was heading to his village of Tasarūt and that when he arrived he would gather up all of the boy's noble cousins and other prominent scholars of the village and demand that his mother return him to his studies. The Shaykh then said, "For I do indeed see the people swarming upon you to follow you, and that there will not exist in all the West a Ṭarīqa loftier than your own."

At the end of that day, Mūlay ʿAbdullāh returned home to find all the noble men of Tasarūt gathered at the door to his house. They spoke to his mother on the boy's behalf, informing her of what would become of him and the great spiritual station he would reach, and how he would develop a following greater than any man in the West. His mother was greatly pleased and returned the boy to his studies.

It is recorded in *al-Rawḍ al-Munīf* by Mūlay Ṭayyib al-Wazzānī himself, that when Mūlay ʿAbdullāh Sharīf's shaykh al-Ṣarṣarī passed away Mūlay ʿAbdullāh entered a place near the country of the Maṣmūdah Amazighs and performed khalwa[15] for a total of fourteen months. In that time nobody was allowed to see the Shaykh except for one man from among his companions, Sidi ʿAbd al-Kabīr ʿAlawāt, who would visit him occasionally to provide him with food and whatever sustenance he needed.

Sidi ʿAlawāt remarked that he never entered upon the Shaykh in all those fourteen months, be it day or night, except that he found the Shaykh standing on his feet reciting, "O Allah, send peace and blessings upon our master Muḥammad, the unlettered prophet, and upon his family and companions."

One day Sidi ʿAlawāt remarked that he entered upon the Shaykh just before sunrise and found him reclining. Sidi ʿAlawāt remarked, "O Sidi, are not the likes of yourself usually in religious practice at this hour?" To which the Shaykh replied, "O ʿAbd al-Kabīr, there is no need for me now to stand or perform my practice. I have received my opening, all thanks be to God. My forefather the Messenger of God ﷺ appeared to me and said, and I do not brag, 'Your affair is now [one] with the affair of God. If you say "Be" then it is.' He spoke to me 34 times as I was awake, not sleeping, and said to me, 'Stretch out your hand and your foot and receive those who come to you—may Allah protect you—and of those who follow you, receive he who is in rebellion [against God] and he who is in obedience alike, you and your children, and I will

15 Spiritual retreat in isolation.

be to them al-Ḍāmin (the guarantor) on the Day of Judgement. Whoever loves you indeed loves me, and whoever has angered you indeed has angered me."

He died in the year 1089 AH and was buried in Wazzān. Buried near to him are his seven major spiritual descendants of the Ṭarīqa Wazzānīyah. From these seven Quṭbs and the other shuyūkh of the Wazzānīyah a great spiritual tradition was born in Morocco. The city of Wazzān became regarded in time as the Dār al-Ḍamānah (the house of security), with the legend being that whoever set foot on its holy soil had secured their place in paradise.

These Quṭbs are:

- Sidi al-Ḥassan al-Hawārī, who was his muqaddam amongst the Maṣmūdah Amazigh tribes of the West.
- Mūlay Muḥammad ibn ʿAbdullāh al-Wazzānī, his son and inheritor (1120 AH).
- Mūlay Tuhāmī, Mūlay Muḥammad's son and inheritor (1127 AH).
- Mūlay al-Ṭayyib ibn Muḥammad al-Wazzānī, Mūlay Tuhāmī's brother (1181 AH).
- Mūlay Aḥmad, Mūlay Ṭayyib's son and inheritor (1196 AH).
- Mūlay ʿAlī ibn Aḥmad, his son and inheritor (1226 AH).
- Maḥmad ibn Aḥmad al-Rahūnī, his student (1230 AH), who was the author of the *Ḥāshiyyat al-Zuruqānī.*
- Al-ʿArabī ibn ʿAlī, Sidi Maḥmad's son, inheritor, and the seventh Quṭb of the Wazzānī Ṭarīqa (1266 AH).

Directions: To get to the tombs of the Shurufā' of the holy house of Wazzān requires taking a visit to the actual modern day city of Wazzān. It is located about halfway between Chefchouan and Fes and so anyone wishing to pay a visit to the saint Ibn Mashīsh may find it convenient to plan these two visits together. The city of Mūlay Idrīs is also somewhat along the way, though it requires a bit of a detour towards the West.

For good speakers of Arabic or French it is an easy enough matter to simply take a bus with CTM from Fes to Wazzān and then ask for directions from any local or local taxi driver to the tomb of Mūlay 'Abdullāh Sharīf, as he is known. The tombsite complex of the Wazzānīs is the largest in all Morocco, located centrally within the city of Wazzān, and well-known to the locals. The grave rests in a public cemetery in the north of the city near a mosque at which locals pray the Friday prayer, and next to the mosque resides the traditional mansion of the Wazzāni Shurufā' who ran the city for centuries and still live there today with their impressive manuscript library, the *Dar al-Ḍamānah*. The tomb becomes quite lively with visitors from the mosque after Friday prayer. Otherwise, for non-Arabic and French speakers, it may be wise to speak to one's hotel in Fes or a hotel in Wazzān and arrange a tour through the help of the front desk.

The city of Wazzān itself sits at the entry to the Rif mountains, the centre of drug production in Morocco. Due to this, and also due to a lack of any particular tourist attractions (and therefore revenue) other than the tombs, Wazzān is not the most pleasant city in Morocco. If one is not able to communicate well in the local tongue it is advisable to plan one's trip in advance and with a guide, even if it costs more, and one may prefer to spend the night in the nearby city of Chefchouan.

Sidi ʿAbd al-Raḥmān al-Majdhūb (976 AH)

His full name was Abū al-ʿAzm Sidi ʿAbd al-Raḥmān ibn ʿIyyād ibn Yaʿqūb ibn Salāma al-Ṣinhājī, though he was popularly known as al-Majdhūb. Sidi ʿAbd al-Raḥmān was the student of Sidi ʿAlī al-Ṣanhājī al-Dawwār, and it is from him he took the Ṭarīqa and relied upon on the spiritual path. In spite of this, it is said that they only in fact met once, in the Qarawiyyin mosque in Fes.

He was the inheritor of a number of the shuyūkh of his time, the first of whom was his shaykh Sidi ʿAlī al-Ṣinhājī and the last of whom was the shaykh Sidi ʿUmar al-Luwāh al-Sarīfī. Sidi ʿAbd al-Raḥmān was also a shaykh of the Malāmatī tradition, like his shaykh Sidi ʿAlī before him and his shaykh Sidi Ibrāhīm Āfahām before him. For this reason he used to display behaviour which shocked people and caused them to flee from him and despise him, while in truth he was upon the ḥaqīqah (reality). In spite of his shocking behaviour he was in truth firmly established in and attentive to the rules of sharīʿah. He took great care to understand and follow the sunnah of the Prophet ﷺ and advised his followers to do the same.

ʿAbd al-Raḥmān died in the year 976 in the middle of a Friday night, on Eid al-Adhā, in the country of Owf. His body was carried to Meknes and buried next to the grave of Sidi ʿImrān ibn Mūsā outside the Bāb ʿĪsā. Afterwards, his student Sidi Yūsuf Abū al-Maḥāsin built a Qubbah over his grave.

Today Sidi ʿAbd al-Raḥmān is best known for his marvellous works of poetry, which continue to be very popular across Morocco. His poetry and the legends surrounding him are so vivid that the lauded Moroccan playwright Tayeb Saddiqi (1938–2016) constructed a play based on the modern oral transmission of these legends, titled *Diwan Sidi Abderrahman al-Majdhūb.*

Directions: Sidi ʿAbd al-Rahman al-Majdhūb has the best real estate of any of the saints in this book—directly in the palace of the Sultan of Meknes! Mūlay Ismaʿīl the Sultan greatly revered this saint and therefore purposely built his own palace and later, tomb, directly around the tomb of al-Majdhūb. The palace of Mūlay Ismaʿīl is a popular tourist destination of Meknes for Muslims and non-Muslims alike, and is to be found to the right-hand side of the open courtyard in the centre of the palace, to the far side of which rests the tomb of the Sultan himself. If one speaks to the guardian of the Sultan's tomb and offers him a small donation he can open up the tomb of al-Majdhūb for you. Access to Meknes itself is exceptionally easy, whether by train, bus, or grand taxi. Taking the train is easiest.

Shaykh al-Kāmil Sidi Muḥammad ibn ʿĪsā (1041)

His full name was Abū ʿAbdullāh Sidi Muḥammad ibn ʿĪsā al-Fahdī al-Sufiyyānī al-Mukhtārī al-Maknāsī, and he is the shaykh and founder of the great ʿĪsawiyya Ṭarīqa in Morocco. It is said that while most saints drank as if out of a spoon from the ocean of the Prophet ﷺ, Sidi al-Kāmil was completely immersed in it, and that the Shaykh did not die until he had reached the station of a complete Quṭb. Shaykh al-Basrī said that there were three shuyūkh in Morocco who had no equal: Sidi ibn ʿĪsā, ʿAbdullāh al-Ghazwānī, and Abū Muḥammad ʿAbdullāh al-Ḥabtī.

Shaykh al-Kāmil took from three shuyūkh, all of whom were direct companions of the famous Shādhilī saint Imam al-Jazūlī, buried in Murrākesh. These were: Abū al-ʿAbbās Aḥmad ibn ʿUmar al-Ḥārithī al-Sufiyyānī (buried in Meknes), then after him and by his orders Shaykh ʿAbd al-ʿAzīz al-Ṭibāʿ, then from Sidi al-Ṣaghīr al-Sahlī.

The Shaykh died in the year 1041 and was buried in a tremendous Qubbah just outside the medina of Meknes. His followers are numerous and spread throughout all of Morocco until today, and upon the occasion of the Prophet's ﷺ birthday the Qubbah is filled with an enormous crowd.

Directions: If one is undertaking a trip to Meknes to visit the tomb of al-Majdhūb and see the city then a visit to the mosque of Muḥammad bin ʿĪsā is a worthy detour. The mosque is massive and can easily be seen on one's way to the old city by taxi from the train or bus station. It is exceptionally well-known in the area and any taxi can take you there. A visit can easily be paid en route to the tomb of al-Majdhūb and the central square of the old city, and the locals sometimes gather after ʿasr. The gatherings here can get a little rowdy, however, so visiting when the tomb is quiet and empty may be preferable.

Mūlay Ismaʿīl, Second ʿAlawite Sultan of Morocco (1727 CE)

The Sultan Mūlay Ismaʿīl was the second king of the ʿAlawite dynasty, which continues to reign until today in Morocco under the current King Muḥammad al-Sādis VI, after its founder and his brother Mūlay al-Rashīd. Mūlay Ismaʿīl rose to power in the year 1672 upon his brother's death, and ruled until his own death in the year 1727. This was a chaotic time in Morocco, in which the ruling Saadian dynasty fell into collapse. Rule of the country fell for a time into the hands of various Sufi orders in an episode called "The Maraboutic Crisis," and competing factions warred for supremacy until the ʿAlawites triumphed.

Mūlay Ismaʿīl himself is most famous for constructing the city of Meknes and filling it with a number of important cultural legacies, and for his immense cruelty and iron fist which earned him the nickname "The Blood-Thirsty". One of his first acts as Sultan was to decapitate and display around the city of Fes some 400 heads, and it is said that over the fifty-five years of his rule he tortured and killed some 30,000 victims. Yet, he is also recognised as one of Morocco's greatest figures, one who inherited a weakened state and transformed it into a powerful nation.

It is famously reported that the wall around the city of Meknes was constructed entirely from Jewish and Christian slave labour, and that when a slave fell ill or was unable to keep up with the work he would merely be buried alive in the wall at the place where he fell. Political opponents were gathered together in an enormous prison constructed beneath the city, which can still be visited today, in addition to the Sultan's own palace and tomb. Furthermore, Mūlay Ismaʿīl instituted a programme to enslave all the blacks in Morocco for his army, regardless of their being free or Muslim. This absolutely contradicts Islamic law and earned him the immense ire of the scholars. These scholars, however, were intimidated into silence. This "blackguard" is said to have constituted as many as 150,000 soldiers. Mūlay Ismaʿīl himself is said to have sired as many as a thousand children from his four wives and 500 odd concubines.

However, it is also known that Mūlay Ismaʿīl loved to visit the tombs of the saints and some question whether he was himself a saint, a tyrant, or perhaps both. The Sultan Mūlay Ismaʿīl is also famous for his peculiar relationship with the saint al-Ḥassan al-Yūsī, considered the greatest scholar of that age in Morocco. It is on the Sultan's request that al-Yūsī devised the "seven saints pilgrimage" ritual now famous in Murrākesh and that al-Jazūlī's tomb was excavated and transferred to Murrākesh to partake in this ritual. Recorded letters also show that Mūlay Ismaʿīl genuinely consulted al-Yūsī on matters of fiqh and Islam. Yet, al-Yūsī also spent a great portion of his life under the Sultan in exile outside Sefrou, and eventually died whilst still in exile. The case of al-Yūsī and Mūlay Ismaʿīl demonstrates the delicate, nuanced, co-dependent relationship that saints frequently held with the governing authorities in Morocco, with one party requiring the favour of the other for spiritual legitimacy amongst the populace, and the latter often at the mercy of the Sultan's armies or beholden to his treasury for subsistence.

Directions: Mūlay Ismaʿīl is buried in his palace in Meknes, which is a well-known tourist destination open to Muslims and non-Muslims alike. From Fes one can take the ONCF trains to Meknes, about an hour away, and from the station it is a short taxi ride into the old city. One can pick up a map of Meknes from the train station, any of which should clearly mark the tomb site.

Mūlay al-ʿArabī al-Darqāwī (1239 AH)

He was among the select few perfect Knowers of God who guide others to God by their actions, words, and all of their states. He became the shaykh of his age, the Kaʿba of the spiritual pilgrims and the example for all travellers of the path. He was born after the year 1150 AH in the Banī Zarwāl, and he died in the year 1239 AH.

In his youth, he only ever took interest in visiting the righteous and reciting the Quran. He mastered the seven styles of recitation before enrolling in the Madrasah Maṣbāḥiyya in Fes in pursuit of knowledge. This continued until he met his shaykh, Sidi ʿAlī al-Jamal.

It is related that before this happened, Sidi al-Darqāwī sat in the mausoleum of Mūlay Idrīs and read through the entirety of the Quran sixty times in pursuit of a *murshid* (spiritual guide). Upon completing the sixtieth recitation he began weeping profusely until his eyes turned red and he exited the mausoleum. On his way out he passed by the Sharīf Ḥamīd, who was a grandson of the great Shaykh ʿAbd al-ʿAzīz al-Dabbāgh and greatly esteemed by al-Darqāwī and the people of Fes. Sidi Ḥamīd said to him, "What has happened that I am seeing you like this?" Sidi Ḥamīd pressed him, and so Sidi al-Darqāwī informed him that he was desperately seeking for someone to take his hand (and lead him on the path to God).

Sidi Ḥamīd then replied, "I will lead you to him, if you promise not to consult the people of faulty viewpoints and weak intellects about him." Sidi al-Darqāwī then said, "And who is he?" To which Sidi Ḥamīd replied, "He is the majestic teacher of Prophetic descent, the *Ghawth al-Jāmiʿ*, the vast ocean, Abū al-Ḥassan Sidi ʿAlī ibn ʿAbd al-Raḥmān al-ʿImrānī, whom the people call al-Jamal (the camel)."

From then on al-Darqāwī himself directly relates:

> It was my custom never to advance upon either an important or trivial matter until I had performed the Prophet's ﷺ prayer for *istikhārah* (seeking guidance), so I prayed the *istikhārah* that night. As I slept, my thoughts revolved around his character. What was he like? What would my meeting with him be like? In the end I couldn't sleep at all that night, and after I prayed the morning prayer I sought him out in his zāwiyah in Ramīlah, where his grave is now a famous and much sought-after pilgrimage site.

> I knocked on the door, and there he stood tidying the zāwiyah as he never ceased to do with his own blessed hands every morning in spite of his old age and lofty station before God. He said to me, "What do you want?" I replied, "I want, O Master, for you to take me by the hand and lead me to God." In response he turned towards me furiously. I suddenly doubted what I had come for as he disguised his station from me, saying, "Who told you this? And who has taken my hand, that I might take you by yours?" He then severely cursed and scolded me. All of this was merely a test of my sincerity. I ran from him, and that night I again performed the *istikhārah* prayer, and after praying the morning prayer I again sought him out in his zāwiyah. I found him as he was sweeping the zāwiyah, may God be pleased with him, and I knocked on the door. It opened for me, and I said, "Will you take me by the hand and lead me to God?" So he grasped me by my hands and said to me, "You are welcome." He then led me into his place in the zāwiyah, taking the utmost pleasure and delight in me.
>
> I said to him, "O Master, how long I have been searching for a shaykh!" To which he replied, "And how long I have been seeking for a sincere student!" He then taught me the *wird*, and said to me, "Go! And come back again!" After that I would come and go every day, and he introduced me to some of the spiritual seekers of the city of Fes, may God protect her from every harm.

Mūlay al-ʿArabī al-Darqāwī then remained in Fes with his Shaykh for another two years before he asked and received permission to depart for his homeland in the Banī Zarwāl. His spiritual path, during that time and afterwards, was one of extreme asceticism, the likes of which very few men are capable of. It is said that he would not leave anything at night for the next day, and during the following day he would not leave anything over for the night in his pursuit of total reliance upon God in every waking moment. He would wear thick, coarse robes that scratched his skin, walk barefoot through the marketplaces and occasionally beg. He never took more than was enough to provide for himself and his family, and by means of that he reached a great station among the Gnostics.

Directions: The final two saints in this guidebook, Shaykh al-Darqāwī and Abū Yaʿzā, are unquestionably the hardest of any in this book to reach. Both lie deep amidst the countryside, nestled amongst trails of the Atlas mountains, the former about four or five hours north of Fes and the second a similar distance south.

The terrain on the road to al-Darqāwī is treacherous and barren, and on a rainy day no taxi will be willing to undertake the trip as the roads become too muddy and dangerous. On a sunny day, however, your average, intrepid grand taxi will be more than willing to undertake the journey for the right price—no less than 800 dirhams for the day.

Not every grand taxi will know this route. However, if one travels to the large intercity bus station near the Bāb Gheesa (a special "baladī", or popular, bus station used by the lesser bus companies of Morocco) one will find a parking lot full of grand taxis that may be contacted for this operation. If you talk to the drivers there they should help you find someone who knows the way if they don't know it themselves.

The Imam Abū Yaʿzā al-Hazmīrī (438–572 AH)

Among the famous pilgrimage sites of Morocco is the zāwiyah of the famous saint and Ghawth, Imam Abū Yaʿzā Yalnūr al-Hazmīrī. His name, Yalnūr, means "the possessor of light," and he was an uneducated black-skinned Amazigh from the countryside (some say Hazmīrah, some Haskūrah, and some otherwise). He lived to an incredibly old age, reportedly dying at nearly one hundred and thirty years old.

Abū Yaʿzā was the Quṭb of his time, and reached a station that only a select few among the Gnostics ever reach. He did not eat anything of the food that people normally ate, but rather subsisted off of raw plants. Indeed, everything about him was miraculous, and the accounts of his *karamāt* (miracles) were transmitted by an overwhelming multitude of people (*tawātur*) such as leaves no doubt to their authenticity.

It is reported he said, "What are these people who doubt the miracles of the saints? By God, if I was near the sea then all of you would witness me walk on water with your own eyes!" His student Abū Madyan also reportedly said, "I read of the miracles reported about all of the righteous from the time of Uways until today, and I did not see anything more miraculous than what is reported of Sidi Abū Yaʿzā."

Abū Yaʿzā spent fifteen years inhabiting the deserts and wastelands. The lions and beasts would sleep by his side, and the birds perched upon him. If he spoke to them, they would understand what he said and act upon it. If he told the lions not to live in this land, then they would gather their cubs and leave altogether, and if he said to the beasts to go to a place and that they would find sustenance there, then they would go there and find it, just as he had said. After a time, he was ordered to return to the cities, and he entered Fes and benefitted a great many people there.

Ibn al-ʿArabī said about Abū Yaʿzā, "If a man fornicated or stole or cursed or performed any forbidden act whatsoever, Abū Yaʿzā would see that limb by which he had performed the act marked with black markings... and, nobody saw him except that they went blind from the light of his face, and among those who went blind upon seeing him was Sidi Abū Madyan. After seeing him he could not perceive anyone unless he wiped his face with Abū Yaʿzā's robe, after which his sight would return, and thereafter again he would go blind. The people of Morocco used to seek rain by him, and the rain would come."

It says in *al-Maʿzā* that 'Abd al-Qādir al-Jīlānī was once asked if he had a peer anywhere on the Earth, and that he responded there was a black man in Morocco whose name was Āl-Nūr Abū Yaʿzā, who had reached a great station that few among either the first or the last generations of humanity had ever reached. It is also narrated that Shaykh Abū ʿImrān Mūsā al-ʿAbdūsī used to greatly praise Abū Yaʿzā to the extent that he once apparently said there was "none among the awliyāʾ like him." The Shaykh Sidi Yaḥyā al-Sirāj (the student of Ibn ʿAbbād al-Rondī) said regarding him, "The water of Zamzam and he who drinks it, Surah Yā-Sīn and he who reads it, and Abū Yaʿzā and he who visits him [are blessed]."

It is recorded that the saint Abū Hafs ʿUmar al-Hasīnī visited the grave of Abū Yaʿzā in Tāghiyyā every year from Meknes by walking barefoot, a two-day journey. He remarked that it was from the baraka of Abū Yaʿzā's tomb that whoever visited the grave could make one request of God per visit and that it would be granted without fail.

Aḥmad Zarrūq wrote that Abū Yaʿzā had more miracles in death than in life, and the accounts of all these stories are recorded in a book called *al-Maʿzā Fī Akhbār Abū Yaʿzā*. Abū Yaʿzā took from about forty shaykhs in total, prominent among whom was the saint Abū Shuʿayb Ayūb ibn Saʿīd al-Ṣanhājī al-Zamūrī, who was called al-Sāriyya (the Pole) on account of the length of time he would spend standing during his prayer. The most famous of those who took from Abū Yaʿzā was the shaykh Sidi Abū Madyan al-Ghawth.

Abū Yaʿzā died in the year 561, or 571/572 according to different narrations. He was buried in the city of Tāghiyyā and his grave became an extremely famous pilgrimage site.

Directions: To reach the maqām of the saint Abū Yaʿzā requires travelling a few hours south to the town named after him today: Mūlay Bouazza. Undertaking this trip requires the aid of a grand taxi, and should cost around 1,000 dirhams. There is no set fare, however, so one will have to haggle. It is advisable that one speaks directly to the taxi drivers next to the CTM bus station in the new city, or those at the baladī (popular) bus station near Bāb Gheesa. It is not a common route so planning the trip requires finding a willing driver first.

The route will pass in the general direction of Sefrou and Ifrane, which are both pleasant cities worth visiting. Sefrou is distinct for its large Jewish population while Ifrane is a beautiful Swiss-modelled town in the Atlas mountains with a fully functioning American university.

▲ The simple and humble tomb of Shaykh Ibn Mashīsh.

◀ The indoor patio chamber to the north of the mausoleum of Sidi Amar Hassanī in Meknes, with a central fountain and marble columns.

▼ The mausoleum of Idrīs I, noticeable by its green roof.

8 Ziyarah

Visiting the Saints: What to Expect

Much of the content of this guidebook revolves around the ritual of ziyārah—visitations to the graves of saints, scholars and other notables. This chapter provides a more legalistic guide to this ritual by the 20th century saint-scholar Muhammad ibn Jaʿfar al-Kattānī, discussing things like the religious permissibility of the ritual itself as well as the proper etiquettes (what to say, where to sit, etc.). While this is certainly useful information, in truth it is not surprising if after reading this section one feels even more perplexed as to the true nature of this ritual.

After all, why should anyone endeavour to visit gravesites in the first place, particularly those located in tumbling ruins past labyrinths of decayed buildings? Al-Kattānī offers his own explanation for this ritual, drawing on quotes and anecdotes from great luminaries of the classical Islamic tradition. Even so, it is a question one fairly assumes may arise in the 21st century spiritual tourist's mind.

While it may seem perplexing, it is in fact difficult to measure the immense value placed on the ritual of ziyārah in Islamic history and ethos. The closest one might get is to quote the Shādhilī saying that *ṣuḥbah* (keeping company with the righteous) is half of Sufism, or to quote the opening line of Shuʿayb Abū Madyan al-Ghawth's *Diwān* where he extols,

> Oh, and what pleasure in life is there other than keeping company with those poor for the sake of God? For they are in truth the Sultans and Princes (of this Earth).

Of course, how exactly does one keep company with the righteous in their tombs after they have passed away? It is said in the Quran:

> And do not speak of those who are slain in Allah's way as dead, nay, (they are) alive, but you do not perceive. (2:154)

From this we can understand that the inhabitants of tombs continue to subsist in their spiritual life until the Day of Judgement, although their physical life has ceased. Indeed, authentic traditions leading back to the Prophet ﷺ inform us that the grave is either a garden in Paradise or a fire-pit amongst the pits of Hell depending on the soul buried inside of it, and the inhabitant either in suffering or peace. Thus, a visit to the tomb of a saint or righteous believer is in fact a visit to the spirit of the tomb's inhabitant, who has continued their life beyond the grave.

The exact nature of this matter is very mysterious, subtle, and esoteric even to the most educated Muslim. Yet, taken in its proper context, the meaning of this reality is that the visit to the tomb of a saint is unlike any other visit paid on earth, where the meeting is one of body to body. Here, the meeting transforms into one of spirit to spirit, and the shackles of the flesh are removed from the equation altogether. Thus, for those who strive to look beyond the material reality of things, they will understand that to visit a saint in his or her grave is of a truly miraculous and profound nature, as at the tomb of a saint we stand at the meeting place of another realm altogether.

In the sanctuary of a saint our footsteps literally echo in one of the gardens of heaven. Furthermore, not only do we visit the walī, but we visit the One to whom he is near, as is related in the famous Hadith Qudsi:

> Allah says, "He who is hostile to a friend of Mine, I declare war against. My slave approaches Me with nothing more beloved to Me than what I have made obligatory upon him; and My slave keeps drawing nearer to Me with voluntary works until I love him. And when I love him, I am his hearing with which he hears, his sight with which he sees, his hand with which he seizes, and his foot with which he walks. If he asks Me, I will surely give to him; and if he seeks refuge in Me, I will surely protect him."

If one contemplates this hadith they may understand the Prophet ﷺ commanded his followers to visit the graves of the deceased, as it would remind them of death. Yet for the spiritual seeker it is necessary to understand this reminder of death in a more comprehensive way, as a reminder of the objective of the spiritual path (*fanā*), a state which is also called death before one's physical death. At the grave we contemplate these realities, are reminded of them, become in awe of them, and God willing, possibly even awaken to something of them.

In this way, ziyārah of the righteous is a valuable ritual with limitless spiritual benefit. Furthermore, in learning about the saints within these shrines, reading about their life, and contemplating the depth of their devotion and love for God, is a powerful cure for the hearts. Just a few sips of it leads one to tears, softens the heart, eases one's suffering, and reminds one of the true meaning, beauty, and value of this life. After all, these saints were people who took on immense suffering and hardship on a scale many of us cannot even imagine; one of rigorous asceticism, hunger, isolation, battle, loss of friends and family. Yet, from this suffering they harvested the loftiest spiritual states, and the greatest joy, gratitude, and love towards their Creator. Their very existence is a miracle, a stupendous contradiction, and visiting them is nothing less than direct contact with that miracle. This reality cannot be stressed enough, and in the words of the Sufis, cannot really be explained. It can only be tasted through experience.

As for the practical matter of visiting these tombs, I must warn you that the experience will vary. In seeking them out it is perfectly likely that you will get more than a little bit lost at times, since the medina of Fes is a sprawling maze. In this case never be afraid to ask the locals for help, for Moroccans hold a deep love for ziyārah and will not hesitate to help a spiritual tourist along his or her way.

Even if one finds the saint they are looking for, however, it may not always be possible to get inside the tomb if the tomb's guardian is not around. Then, even if one gets inside, the condition of the interior may be shocking. Men who centuries ago were the pride of Morocco often languish today in mausoleums neglected to the point of absolute disrepair. Even some of the marble stones that once marked their tombs have been stolen by thieves.

Others, by contrast, have been recently renovated and restored, or remain more or less in working condition from the time of their disbandment as zāwiyahs. Others, like the Tijānī zāwiyah, are so grand and elegant that one would think they were visiting the tomb of a prince.

A visit to any of the tombs of the saints of Morocco thus varies greatly in flavour. This holds true not only in relation to the condition of the tomb, but to the saint's own experience. At the beginning of my own time in Morocco, for instance, I used to prioritise visiting the tombs of purported Quṭbs and high-ranking saints, to the neglect of the less-esteemed saints. As I matured along the spiritual path, however, I began to realise the error of this. In time I realised that, as the Sufis say, every saint has been gifted a *sirr* (secret) from God upon their becoming a saint. This secret is none other than the beautiful qualities manifested in their individual souls by the unique flavour of their spiritual path, their life, and their wayfaring. Each saint, no matter how esteemed or obscure, manifested through their individual existence a sublime quality of humanity that was unique to them. Some saints, for instance, walked a path of blame, and others of love. Some walked a path of discipline and ascetic rigour, and others of gratitude and ease. Some laughed with a divine humour and delighted in brotherhood, while others sat in Godly silence, in isolation from all mankind until the day they died.

Some were warriors, others teachers, or poets, or princes, or simple cobblers and tailors. Some sought out the spiritual path after losing everything they loved and being broken to their core. Others were princes of rich kingdoms who gave it all away to seek God. All of these paths are a path to God, and in the context of a saint, their secret. It is this secret which became the special gift by which they established a spiritual connection to their Lord, and which defined them as a walī.

When I understood this I realised that what matters isn't visiting the Quṭb. Rather, it is finding the saint whose reality mirrors one's own, so that through ṣuḥbah of the saint one is invigorated in their own spiritual seeking, seeing in the saint a master of the same challenges one is destined to struggle with. Furthermore, the greatest joy of ziyārah is not finding the greatest saint, but visiting as many as possible, basking in the miracle of each of their beautiful, multifaceted lives. Experiencing what transcends the human potential, in all its forms and flavours, is the greatest reward of ziyārah.

In this vein I encourage the readers of this book to keep an open heart and view the ancient city of Fes, even in its ruined state, as a trove of buried spiritual treasures. Whatever the length of your stay, view that as the time limit imposed upon you by fate for this treasure hunt, before which time you must seek out as much of these spiritual gifts as you can. Bring these spiritual jewels back with you to wherever you call home and keep them with you for the remainder of your life. I urge you, do not waste even a minute of this unique opportunity that God has given you. The chance to meet the Godly men and women of Fes may never come again.

Rulings on Visiting the Saints by al-Kattani

Today the subject of ziyārah has become something of a controversial topic in Islamic discourse. While some feel that the practice has immense spiritual benefit and is clearly established within the Islamic tradition, other commentators claim that the shrines of saints have become hotbeds of innovation, superstition and un-Islamic rites. For this reason, it is perhaps appropriate to discuss the proper etiquette to observe during visitations in order to guard it as a pure and legitimate expression of Islamic spirituality. Additionally, it is useful to examine the many strong arguments put forward by various prominent scholars throughout history that advocate the practice, or indeed, extol the virtues of visiting saints' tombs, provided this is done in an appropriate manner.

In *Salwat al-Anfās*, Muhammad ibn Jaʿfar al-Kattānī wrote a compelling defence and detailed manual of ziyārah, clearly responding to the criticisms of ziyārah which had begun to mount by his time. We saw fit to summarise this in our own modern rendition of his book, along with some helpful commentary. The article, an exposition of the Maghrebī Sufi tradition, sheds light on the way that Moroccan scholars for centuries defended and approached the precious ritual of ziyārah.

To begin with, al-Kattānī confirms that scholars have determined visits in general fall into five categories—the same number as those found in standard sharīʿah rulings. These are, in his own words:

Obligatory: Such as a person visiting his parents according to their right. The author comments that this is especially the case if one's parent has accumulated much knowledge, wealth, and good works throughout his life. In this case, al-Kattānī expounds that one should visit their parent in order to inherit all of these. It is likewise the case for visiting one's shaykh from whom one benefits in worldly and spiritual knowledge, especially if the shaykh is knowledgeable of the intrigues of the ego-self and the proper methods for countering them. Indeed, al-Kattānī holds that it is completely obligatory for a person who has found a truly realised shaykh to constantly stay by his side and not to separate from him until the shaykh grants him permission or his Inner Sight (*baṣīrah*) opens.

Recommended: Such as visiting relatives other than one's parents, and righteous people aside from one's shaykh.

Permissible: Such as visits to other than those already mentioned, so long as there is no harm in one's knowing them.

Disliked: Such as visiting evil people, with whom one fears his or her religion may become corrupt due to associating with them.

Forbidden: Such as visiting unbelievers who are open enemies of the religion, on the pretext of befriending them.

Al-Kattānī then proceeds to furnish his defence of ziyārah by employing a popular technique of Islamic scholarship: referencing other well-known scholars of the past and present more reputable than the author himself to legitimise his point. Al-Kattānī begins this endeavour with several references to Ibn al-Ḥājj,[16] a well-known Mālikī scholar from Fes who travelled to and eventually passed away in Cairo in the year 737 AH. Ibn al-Ḥājj was most famous for his book *al-Madkhal*, a four-volume text which deals with what the author perceived to be innovative and illegitimate practices in the Muslim community of the day. Al-Kattānī quotes at length from this text in his own introduction to ziyārah, clearly enjoying capitalising on the irony of defending ziyārah, often accused of being an innovation itself, with a well-known text written to expose innovations. Al-Kattānī recounts that Ibn al-Ḥājj consistently praised and advocated for the permissibility of ziyārah, sometimes saying merely, "It is desirable" and other times going so far as to proclaim "It is one's duty." Al-Kattānī in particular quotes a lengthy discourse where Ibn al-Ḥājj extols the benefits of visitation. He says:

> One should not deprive oneself of the spiritual practice of visiting the righteous whom by the sight of which God revives dead hearts just as the heavy showers of rain revive the dead earth, and by whom hardened hearts expand and find joy. Just

16 His full name is Muḥammad Ibn al-Ḥājj al-ʿAbdarī al-Fāsī, and he should not be confused with al-ʿAbdari al-Hihi, another scholar who wrote a lengthy account of his travels. The full name of his book is *al-Madkhal ilā Tanmīya al-ʿAmāl bi Taḥsīn al-Nīyāt wa Tanbīh ʿala baʿḍ al-Bidaʿ wa al-ʿAwāʾid* (The introductory textbook to the refinement of actions, perfection of intentions, and caution towards some of the innovations and customs).

> by seeing them, difficult matters become easy for they stand at the door of the Gracious Benefactor (*al-Karīm al-Manān*). Do not fail to sit with them, to know them and to love them. They are the door to God Most Exalted which has been opened to his servants, and whoever is such as this it is (clearly) obligatory to undertake seeing him.

Following Ibn al-Ḥājj, al-Kattānī references another series of prominent shaykhs from history, the vast majority of which, like Ibn al-Ḥājj, if not buried in Fes at least grew up in Fes, and studied in the Qarawiyyin. In this, al-Kattānī displays his peculiar preference for quoting shaykhs of the Moroccan tradition, almost as if the author is trying to convince his Moroccan audience that the practice of ziyārah is well-established in their own history, in spite of criticisms they may have heard from scholars further abroad in the East. Al-Kattānī's choice of quotations places his treatise uniquely in the heart of Moroccan tradition and legacy.

To start with, al-Kattānī quotes Imam Abū ʿAbdullāh ʿAbd al-Qādir al-Fāsī, one of the pre-eminent Shādhilī Sufis of Fes and a latter entry in this guidebook, who in his commentary on *ʿIdah al-Ḥiṣn al-Ḥaṣīn* quotes another luminary of Fes, Aḥmad Zarrūq, as saying, "Visiting the scholars and righteous is recommended so long as you give up performing any of the forbidden or disliked things clearly defined in the principles of the Revelation." Al-Fāsī, in his own book *al-Ajwiba al-Nāṣiriyya,* further says that, "Visiting the graves of the saints is an antidote for hearts, and it is among the best of recommended actions." The Shaykh and Imam Abū ʿAbdullāh ibn Nuʿmān wrote in his book *Safīnah al-Najāʿ*, a biography of another Moroccan scholar:

> It has been proven to be true to those revered masters with Inner Sight in the community that visiting the tombs of the Righteous to thoughtfully seek blessing is beloved to God.

> For the spiritual grace of the Righteous continues to flow after their death, as it did in their lifetime, and prayer at these tombs as well as seeking intercession with God through them was practised by our indubitable scholars and realised Imams of religion.

Pausing from his references to exclusively Moroccan Mālikī scholars, al-Kattānī draws his most compelling defence of ziyārah of all, perhaps, from the great Imam al-Ghazālī himself. Al-Ghazālī, an Abbasid era scholar of tremendous international renown is quoted by al-Kattānī as firmly supporting the practice in a section of his famous *Iḥyāʾ ʿUlūm al-Dīn*. Al-Kattānī references Abū Ḥāmid al-Ghazālī's writing in his book on *The Proper Manners of Travelling*:

> And included in travelling for the sake of worship is: visiting the tombs of the Prophets عليهم السلام, the Companions, the followers, and all the rest of the knowledgeable and saintly. All those who one finds blessings in witnessing during their lifetime, there is blessing in visiting them after their death. It is permissible to undertake pilgrimage to this end and the Prophet's ﷺ Hadith does not forbid it, when he said, "Do not undertake a pilgrimage but to these three mosques: The Masjid al-Ḥaram, my mosque, and the al-Aqsā Mosque." That is because this saying is only in regards to mosques. Other than these three mosques all mosques are the same in rank. So, there is no difference in the permissibility and ruling of visiting the graves of the Prophets عليهم السلام or the scholars and the saints, though they may have a great difference in ranks before God.

Al-Kattānī then returns to the writings of Aḥmad Zarrūq, who, commenting on this article by al-Ghazālī, further says:

> All with whom it was permissible to seek blessings from in their lifetime it is permissible to seek blessings from after their

> death. As much was said by al-Ghazālī in the book *The Proper Manners of Travelling*. He said, "It is permissible to undertake a pilgrimage to this end, and this is not opposed by the Hadith: 'Do not undertake a pilgrimage but to the three Mosques.' This is due to the equivalence in rank between all other than the three mosques (among mosques), but the discrepancy in rank between the Righteous and the Scholars." So, it is permissible to travel from a benefactor to a greater benefactor, and you can recognise their rank from their miracles, their works and their knowledge. In particular, those from whom miracles manifested after their death, miracles much like those that manifested during their lifetime, such as (Abū al-ʿAbbās) al-Sebtī. Or, those for whom manifested even greater miracles than in their lifetime, such as Abū Yaʿzā. Also, this goes for whosoever's tomb possesses the miracle of unfailing divine-response to supplications made in its vicinity—and there are many such cases across the globe. Shaykh al-Shāfiʿī indicated this miracle when he said, 'The grave of Mūsā al-Kāẓim is a tested remedy.' Such was transmitted by the commentators of *al-Ḥusn* and likewise by ʿAllāmah Abū Zakariyya.

Having successfully established his point with references not only to scholarly heroes of the Moroccan tradition but such giants of the Islamic tradition in general as Imam al-Ghazālī, al-Shāfiʿī, and others, al-Kattānī ends this section of quotations by famous spiritual and scholarly luminaries of the past by bringing them home to yet another luminary of Fes, the seminal Shādhilī shaykh Abū al-Maḥāsin Yūsuf al-Fāsī. Al-Kattānī himself quotes, and then comments:

> Abū al-Maḥāsin wrote, "That which the majority of people are upon and even those in the furthest reaches of the planet practice is: visiting the tombs of the Righteous to benefit from them and to ignite with the fire of their baraka, for they are the Doors to God." He then verified that with references to the

> words of al-Ghazālī in his *Iḥyā*, as well as al-Abī, al-Barzālī, Ibn Ḥajar al-ʿAsqalānī, Abū Qāsim al-ʿAbdūsī, Shaykh Zarrūq, and the author *al-Madkhal*...

He furthermore wrote,

> As for the speech of those who say there is no benefit except in visiting him (The Prophet) ﷺ, they are outnumbered and contradicted by the majority... Visiting the saints and scholars is in fact a means of connecting with him ﷺ. For, every blessing and good thing in this world, be they few or innumerable, are obtained from him, and by his rising into being manifested. How could they not be? For all of the other scholars and saints are but detailed images of him, his inheritors and manifestations of his particulars. There is not one of them (saints and scholars) but who is swimming in his light, and extending out from his Ocean, in accordance to their station. For he ﷺ gathers together in himself the various qualities, and he is the Messenger to all!

Al-Kattānī concludes thus that, from Abū al-Maḥāsin's words and the words of those he mentioned before them, not only is it both permissible and desirable to visit the graves of the Prophets, the Companions and the saints, so too is it desirable to visit the tombs of the pious scholars, even if they were not famous for sainthood or righteousness. This perspective of al-Kattānī's in fact takes over the next part of his discourse with unusual emphasis, reflecting perhaps some inexplicable polemic that al-Kattānī wished to prove to his audience about the spiritual authority of the scholar. Under the shadow of secularist French occupation and in an era of consequently diminished national authority for the once proud Moroccan scholars, it is possible al-Kattānī felt particularly compelled to prove this point. Al-Kattānī equivocates to that effect, "Knowledge in conjunction with good works is the very definition of righteousness, and the evidence of a profitable life and success in the hereafter, and uprightness is better than a thousand miracles. For God said in His Book, the Quran, 'The most noble of you in the sight of your Lord is the most pious of you' (49:13)."

Al-Kattānī further relates on this subject of visiting the scholars that "some sages" (we are left to guess whom) were recorded to have said: "Would that I knew! What has the man achieved, who has neglected knowledge? And what does the man lack, who has achieved knowledge?"

Furthermore, referencing the *Tanbīh al-Mughtarīn* of Imam al-Shaʿrānī, the author transmits a saying of the venerable Ḥassan al-Baṣrī:

> The scholars are the Lights of the Ages. Every knowledgeable person is the Lamp of his time by which his contemporaries seek to find guidance, and if it were not for the scholars then humanity would have become like the beasts.

And, in another narration:

> If it were not for the ʿAbdāl then the Earth would have swallowed up all those who are on it; and if it were not for the righteous then the Earth would have indeed fallen into corruption; and were it not for the scholars the people would have been illiterate like the beasts; and were it not for the Sultan the people would have turned on and consumed one another; and were it not for the imbeciles, the earth would have collapsed in ruin; and were it not for the wind, then all that is between the heavens and the earth would have rotted.

Yet, in spite of this avid defence of the blessings inherent in visiting the knowledgeable regardless of their piety or saintliness, al-Kattānī concludes by admitting the superiority of one who has knowledge of God compared to one who has simple exoteric knowledge of religious rites and rituals. Offsetting the danger poised by granting too much glory to the exoteric scholars, many of whom were by his time critics of ziyārah, al-Kattānī is quick to reaffirm the overarching spiritual superiority of the saint. To this end he quotes Ibn Rushd who in his *al-Miyār* responded to a question saying:

> As for the superiority of the Knowers of God over the Knowers of God's Rulings (*Aḥkām Allah*), the opinion of Abū Ḥāmid al-Ghazālī and the Teacher (al-Qushayrī) are agreed upon, and no rational person should doubt that one who is knowledgeable of what we should ascribe to God of Majesty and Perfection is better than one who is simply knowledgeable of rulings. Nay, the Knowers of God are better than all the scholars of the principles (*uṣūl*) and rulings (*furūʿ*), for knowledge only gains its nobility in commensuration to the nobility of that which is being Known.

Al-Kattānī follows this up with another quote by Shaykh Abū ʿAlī Sidi al-Ḥassan Ibn Raḥāl al-Maʿdanī who in his book *Ruʿūd al-Yāni* writes:

> A group of jurists asked Shaykh ʿIzz al-Dīn Ibn ʿAbd al-Salām: "What do you say about al-Khiḍr عليه السلام, is he alive?" To which the Shaykh replied, "What would you all say if Ibn Daqīq al-ʿIdd informed you that he had seen al-Khiḍr with his own eyes? Would you say he was telling the truth or accuse him of lying?" They replied, "Nay, we would of course say he was telling the truth." The Shaykh said, "Seventy truthful men have all reported seeing al-Khiḍr with their own eyes, each one of them better than Ibn Daqīq al-ʿIdd." Some of the Imams said, "And this is the opinion selected as true by the verified, realised scholars: that the Knowers of God (Gnostics) are greater than the knowers of God's Rulings (*al-Aḥkām*), and as much was said by the aforementioned Shaykh ʿIzz al-Dīn and others..."

To conclude this final thought on the preeminent position of the saint above all believers, be they scholars or otherwise, al-Kattānī cannot resist once again bringing home the discussion with a reference to one final Moroccan luminary. Al-Kattānī records that Shaykh Abū al-ʿAbbās Ibn ʿAjība (d. 1224 AH), a well-known student of the famous Shādhilī shaykh Mūlay al-ʿArabī al-Darqāwī, wrote in his famous exegesis of the Quran, *al-Baḥr al-Madīd*, on the verse "God raises those who believe from among you and those to whom came knowledge to Ranks..." (58:11):

> So the sincere scholars who know God by way of (logical) proofs trail in rank those saints who are people of Eye-Witnessing (of the Divine Truth), then the pious Righteous, then the general believing masses. Whoever says other than this is simply ignorant of the ranks of wilāyah. And God knows best.

The Benefits of Visiting the Tombs of the Righteous

Having exhausted the subject of the permissibility of visiting the saints and scholars and the various ranks of benefits attached to them, al-Kattānī follows up his introduction to ziyārah by providing an exposition of the many "secret" and "noteworthy benefits" of the practice. Among these, al-Kattānī relates, is simply remembering the inevitability of death due to viewing the saints' graves and burial grounds, and knowing that death is a path we all must walk and which no one can avoid traversing. For if they—those who were in a station of nearness to their Lord and security from Him—had to face death, then how could the rest of us possibly avoid it?

By remembering this and contemplating it, al-Kattānī enthuses, the veils lift from hardened hearts, their state of affliction is removed, and they develop a repulsion for the material world and a devotion to the afterlife. For this reason the Prophet ﷺ said: "First I forbade you from visiting graves, so visit them now; for, doing so is to withdraw from the lower world, and remember the afterlife." Al-Kattānī also references another narration in which he ﷺ states: "So visit them, for doing so cures the heart, compels the eye and reminds one of the afterlife."

Another benefit according to al-Kattānī is that it allows the visitor to draw from the ocean of the saint's generosity, and to drink from the overflowing fount of their (spiritual) gifts. Moreover, the visitor becomes exposed to the breezes of Divine mercy, and the requisite exposure to the Knowers (Gnostics) of the highest order truths, for they are the doorways to God Most High, and the gatekeepers to His Divine Presence. At their tombs exists Divine mercy and blessings unlike that found anywhere else.

Furthermore, the visitor is able to make intercession via them to God, and to seek intercession through them to Him, for the saint's intercession is unfailingly accepted. Their standing before God is significant, to the extent that just about nobody who intercedes with them with sincerity falls into ruin. On this point al-Kattānī references a saying of Shaykh al-Tawdī, "As for the secret of visiting the Righteous: it is because they are God's sincere servants and his intimate Friends. So, for that they are a door from among the doors to His Mercy, the inheritors of prophecy, and one of its secrets. Its rank has been unfolded to them and so by them we can seek intercession (*tawassul*) with God."

Al-Kattānī mentions as well a segment of *Minhāj al-Falāḥ* by Ibn ʿAtā Allāh al-Iskandarī, where he writes, "And I warn you not to believe that He can't be interceded with by way of His Prophets and the Righteous, for God has made them an intermediary between us and Him, and every miracle that appears from them is but a confirmation of the Prophet ﷺ." Finally, al-Kattānī ends this segment of his treatise with a reference to Abū Sālim and

Abū Isḥāq Sidi Ibrāhīm bin Muḥammad bin ʿAlī at-Tāzī,[17] whom he calls "the famous and illustrious saint, the most knowledgeable of the knowledgeable, the pious and ascetic master, the emir of the saints of his time," who purportedly wrote the following lines of poetry:

Visiting the Masters of Godliness is a salve that cures
And a key to the doors of guidance and goodness.

Etiquettes of Ziyarah

When visiting the graves of the saints, maintaining the following etiquettes is of paramount importance for a spiritually invigorating experience. In paying the proper respects due to the saint, the visitor can hope for supplication on their behalf and nearness to God through His most intimate and beloved friends.

1) **To go when one has spare time and is not busy with something that needs to be carried out, whether it be related to work, family, or the rights of God and His servants.** The spiritual tourist should only perform visitations at a time when one is free of all other important preoccupations, which could harm one in their material and religious life if neglected. If one is not free from all important preoccupations or has to perform one of God's rights or those of His servants (such as praying one of the five daily prayers or visiting a sick neighbour), then abandoning these in order to perform a visitation would be considered sinful. This is illustrated by Shaykh al-Dabbāgh in *al-Ibrīz*, a classic biographical work recording the sayings of this well-known scholar. He states, "It is plainly evident what is in it (the

17 A saint who resided in the city of Oran and was buried in his zāwiyah in the year 866 AH.

sin of ignoring religious obligations to partake in visitations) of darkness and severance (from the Divine)." Ziyārah, therefore, is an act that is meritorious but certainly not obligatory, and must always take second place to the obligatory practices incumbent upon every Muslim.

2) To visit for the sake of God alone and not for worldly matters. Therefore, the visitor should not carry anything that is not necessary. It is important that the visitor has a sincere intention to seek only God's countenance and not wealth or the material world. This is quoted in *al-Dar al-Nafīs* by al-Qurtabī, who states that the visitor should "keep his heart present throughout the course of it so that his portion from the visit should not just be to have walked around tombs in circles. Rather, one should seek the countenance of God and the rectitude of his heart." One should also be free of carrying anything that is not necessary, excluding basic provisions.

3) To be in a state of ritual purity. It is encouraged to be in a state of minor purity (*wudu*) as this is desirable upon greeting kings and great men, and the people of God are even more deserving of such veneration. Outer purification also has an effect on inner purity and is a protection from all evil, such as one's resolution abating. Wudu is considered the weapon of the believer by which he defends himself from shaytan.

4) To wear one's best clothes out of respect for the saint that one is visiting.

5) To empty one's mind and heart of anything related to earthly matters that are not connected to the visit. One should empty his heart from all lowly matters of the material world and what does not relate to the visit, in order for his heart to be in a sound state. It is an established fact to the Realised Sufis that a heart preoccupied with the lower world, such as one's appetites and desires, is not in a state to receive spiritual support. If one sincerely strives to remove this from one's heart but fails, there is no blame on that person, and he should request the compassion of the saint to forgive and overlook his shortcomings.

6) To visit the living before the dead if one is a traveller. However, if one happens to pass by the graveyard on the way to visiting those resident in the area, he should visit the dead first.

7) To give charity before the visit. It should be given to someone in need, or if there is no one present, one should put it in the shrine's collection box. Many people bring a sum of money for the saint they are visiting, as part of their effort to fulfill what they are seeking during the visitation. This is a valid practice; however, if one should come across somebody at the mausoleum or on the way who is in greater need of that charity, then one should give precedence to that person over the saint. He should do this whilst intending that the reward for this charity should be given as a gift to the walī. In this way, the person earns an even greater reward than if he had simply given the money to the walī.

8) To go to the graveyard on foot out of humility and if one goes by any other means, one should not enter the graveyard itself in this mode of transport. It is more appropriate to visit the graveyard on foot, if possible. This custom is supported by the hadith, "Whoever raises dust (from travelling) and casts it upon the way of God, (meaning, a path by which he is seeking God's pleasure) God shall forbid him from (touching) the fire." If one should be compelled to use another mode of transport, the visitor should descend upon reaching the shrine and enter it by foot.

9) To visualise the saint alive in his grave and bear in mind that he/she is aware of your presence. This is as God says: "And do not consider those who were killed for the sake of God as dead. Nay, they are alive." (3:169) It is thus important to behave with politeness before the saint as if they were still alive in the material world.

10) Give priority to greeting the saint over making supplications. The Prophet Muḥammad ﷺ commanded us to greet the martyrs upon passing their graves. As the saints are considered to be aware of the presence of visitors, it is important to send greetings before engaging in anything else.

11) To greet the mosque by praying two rakahs before greeting the saint if he is buried in a mosque. Priority should be given to *taḥiyyat al-masjid* (greeting the mosque by praying two rakahs upon entering) over greeting the walī, should the saint be buried in a mosque. This is because what relates to God has priority (in all cases) over what relates to other than Him of the creation. This practice is also requested of those visiting the tomb of Prophet ﷺ, thus it is necessary when visiting the graves of those other (lesser) than him. If upon entering the mosque, one sees people praying an obligatory prayer that he has yet to perform, then he should join them. Doing so suffices the requirement to greet the mosque and will garner the reward for both the obligatory prayer and the prayer for taḥiyyat al-masjid, so long as he makes the intention for this upon joining the congregation.

12) As one draws near to the saint, one should supplicate. It is recommended to recite the following supplication upon entering the saint's rawḍa:

اللّهُمَّ هذا حَرَمُ وَلِيّ مِنْ أَوْلِيَائِكَ فَاجْعَلْهُ لِي وِقَايَةً مِنَ النَّارِ وَأَمْنًا مِنَ الْعَذَابِ

Allāhumma hādha ḥaramu walīyyin min awliyā'ika faj'alhu lī wiqāyatan mina an-narr wa amanan mina al-'adhāb.

'O God, this is a sanctuary of one of your beloved righteous servants, so make it a means of protection for me from the Fire and a sanctuary from the punishment.'

Other supplications are also encouraged. These should be made analogous to what one might say upon seeing the noble city of Madina. This is affirmed in *Mu'atamid al-Rāwī*: "And should there be a mosque upon it, there is no harm for one to stop at the door. Should one desire to enter—and that is best—it is *mustahab* (recommended) for him to enter by his right foot first and to say, 'Bismillah. O God, send your prayers upon Muḥammad and the family of Muḥammad. My Lord, forgive me my sins and open for me the doors of Your Mercy,' as it is recommended to say upon entering any mosque."

13) To believe the saints are attached to the presence of the Prophet ﷺ. It should be understood that the saint's spiritual support is derived from the essence of the Prophet ﷺ. For in truth, he is the one being visited, and the saints are merely the doorways to him and servants imparting his gifts and spiritual essence. He is the one supporting all of them, and the true source for what each of them imparts to those who seek them out, in accordance with the capacity of the visitor and the one being visited.

14) One should ask God using the saint as a means and not ask the saint himself. One should begin by asking God directly using the Prophet ﷺ as a means, then the saint, and then those that follow in their footsteps until the Last Day.

15) To approach from the feet of the grave until one reaches the head of the grave. This etiquette is derived from Shaykh

Aḥmad Zarrūq in his book *al-Jāmī*. It is generally considered more polite to approach from the feet of the grave than from the direction of the head. After approaching from the feet, one should sit near the head of the saint and orient oneself towards his or her face if possible.

16) To sit at the head of the saint facing the direction of the grave with one's back to the direction of prayer. Ibn al-Ḥājj in his *al-Madkhal* advises in his own manual on visiting the deceased: "Then sit facing in the direction of the deceased, your gaze meeting them about the face area. Doing so is better than to sit at the deceased's legs while facing in the direction of his head or (to sit) opposite his face." Al-Kattānī, however, claims that perhaps sitting opposite the face is best, as it is a more respectful position for greeting the saint, and also limits saints other than the one being visited from occupying one's vision.

Al-Kattānī also considers it a display of bad manners to pray for the saint and beseech him from behind, just as the spiritual tourist would consider it bad manners for somebody to demand something from them whilst facing their backs. Greeting a Muslim in all cases—especially one perfect in faith—is better even than greeting the Kaʿba in al-Kattānī's view; for the sanctity of a believer is greater before God than the sanctity of the Kaʿba, and to honour a believer is better than to glorify the Kaʿba, while to quarrel with a believer is worse even than to raze and demolish the Kaʿba.

17) To sit as if one were sitting in prayer or to sit on one's knees. This is preferable to sitting cross-legged or leaning on one's side. Sitting is preferable unless it is difficult to do so due to time constraints or the area being filthy. It is preferable to stand for brief visits and sit for longer ones. In al-Kattānī's view, politeness is relative to the customs of the place, and the

Moroccan custom indicates that it is more polite to sit than to stand, if this is possible.

18) To remove one's shoes out of humility as long as it is feasible to do so. This is a practice that is carried out by the most pious. To take off one's shoes is nearer to the state of modesty desired in such places and more reverent and meaningful a gesture. This is supported by the opinion of Ibn ʿAtiyya in his exegesis of the following Quranic verse: "So remove your shoes, for you are in the holy valley of Tawa." (20:12). He suggests that the order to remove his shoes was a show of politeness before a place in which one would partake in an intimate discussion with God.

19) To stand an arm's length away from the grave. One should refrain from pressing one's body against the grave itself. One should draw close to the grave so that there exists between oneself and the tomb a *dhiraʿ* (cubit or arm's length), and not move very far from it nor physically cling to it. This view is expressed in numerous books of the Mālikīs. According to the Shāfiʿīs, a greater distance between oneself and the tomb is better. Ibn Hājar al-Haythumī states in *Jawhal al-Munadham* that, "The further away (that you are) the better, as sitting at a distance is better manners."

20) To avoid stepping on the grave or sitting on it, as one should display as much etiquette as possible. However, if it is necessary, then there is no harm in sitting or walking across the graves. Care must be taken not to step or sit on the grave, as that ground should be respected and treated with the best of manners. For this reason, numerous scholars and others disliked entering the Idrīssī Qubbah as doing so entails stepping on the graves of the scholars, the ashrāf and the righteous men and women buried inside of it. However, as this is commonly considered the most blessed and illustrious tomb in Fes, al-Kattānī defends the case for disregarding the norms in this case.

It is indeed permissible to enter the Qubbah as the reason behind the rulings mentioned is only valid if some necessity of the sharīʿah does not require one to do so. If the ground under which the grave lies is not connected to some religious objective which the Divine Law has charged us with performing in that place, such as salāt, then it is forbidden to sit or step on the tombs. Conversely, if it is connected to such a practice then it is permissible to sit and step upon the ground over the grave to fulfill that religious obligation.

Before anyone was buried in the Qubbah, it was originally a mosque; thus, the rulings pertaining to mosques still apply. It is therefore permissible to sit and walk across the graves should one wish to pray there, perform invocations, or any other type of worship.

Moreover, the Idrīssī Qubbah is a place filled with *baraka* (divine grace), *khayr* (goodness), *fadl* (benefit), and *qubul al-daʿwā* (unfailing divine response to supplication), among other things. It is rarely empty of pious and righteous people. Its spiritual grace is so potent that a heart overcome with longing for the Divine cannot be cured except by entering into the Idrīssī Qubbah, and so one cannot be forbidden from doing so. It is reported that some of the greatest knowers of God had visions of Mūlay Idrīs in which he is reported to have said: "Don't let anyone neglect to enter my Qubbah except for those specifically debarred from entering mosques (*al-mahrūm*)."

21) To look towards the ground so as not to see something that is forbidden or anything that is a distraction.

22) One should remain focused on why one is there and should not raise one's voice. One should maintain humility

throughout the visit. One should not shout at the saint in their grave, just as it would be unacceptable to shout at them if they were sitting in front of you. Likewise, care should be taken to abstain from all behaviour unbefitting to display before a saint. One should be humble and self-effacing before them and their high stature, rather than arrogant. This is because one visiting the tombs will achieve by abasement that which cannot be achieved by pride. Al-Kattānī asserts that Lordly Gifts do not settle except in broken hearts and humbled souls.

23) Not to pry as to what is under the box on top of the grave. One should not look under the box or put one's hand underneath it. Care should be taken not to enter the grave stone, i.e. the place in the saint's tomb reserved especially for the saint. This includes the darbūz (box structure) which sits over his grave. One should not stick one's fingers or hands into the darbūz covering the graves, as this contradicts the sunnah.

Al-Kattānī quotes from *al-Dars al-Nafīs* that somebody once did this with the darbūz of Mūlay Idrīs and he felt as if something had bitten or stung him. He withdrew his hand and found it to be dripping blood. He stuck his hand in again, and found it to be injured in another place. Somebody else also once stuck their hand in the darbūz on another occasion, and was stung by a scorpion. That was to teach him and others like him to never do such a thing again. Likewise, one should not hit the darbūz as many "ignorant fools" do. Some strike it so hard it nearly breaks, which is immensely disrespectful towards God's awliyāʾ.

24) It is impermissible to bow before the tomb. This practice is utterly condemned. It is worse yet to kiss the ground between the hands of the saint, and even worse to prostrate before the tomb by placing one's forehead all the way to the ground or to bow to such an extent that it becomes rukuʿ. It is these types of things, al-Kattānī warns, which steal the breath from those who hear of them, and all but break the hearts of those who witness them. It is also advisable to stop other people from performing such innovations.

25) It is impermissible to pray on top of or towards the tombs, unless this is done with the intention of facing the qiblah. The issue of standing or praying on tombs is a delicate one. Regarding this, al-Kattānī agrees that it is impermissible to pray standing over the tomb of a saint (or anyone) or towards it, whether it is for the purpose of seeking baraka from the saint or to venerate him. Shaykh al-Zarrūq affirms this in his book, *al-Jāmiʿa*: "Do not pray upon the tomb in your seeking its blessings, for the Prophet ﷺ said, 'God's wrath was severe towards a people who had taken the tombs of their prophets and righteous as mosques.'"

However, if one should pray over a tomb or in its direction simply because that is the direction of the qiblah, and not for the purpose of glorifying the tomb but with the purpose of drawing near to God in the vicinity of one of his intimates, then there is no harm in that. Rather, it is desirable to do so. He adds that Islamic jurists have generally affirmed the permissibility of praying on or in the direction of a graveyard so long as the area is pure (and free of ritually impure filth).

26) It is recommended to read some of al-Bukhārī at the tomb. One of the unique characteristics of al-Bukhārī is that whoever opens one of his books at the tomb of a walī and reads just one hadith that his eyes fall on, then seeks tawassul from God via all the men in its line of transmission up to the Prophet ﷺ that God should fulfil a need of his, then God will fulfil it, if He wills.

27) It is recommended to recite 'Qul Hu Allahu al-Aḥad' a thousand times. It states in the autobiography of the erudite teacher Abū ʿAlā Sidi Idrīs ibn Muḥammad al-Manjarī: "Whosoever wants to be drawn near to a saint from among God's saints, then he should recite Qul Hu Allahu al-Aḥad [Surat Ihklas, Verse 1-4] a thousand times and gift the reward to the saint, should he be already deceased, for he will obtain nothing but joy from this. If the murīd recites this number and gifts the reward for it to his shaykh, be that shaykh alive or deceased, then he will certainly obtain the pleasure of his shaykh."

28) To depart left foot first, and one should not walk backwards when departing with the intention to not turn one's back on the saint.

How to perform Ziyarah

There is a time-honoured and extremely simple tradition of visitation passed down to al-Kattānī by the dignitaries of Fes, and through him to us in the 21st century.

First, the saint should be greeted before supplicating, by saying:

اَلسَّلَامُ عَلَيْكُمْ دَارَ قَوْمٍ مُؤْمِنِينَ وَأَتَاكُمْ مَا تُوعَدُونَ وَإِنَّا إِنْ شَاءَ اللّٰهُ بِكُمُ اللَّاحِقُونَ

Assalāmu ʿalaikum dār qawmin muʾminīn wa atākum mā tūʿadūn wa innā in shā allāhu bikum ul-lāhiqūn.

'Peace be upon you, fellow believers. You have received that which you were promised and we will eventually join you, God willing.'

Then one should read verse 62 from Sūrah Yūnus:

﴿أَلَآ إِنَّ أَوْلِيَآءَ ٱللَّهِ لَا خَوْفٌ عَلَيْهِمْ وَلَا هُمْ يَحْزَنُونَ ٦٢ ٱلَّذِينَ ءَامَنُوا۟ وَكَانُوا۟ يَتَّقُونَ ٦٣ لَهُمُ ٱلْبُشْرَىٰ فِى ٱلْحَيَوٰةِ ٱلدُّنْيَا وَفِى ٱلْءَاخِرَةِ لَا تَبْدِيلَ لِكَلِمَٰتِ ٱللَّهِ ذَٰلِكَ هُوَ ٱلْفَوْزُ ٱلْعَظِيمُ ٦٤﴾

A lā inna awliyā' ullāhi lā khawfun 'alaihim wa lā hum yaḥzanūn aladhīna āmanū wa kānū yattaqūn la hum ul-bushrā fī ḥayāt id-dunyā wa fi il ākhirah lā tabdīla li kalimāt illāh dhālika hu al-fawz ul-'Aẓīm.

'Surely God's friends—no fear shall be on them, neither shall they sorrow. Those who believe, and are God-fearing for them is good tidings in the present life and in the world to come. There is no changing the words of God; that is the mighty triumph.'

Then one should read the Tashahhud (which one reads in prayer) until one arrives at the end of the greeting on the Prophet ﷺ. Then one should repeat the greeting either three, five or seven times. After, one should complete the Tashahhud intending when greeting every righteous servant of God in the heavens and the earth. Then say:

اَلسَّلَامُ عَلَيْكُمْ يَا سَيِّدِي ـــــ

Assalāmu 'alaika yā sayyidī .... (mention the saint's name here).

Then say:

أَشْهَدُ أَن لَّا إِلٰهَ إِلَّا اللَّهُ وَحْدَهُ لَا شَرِيكَ لَهُ وَأَشْهَدُ أَنَّ مُحَمَّدًا عَبْدُهُ وَرَسُولُهُ صَلَّى اللَّهُ عَلَيْهِ وَسَلَّمَ وَعَلَى آلِهِ

Ashhadu allā illāh illallāhu waḥdahu lā sharīka lah wa ashhadu anna muḥammadan 'abduhu wa rasūluh ṣallāhu 'alaihi wa sallama wa 'alā ālih.

'I testify that there is no deity worthy of worship except God alone. He has no partner and I testify that Muḥammad is His servant and His messenger, may He bless him and give him peace.'

According to al-Kattānī, after this point the walī sits cross-legged in his tomb and attends to fulfilling the needs of his visitor, and also repeats everything (all prayers) his visitor says for his sake back to him until the time his visitor departs.

After this, intend the reward of whatever you are going to recite for the saint before recitation. Then recite whatever you wish from Quran or dhikr. It is highly recommended to recite Surah Yāsīn once and Sūrah al-Ikhlaṣ, which should be recited eleven times for the deceased. Once one has finished reciting he should say:

اَللّٰهُمَّ أَثِبْنِي عَلَى مَا قَرَأْتُ وَذَكَرْتُ وَاجْعَلْ نَظِيرَ ثَوَابِهِ هَدِيَّةً مِنَّا لِكُلِّ عَبْدٍ صَالِحٍ فِي السَّمَاءِ وَالْأَرْضِ هَدِيَّةَ الْفَقِيرِ لِلْأَمِيرِ

Allāhumma athibnī ʿalā mā qarātu wa thakartu wa jʿal naẓīra thawābihi hadiyyatan minnī li kulli ʿabdin ṣāliḥīn fi is-samāʾi wa al-arḍ hadiyyata al-faqīr li il- amīr.

'O God, reward me for what I have recited and make its equivalent reward a gift from me to every righteous servant in the heavens and earth, a gift from the needy to the master.'

Or one may read:

اَللّٰهُمَّ إِنْ تَفَضَّلْتَ عَلَيَّ بِثَوَابِ هٰذِهِ الْقِرَاءَةِ أَوْ هٰذَا الذِّكْرِ فَاجْعَلْهُ فِي صَحِيفَةِ سَيِّدِي ــــ هَدِيَّةً مِنَّا هَدِيَّةَ الْفَقِيرِ لِلْأَمِيرِ

Allāhumma in tafaḍḍalta ʿallayya bi thawābi hādhihi il-qirāʾah (or hādah al- dhikr) fa jʿalhu fī ṣaḥīfati Sidi ......(and mention the walī's name) hadiyyatan minnī ilaihi hadiyyata al-faqīri li il-amīr.

'O God, if you honour me by rewarding me with this recitation or invocation, then place it in the record of Sidi... then mention the saint's name... as a gift from me to him, a gift from the needy to the master.'

Then one should supplicate for oneself and the saint as he wishes. He should ask for an increase in blessing and provision and then supplicate for his parents, teachers, family, relatives and loved ones and for all the Muslims in general, both living and deceased. One may say:

اَللّٰهُمَّ بِحَقِّ الَّذِينَ نَظَرْتَ إِلَيْهِمْ سَكَنَ غَضَبُكَ وَبِحَقِّ سَيِّدِنَا مُحَمَّدٍ صَلَّى اللّٰهُ عَلَيْهِ وَسَلَّمَ وَبِحَقِّ وَلِيِّكَ هٰذَا اقْضِ حَاجَتِي وَاجْعَلْ لِي مِنْ أَمْرِي فَرَجًا وَمَخْرَجًا يَا ذَا الْجَلَالِ وَالْإِكْرَامِ يَا أَرْحَمَ الرَّاحِمِينَ يَا رَبَّ الْعَالَمِينَ

Allāhumma bi ḥaqqi illadhīna idhā naẓarta ilaihim sakana ghaḍabuk wa bi ḥaqqi sayyidinā muḥammad ṣalla allāhu ʿalaihī wa sallama wa bi ḥaqqi walīyyika hādhā iqḍī ḥājatī wa jʿal lī min amrī farajan wa makhrajan yā dha al-jalāli wa al-ikrām yā arḥama ar-rāḥimīn yā rabba al-ʿālamīn.

'O God, by the station of those of whom when You look upon them, Your anger ceases and by the station of our master Muḥammad, may You bless him and give him peace, and by the station of this beloved righteous servant, fulfill my need and ease my hardship, O Magnificent and Generous, O Most Merciful, O Lord of the worlds.'

Then one recites Fātiḥah three times.

On gifting the reward for recitation to the deceased

After saying all of the previous, according to al-Kattānī the visitor should read what he can of the Quran, or perform some other verbal practice which is beneficial such as praising God, or sending prayers on the Prophet ﷺ. Then, he should direct the reward for that recitation to the walī.

Al-Kattānī cautions his reader not to trespass the bounds of proper etiquette by saying, "This is a charity for you, o Sidi so-and-so!" This is the utmost bad manners. Rather, one should say, "This is a gift from me to you, o Sidi so-and-so. A gift from the *faqīr* (poor man) to the *emīr* (King)." Or, to supplicate for the reward of one's recitation to reach the walī is even more proper, which one can do by saying: "O God, if you favoured me with a reward for this recitation, or in this dhikr, or in these blessings upon the Prophet ﷺ then please put that reward in the book of Sidi so-and-so, or this saint, as a gift from me to him, the gift of the faqīr to the emīr."

Al-Kattānī explains this is because prayer reaches the deceased and benefits them, without doubt (or controversy of opinion), as is supported by *al-Madkhal* and other texts. There is some dispute, however, as to whether or not the prayer benefits the deceased if the one supplicating does not specifically request the reward of his prayer to be given over. What al-Kattānī calls the *muḥaqqiqūn* (realised) of the community are related by al-Kattānī to be of the opinion that the rewards for such prayer reach the deceased as well, so long as the one reciting has the intention (in his heart) before he begins reciting that the rewards for his actions should be given to the walī.

As proof of this al-Kattānī references al-Abī, who in his book *Sharḥ al-Muslim*, during his discourse on the subject of giving charity to the deceased in the book of *Zakat,* writes:

> I came of the opinion that one who performed recitation for the sake of one other than himself, so long as he clearly stated out loud or intended in his heart that the reward of his recitation should belong to that other person he was reading for, then the reward was indeed transferred to them. On the other hand if he made the intention for the reward to be transferred after he had already finished reciting then it does not transfer. This is because the reward has already been obtained by the one reciting, and once a reward has been obtained it cannot be transferred. This *madhhab* (opinion) was the one chosen by the Shaykh—and by that I mean: Ibn Arfa.

Likewise, al-Kattānī quotes Shaykh Abū ʿAbdullāh al-Haffār al-Granāṭī as commenting:

> If one performs a recitation with the intention of reciting in place of a deceased, then, the correct opinion is that the deceased person will not benefit from his recitation. That is because recitation is a physical act of worship, and nobody can perform a physical act of worship in place of another person. On the other hand if one simply makes the intention to recite for himself, but to bestow the rewards for that recitation to the deceased, then this category of actions does indeed benefit the deceased.

Al-Kattānī further quotes Shaykh Abū ʿAbdullāh al-ʿAbdūsī al-Fāsī (another luminary of Fes) as saying one should make the intention for that (transfer of reward) at the start of recitation or before it, but not after. Then, after one has completed their recitation al-Kattānī writes that they should supplicate for themselves, asking for whatever good things it is they desire from this world and the next, as well as for their parents, their relatives, the rest of their loved ones, and all of the ummah (nation) of Muḥammad ﷺ. One of the supplications al-Kattānī recommends to perform is, "O God, by the right of those whom when you look at them your wrath is calmed, and by the right of those surrounding the throne; by the right of your awliyā' wheresoever they are, be it in the East or West or North or South; by the right of Muḥammad ﷺ and by the right of your walī here, I beseech you; provide me my need and grant me relief from my affair, O You who Possess all glory and providence, O Most Merciful of the Merciful, O Lord of the Worlds..." Then, al-Kattānī instructs one read the Fātiḥah three times.

Following this prayer manual, al-Kattānī relates an extremely obscure anecdote by ʿAbdullāh al-Khayyāṭ al-Hārūshī, whose meaning was more clear perhaps to al-Hārūshī and al-Kattānī than to the general masses. Al-Hārūshī writes in *al-Fatḥ al-Mubīn*, "My brother in God Sidi ʿAbd al-Salām al-Majdhūb al-Ṭarābulusī (may God have mercy on him) said to me: the Friends of God (*awliyā'*) said that first, there is the egg; second, the hatchlings; then third, the growth of feathers. With feathers the bird flies, and once it has flown then it does not stop except where Allah has willed it, so understand."

Transitioning from this, al-Kattānī continues by insisting that everything he has mentioned in this section about recitation at tombs was in his time standard practice in both the East and the West. That is because, he explains, God's mercy descends upon doing this practice. To prove his point he again references other scholars, this time al-Tibrānī and al-Bayhaqī, who transmitted in his *Kabīr* and the book *Shaʿb* from Ibn ʿUmar, respectively, that, "If one of you dies then don't set him aside, but rather rush him to his grave. At his head read the Fātiḥah, and at his feet recite the final portion of Surah al-Baqarah in his grave." Furthermore, al-Kattānī notes that Aḥmad, Ibn Dawūd, Ibn Mājiḥ, Ibn Ḥibān and al-Ḥākim (all authors with their own famous *sunan*, or hadith compilations) transmitted in their respective authenticated hadith collections on authority of Maʿqal ibn Yassār, the Prophet ﷺ

saying, "Read Surah Yāsīn over your deceased." At this al-Kattānī acknowledges the argument of some that the intended meaning of "deceased" here is those for whom death has come (but not yet taken them). Yet, he emphasises that others held it means those who have already died, and in his view this is the apparent meaning from the wording of the hadith. He follows up that Ibn Abū Shaybah and others also transmitted on authority of al-Shaʿbī, "The Ansār used to read Surah al-Baqarah over their deceased."

Al-Kattānī relates from the commentary *al-Kabīr* of Shaykh Mīyārah, on the *Murshid* of Ibn ʿĀshir,[18] "Ibn ʿUrfa accepted the arguments of some of the scholars in favour of the permissibility of reading at the graves according to the hadith of the Jaridatayn." Al-Shāfiʿī also took that opinion, and it says in the *Iḥyāʾ* that "There is no harm in reciting over a grave." Al-Muwāq transmitted this as well in *Tāj wa al-Iklīl,* adding to the end of it a longer story about Ibn Ḥanbal to the following effect:

> ʿAlī bin Mūsā said: '"I was with Aḥmad bin Ḥanbal at a funeral and Ibn Qudāmah was with us. When they had buried the deceased a righteous man came and began to recite over the tomb. Aḥmad said in response to that: 'This is an innovation!' So Ibn Qudāmah said to Aḥmad, 'What do you have to say about Mubashir bin Ismaʿīl?' Aḥmad replied, '(His narrations are) reliable.' Qudāmah said, 'Have you written anything (narrations) from him?' To which Aḥmad replied again, 'Yes.' Qudāmah then said, 'He informed me on authority of ʿAbd al-Raḥmān Abū al-ʿAlā bin al-Jalāj, who heard from his father, who advised him: if he should die, then they should read the opening and closing āyāt of Surah al-Baqarah over him near his head. He said also that he had heard Ibn ʿUmar advise as much.' Upon hearing that, Aḥmad responded, 'Iṇ that case, go back to that man and tell him to recite...'"

18 A famous text of Moroccan Mālikī jurisprudence, theology and mysticism still used today in the Qarawiyyin and respected the world over by Mālikī scholars.

Al-Kattānī further relates that *Sunan al-Muhtadīn* speaks at length about this subject and mentions numerous accounts which indicate the permissibility of reading over the graves, originating from numerous imams of the Mālikī and Shāfiʿī madhhabs. This, al-Kattānī advises, may be referenced if one has any doubt. As for what is the most well-known opinion among the Mālikīs, it is that reading over the tombs is *makrūh* (disliked). This is as the gnostics Ibn Abū Ḥamzah al-Khalīl reported, as well as what Ibn al-Ḥajj opines in his *Madkhal*. He writes, "The one visiting a tomb should not recite over the grave of the deceased. This is due to his prior preoccupation with what we have already mentioned of engaging in contemplation (about the afterlife and the fleeting nature of life), for reading the Quran requires that one attend to and contemplate over what he is reading but a single heart simply cannot occupy two trains of thought at one time."

The gnostic al-Shaʿrānī also mentions in *ʿUhūd al-Mashāyikh*:

> Someone who recites with the intention of visiting a walī from among God Most High's awliyāʾ should say after they have finished their recitation: 'O God, please put a reward equivalent to that of my recitation in the scrolls of such and such righteous walī.' Do not say, 'O God, give him the reward from this recitation.' For whoever deprives his soul of one of the works it has performed has oppressed himself. Furthermore, why should Allah grant him the reward for that action? The value of that reward is expiation from what he has reaped of his mistakes. It is not proper for a servant to give the rewards for his actions away when he is in need of them himself, except in the case of a person for whom rewards are overflowing and he has access to the full store of them. In that case he can give the surplus as charity, such as one does of material possessions, but who is like that? Except for those who have achieved true unveiling.

> Truly, the exception to this is the Messenger of God ﷺ and whosoever he has guided to do as much from among the knowledgeable shaykhs, for it is his right to deposit the reward for his actions in their scrolls as he pleases.

Al-Kattānī remarks, following this long quotation, that in his view the knowledgeable and the righteous are the vicegerents of the Prophet ﷺ and his representatives amongst us. He directs the rewards for his actions to them in veneration and honour of them since they are his vicegerents and representatives. Yet in truth, it is directed by the Messenger of God ﷺ and not them, and it is not strange to think that God might reward him for doing all this with a reward even greater than the reward he has gifted to them.

Also, he may achieve on account of that what is greater than the affection and pleasure of that walī, being his aid and his intercession between him and our Master (glory be to Him) and the Messenger ﷺ. As much is befitting for the brethren of nobility and generosity, that they should accept an easy and paltry thing by which its performer sincerely intended to venerate things of far greater value, deserving of veneration. At that point the performer is profiting rather than losing, achieving increase in his rewards rather than decrease in them. It cannot possibly be said of one who achieves such a thing, "He is oppressing himself." The reward, even if it is not necessarily due to him, is sought after from the door of God's generous gifts rather than the door of merit, and God is the possessor of limitless generosity towards His servants.

For that reason, we can relate directing one's reward to the walī to God's bounty and the human gift of free will, and say, "O God, if you willed to grant me a reward..." until the end of the aforementioned supplication. Even if one is greatly in need of the rewards for their actions, in truth it is only a small payment, while what he gets in return from his gift is immense, due to his veneration of that walī, his striving in service, and God's granting him a great reward as a consequence. What he takes from the walī does not even leave a mark on the walī, for the walī is firmly grounded in God's limitless bounty. Whosoever is covetous of what the walī has should supplicate to God for the likes of it.

Furthermore, there are many hadith on the desirability of reciting some of the Quran and directing the reward to the deceased in general terms, so what of directing the reward to the deceased saints and scholars?

Shaykh al-Ra'ūf al-Manāwī wrote in *Sharḥ al-Arba'īn al-Nawawī*:

> Al-Ṭūfī said: "And he mentioned by some of the scholars and righteous that he used to recite the Quran, remember God's name and glorify Him and direct the reward for all of that to every righteous servant of God in Heaven and on the Earth, and it is suitable for those who succeed to have done that... He said: and it was stated by some of those who used to do that, with absolute certainty in which there is no doubt, that he one day had a dream. In it, he saw himself lifted to the heavens and all those who were in them of Prophets and Angels came out to meet him. He saw this as a confirmation that what he had directed to them of his rewards had indeed reached them... so a person should not slack in reading Surat al-Ikhlāṣ, for instance, for it equals the whole of the Quran. Or, to glorify Him, or to praise Him, or to magnify Him or declare His unity, say: 'O God, please reward me for what I have recited and remembered (of Your Name). Then, grant the reward for it as a gift from me to every righteous servant in Heaven and on the Earth.' For, if this prayer is accepted it will arrive to all of them."

The text also states:

> Some of our Sufi shaykhs used to say: "Every time a person passes by the grave of a walī or a hard-working scholar, he should recite the Fātiḥah and direct the reward of that to them, and make that an exchange between himself and that walī. For the walī will admit to what that person has done for him when difficulty descends upon him and lend him his aid; and the effect of that will manifest upon him."

While Abū ʿAbdullāh al-Amīn al-ʿAttār (who is buried on Jabal Zorhūn in northern Morocco) says in *Mumtiʿa al-Asmāʾ*:

> He (Abū ʿAbdullāh) had a connection to ʿAbd al-Qādir al-Jīlānī, and saw them in his sleep upon which they helped him. Because of that he contracted with God that for every supererogatory act of worship he performed, the reward should be given to those two saints. Thereafter he beheld another vision of them while he was at the grave of Abū Yaʿzā. In it, they gave something to him and suddenly there manifested to him all manner of miracles and unveilings. He (Abū ʿAbdullāh) is among the men that Shaykh Aḥmad Zarrūq recounts meeting.

Next, al-Kattānī relates that the erudite scholar Ibn Zakariyya in his commentary of the *Ṣalāt* of the Quṭb Mawlana ʿAbd al-Salām, comments after relating what was previously mentioned about ʿAbd al-Wahhāb al-Shaʿrānī, that he once asked his shaykh, ʿAlī al-Khawāṣ, "Should I recite and fast, then give the reward for that to Adam عليه السلام?" and that his teacher replied, "Never take an intermediary between you and God, be it a Prophet or otherwise!" Following this, Ibn Zakariyya states:

> Don't let the matter of this account frighten you in spite of what we have demonstrated. As for the question of directing one's reward to the Prophet ﷺ and other prophets and saints, the evidence in favour of that has already been presented in

> various hadith and in the practice of the famous imams whom we (all) follow, and what was said by Shaykh al-Zarrūq. This is verified and discussed in the interpretation of ʿAbd al-Salām's saying: "Prayers befitting of you, from you, to him." As for the matter of being self-sufficient beyond the need of his ﷺ mediation with God, there is no way to God (except via the Prophet as an intermediary), even if you were to reach what he reached.

That is the end of his speech, and al-Kattānī holds it is among the greatest attestations to what he argues here. What is the summary of all this? Al-Kattānī concludes that what should be taken is that all of the preceding quotations on reciting at saints' tombs demonstrates that as much was in fact in al-Shaʿrānī's Ṭarīqa, in spite of the admonition from his teacher against taking intermediaries. We have mentioned his view of it, as well as the ṭarīqas of those other than him—and they amount to the majority of the scholars and Sufis—permitting one to direct the same reward to the saint being visited. And God knows best.

And may God be pleased with our Imam Mālik, the Imam of the abode of the Immigrants (Madina), when he said, "All speech about this is either accepted or refuted, except what was said by the owner of this grave," and he pointed to the Prophet's ﷺ tomb. Furthermore, in the publications of some:

> Sidi ʿAlī al-Khawāṣ forbade his student ʿAbd al-Wahāb al-Shaʿrānī (may God be pleased with them) when he said, "Never take an intermediary between you and God, be they a prophet or otherwise...!" Amongst the saying "prophets" here is included the master of all the universe (Muḥammad), as he would be included within the general meaning of what was said since the speaker did not exempt him. Except, there is no way for anyone—no matter who they may be—to God except through him as an intermediary, even if they were to reach what he reached.

Itineraries and gatherings

Proposed Itineraries

Fes is a city that takes years, if not decades, to explore fully. From the historical treasures to be discovered to the rich contemporary city to be explored, there is a lot to see and do in Fes. For those who have several weeks or months in Fes, this guide can be used flexibly, and your own itineraries can be planned at ease, allowing you to visit all of these sites over the course of your stay.

For those who are only visiting for a few days, however, time is of the essence. Below are some proposed itineraries for your visit. If you are interested in attending religious gatherings, please refer to the index of gatherings for the days you will be in Fes to see what might be available on the days of your stay.

Day 1:

If you have one day in Fes, you will not be able to see everything, but you will get a taste of the treasures of Fes, both cultural and spiritual.

Morning: Begin your day with a visit to the Madrasa Bu Inaniya, one of Fes's most exquisite architectural masterpieces. This Islamic school is renowned for its intricate cedar wood carvings and beautiful zillij (Moroccan ceramic tilework). It's a live museum that showcases the splendour of Merinid architecture.

Afternoon: After lunch in a nearby traditional Moroccan restaurant, head to the Zāwiyah of Mūlay Idrīs, an important religious site dedicated to the founder of Fes. Next, visit the Aḥmad Tijānī Mosque, part of the Zāwiyah of Sidi Aḥmad Tijānī.

Evening: Head to Riad Zahra for the evening. Enjoy dinner at your riad or explore local dining options. Riads in Fes often have stunning terraces that offer magnificent views of the city, making for a peaceful evening.

Day 2:

Morning: Start your day with a visit to the Qarawiyyin University, the oldest operating educational institution in the world. While the university itself is not open to tourists, you can admire its architecture from the outside. The library has been recently renovated and is sometimes accessible to the public through special appointments or tours.

Afternoon: After lunch, make your way to the famous tanneries of Fes, where you can witness the traditional leather-dyeing process. The Chouara Tannery is the most well-known and offers a fascinating glimpse into this ancient craft. Be prepared for the strong smell!

Evening: Attend a dhikr gathering. Refer to the index of gatherings on the next page to see what is available during your stay.

Day 3:

Morning: Madrasa as-Sahrij & Madrasa al-Atarine are worth exploring for their beautiful Islamic architecture and art.

Afternoon: Dedicate your afternoon to visiting another exquisite example of Moroccan architecture at Madrasa Sefarayn. It's one of the lesser-known educational institutions in Fes, offering a more tranquil atmosphere to appreciate the detailed workmanship.

Evening: Spend your final evening in Fes leisurely wandering through the medina, shopping for souvenirs, or relaxing in one of the city's many beautiful gardens. Reflect on the rich cultural and historical experiences you've absorbed over the past three days.

Tip: When travelling in a grand taxi, the taxi will not leave until all seats are filled. To leave sooner or for comfort, consider buying two seats. Grand taxis can be very crowded and are uncomfortable by Western standards. Especially on longer journeys, purchasing two seats may be preferable. If you buy two seats, try to take the front seat.

Index of Gatherings

In this section there is a comprehensive list of all the major religious, dhikr, and samaʿ gatherings throughout the week in Fes. This excludes special gatherings, such as during Rabiʿ al-Awwal in commemoration of mawlid and Ramadan, and private gatherings in people's homes. Three enduring elements of the Moroccan tradition become apparent in these gatherings: preservation of the Quran, salutations upon the Prophet Muḥammad ﷺ and dhikr Ullah.

When attending these gatherings as a visitor, endeavour to maintain the highest adab. Some of these gatherings are used to welcoming foreign visitors on a weekly basis, and others rarely receive visitors from abroad. If you intend to visit as a large group, visit the zāwiyah in advance and ask permission to attend.

Through these gatherings, you will encounter some of the enduring elements, texts, recitations, and styles of the Moroccan Sufi tradition. May it be a window to many further openings.

Monday	
After Fajr	- Hizb of Quran recited communally in most masajid
After Dhuhr	
After Asr	- Tijānī Wazīfa - Reading of Dalā'il al-Khayrāt (Masjid Hayy Fadila: Ville Nouvelle) - Readings of Dalā'il al-Khayrāt or Quran in Zāwiyah Aḥmad al-Saqali (occasional)
After Maghrib	- Dhikr in Zāwiyah Butchichia - Hizb of Quran recited communally in most masajid
After Isha	

Tuesday	
After Fajr	- Hizb of Quran recited communally in most masajid
After Dhuhr	
After Asr	- Reading of Dalā'il al-Khayrāt (Masjid Hayy Fadila: Ville Nouvelle) - Tijānī Wazīfa - Readings of Dalā'il al-Khayrāt or Quran in Zāwiyah Aḥmad al-Saqali (occasional)
After Maghrib	- Hizb of Quran recited communally in most masājid - Dhikr in Zāwiyah Butchichia
After Isha	

Wednesday	
After Fajr	- Hizb of Quran recited communally in most masajid
After Dhuhr	- Dalāʾil al-Khayrāt - Mūlay al-Arabi al-Darqāwī
After Asr	- Reading of Dalāʾil al-Khayrāt (Masjid Hayy Fadila - Ville Nouvelle) - Tijānī Wazīfa - Readings of Dalāʾil al-Khayrāt or Quran in Zāwiyah Aḥmad al-Saqali (occasional)
After Maghrib	- Hizb of Quran recited communally in most masajid - Dhikr in Zāwiyah Butchichia
After Isha	

Thursday	
After Fajr	- Hizb of Quran recited communally in most masajid
After Dhuhr	
After Asr	- Reading of Dalāʾil al-Khayrāt (Zāwiyah Wazzānīya - Ayn al-Zlaytin, Medina) - Reading of Dalāʾil al-Khayrāt (Masjid Hayy Fadila - Ville Nouvelle) - Tijānī Wazīfa - Readings of Dalāʾil al-Khayrāt or Quran in Zāwiyah Aḥmad al-Saqali (occasional)
After Maghrib	- Dhikr in Sidi ʿAlī al-Jamal - Hizb of Quran recited communally in most masajid - Dhikr in Zāwiyah Butchichia
After Isha	- Dhikr in Zāwiyah Wazzānīya (Darb al-Houra) - Dhikr in Zāwiyah Naqshbandiya-Haqaniya - Dhikr in Zāwiyah Ben Souda - Dhikr Mūlay al-Arabi al-Darqāwī - Dhikr Sidi Qāsim ibn Raḥmūn in Talaʿa Saghira

Friday	
After Fajr	- Visiting ʿAbd al-Aziz Al-Dabbagh and other awliyāʾ of Bāb Futuh - Hizb of Quran recited communally in most masajid
Jumʿa Prayer	- Before: Burda, Qasȃid in Masjid Imam Mālik - Reading hizb Quran in most major mosques
After Asr	- Dalāʾil al-Khayrāt in Mūlay Idrīs - Dalāʾil al-Khayrāt in Ben Suda - Dhikr and dars - Zāwiyah Makhfiyya - Dhikr in Zawiyah of Sidi ʿAbd al-Qadir al-Fāsī - Tijānī Wazīfa and hadra - Recitation of Surat al-Kahf and dhikr at al-Zawiyah al-Fassiyyah (aka Zawiya de Sidi Abdelkader El Fassi) - the dhikr includes al-Wazīfah al-Zarrūqiyyah and Hizb al-Imam al-Nawawi
After Maghrib	- Hizb of Quran recited communally in most masajid - Dhikr in Zāwiyah Butchichia
After Isha	

Saturday	
After Fajr	- Hizb of Quran recited communally in most masajid
After Dhuhr	
After Asr	- Dalāʾil al-Khayrāt - Zāwiyah Aḥmad Mansūr - Tijānī Wazīfa
After Maghrib	- Dhikr and suhba (Zāwiyah Naqshbandiyya-Haqqaniya) (occasionally) - Hizb of Quran recited communally in most masajid - Dhikr in Zāwiyah Butchichia
After Isha	

Sunday	
After Fajr	- Hizb of Quran recited communally in most masajid
After Dhuhr	
After Asr	- Tijānī Wazīfa
After Maghrib	- Hizb of Quran recited in most masajid - Dhikr in Zāwiyah Butchichia (every day after Maghrib)
After Isha	

Litanies and Supplications of the Moroccan Tradition

Included below are several texts and excerpts which are important in the Moroccan Islamic tradition. They include litanies of several important Sufi turūq of Morocco, general invocations developed by Moroccan scholars and awliyā', and excerpts from classic spiritual texts.

The General Litany of Mūlay al-'Arabi al-Darqāwī

The general litany of the Darqāwīs is not much different from the general litany (wird) performed by Shādhilīs. Indeed, various sects of the Shādhiliyya generally do not stray far from the mother litany of their shaykh, altering a few words at most. Recited after sunrise and sundown, the murid is encouraged to say the following:

أَسْتَغْفِرُ اللهَ الْعَظِيمَ

Astaghfir Allāh al-'adhīm (x 100)

اَللّٰهُمَّ صَلِّ عَلَى سَيِّدِنَا مُحَمَّدٍ

Allah Humma Ṣali 'ala Sayyidina Muḥammadin (x 100)

لَا إِلَهَ إِلَّا اللهُ

Lā ilāha illallāh (x 100)

The General Wird of the Wazzānī Ṭarīqa

Also a subsect of the Shādhiliyya, the wird of the Wazzānī Ṭarīqa is a good example of the way in which factions slightly alter the wording of the general litany without seriously affecting the content or substance.

أَسْتَغْفِرُ اللهَ إِنَّ اللهَ غَفُورٌ رَّحِيمٌ

Astaghfirullāh innallāh ghafūrun raḥīm (x 100)

سُبْحَانَ اللهِ وَبِحَمْدِهِ

Subḥānallāhī wa biḥamdiḥī (x 100)

اللهُمَّ صَلِّ عَلَى سَيِّدِنَا مُحَمَّدٍ نَّبِيِّ الْأُمِّيِّ وَعَلَى آلِهِ وَصَحْبِهِ وَسَلِّمْ

Allāh humma ṣalli ʿala sayyidina Muḥammidinin nabiyyil ummiyyī wa ʿala ālihī wa ṣaḥbihi wa sallim (x 100)

لَا إِلَهَ إِلَّا اللهُ

Lā ilāha illallāh (as many times as possible)

(In addition, in the morning they would add the following:)

اللهُمَّ صَلِّ وَسَلِّمْ عَلَى سَيِّدِنَا مُحَمَّدٍ نَّبِيِّ الْأُمِّيِّ وَأَزْوَاجِهِ وَذُرِّيَّاتِهِ

Allāh humma ṣalli wa sallim ʿala sayyidina Muḥammadin nabiyyil ummiyyī wa azwājihī wa dhuriyyātihī (x 50)

(Furthermore, upon completing every obligatory prayer:)

لا إِلَهَ إلا اللهُ مُحَمَّدٌ رَسُولُ اللهِ صَلَّى اللهُ عَلَيْهِ وَسَلَّمَ وَعَلَى آلِهِ

Lā ilāha illallāhu Muḥammadun rasūlallāh ṣallallāhu ʿalayhi wa sallim wa ʿala ālihī (x 10)

Litany of the Tijāniyya Ṭarīqa

Before he founded his own Ṭarīqa, Aḥmad al-Tijānī operated as a muqaddam of the Shādhiliyya Khalwatiyya. This is reflected in his litany which once again follows the general sequence and theme of the Shādhilī litany. The main difference is the emphasis on using (for the second recitation focused on the Prophet ﷺ) a prayer which al-Tijānī was gifted by his Shaykh who received it directly by the Prophet ﷺ in a dream. This prayer is called the Ṣalat al-Fātiḥ. Regarding this special prayer, Aḥmad al-Tijānī once supposedly claimed that if thousands of people from thousands of tribes recited all other known forms of prayers on the Prophet ﷺ thousands of times, it would not equal the weight of even one Ṣalat al-Fātiḥ. Thus:

أَسْتَغْفِرُ اللهَ

Astaghfirullāh (x 100)

اللّهُمَّ صَلِّ عَلَى سَيِّدِنَا مُحَمَّدٍ الفَاتِحِ لِمَا أُغْلِقَ و الخَاتِمِ لِمَا سَبَقَ نَاصِرِ الحَقِّ بِالحَقِّ و الهَادِي إِلى صِرَاطِكَ المُسْتَقِيمِ و عَلَى آلِهِ حَقَّ قَدْرِهِ و مِقْدَارِهِ العَظِيمِ

Allāh humma ṣalli ʿala sayyidina Muḥammadin al-fātiḥ li mā ughliqā, wa al-khātim li mā sabaqa, nāṣiril ḥaqqi bil ḥaqqi wa al-hādī ilā ṣirātikal mustaqīm, wa ʿala ālihī ḥaqqa qadrihi wa miqdārihil ʿadhīm (x 100)

لَا إِلَٰهَ إِلَّا اللهُ

Lā ilāha illallāh (x 100)

Ṣalāt al-Mashīshīyah

When Abū al-Ḥassan al-Shādhilī stayed with ʿAbd al-Salām ibn Mashīsh in order to learn the mysteries of the Sufi way, it is said that al-Shādhilī used to observe ʿAbd al-Salām descend to a rock on the mountainside near where he lived every morning and recite a simple prayer he had composed himself. This prayer today is known as the Ṣalāt al-Mashīshiyya and is considered one of the most sacred, and succinct, expressions of the spiritual way, as well as one of the most eloquent odes to the Prophet Muḥammad ﷺ.

Numerous commentators throughout history have written full books explaining the concepts contained within this prayer of barely a few paragraphs. The first to comment on the Ṣalāt, however, was arguably al-Shādhilī himself, who wrote an extended version of the prayer that later came to be known as the Wazīfa of the Shādhilī Ṭarīqa, and which is considered by Shādhilīs to contain the entire essence of their teachings.

Ibn ʿAjība in his commentary on the Ṣalāt notes that when Ibn Mashīsh asks God to "Listen to my call, just as you listened to the call of your servant Zakariyya," this was in fact an entreaty to God to grant him an heir just as Zakariyya was miraculously granted an heir in old age. Thus, while al-Shādhilī may not have perceived it at the time, in truth it was he who was the answer to Ibn Mashīsh's Ṣalāt.

اللَّهُمَّ صَلِّ عَلَى مَنْ مِنْهُ انْشَقَّتِ الْأَسْرَارُ ، وَانْفَلَقَتِ الْأَنْوَارُ ، وَفِيهِ ارْتَقَتِ الْحَقَائِقُ ،
وَتَنَزَّلَتْ عُلُومُ آدَمَ فَأَعْجَزَ الْخَلَائِقِ ، وَلَهُ تَضَاءَلَتِ الْفُهُومُ فَلَمْ يُدْرِكْهُ مِنَّا سَابِقٌ وَلَا لَاحِقٌ

، فَرِيَاضُ الْمَلَكُوتِ بِزَهْرِ جَمَالِهِ مُونِقَةٌ ، وَحِيَاضُ الْجَبَرُوتِ بِفَيْضِ أَنْوَارِهِ مُتَدَفِّقَةٌ ، وَلَا
شَيْءَ إِلَّا وَهُوَ بِهِ مَنُوطٌ، إِذْ لَوْلَا الْوَاسِطَةُ لَذَهَبَ كَمَا قِيلَ الْمَوْسُوطُ ، صَلَاةً تَلِيقُ بِكَ مِنْكَ
إِلَيْهِ كَمَا هُوَ أَهْلُهُ ، اَللَّهُمَّ إِنَّهُ سِرُّكَ الْجَامِعُ الدَّالُّ عَلَيْكَ ، وَحِجَابُكَ الْأَعْظَمُ الْقَائِمُ لَكَ بَيْنَ
يَدَيْكَ ، اَللَّهُمَّ أَلْحِقْنِي بِنَسَبِهِ ، وَحَقِّقْنِي بِحَسَبِهِ ، وَعَرِّفْنِي إِيَّاهُ مَعْرِفَةً أَسْلَمُ بِهَا مِنْ مَوَارِدِ
الْجَهْلِ ، وَأَكْرَعُ بِهَا مِنْ مَوَارِدِ الْفَضْلِ ، وَاحْمِلْنِي عَلَىٰ سَبِيلِهِ إِلَىٰ حَضْرَتِكَ ، حَمْلًا مَحْفُوفًا
بِنُصْرَتِكَ ، وَاقْذِفْ بِي عَلَى الْبَاطِلِ فَأَدْمَغَهُ ، وَزُجَّ بِي فِي بِحَارِ الْأَحَدِيَّةِ ، وَانْشُلْنِي مِنْ
أَوْحَالِ التَّوْحِيدِ ، وَأَغْرِقْنِي فِي عَيْنِ بَحْرِ الْوَحْدَةِ ، حَتَّىٰ لَا أَرَىٰ وَلَا أَسْمَعَ وَلَا أَجِدَ وَلَا
أُحِسَّ إِلَّا بِهَا ، وَاجْعَلِ الْحِجَابَ الْأَعْظَمَ حَيَاةَ رُوحِي ، وَرُوحَهُ سِرَّ حَقِيقَتِي ، وَحَقِيقَتَهُ
جَامِعَ عَوَالِمِي بِتَحْقِيقِ الْحَقِّ الْأَوَّلِ ، يَا أَوَّلُ يَا آخِرُ يَا ظَاهِرُ يَا بَاطِنُ ، اِسْمَعْ نِدَائِي بِمَا
سَمِعْتَ بِهِ نِدَاءَ عَبْدِكَ زَكَرِيَّا ، وَانْصُرْنِي بِكَ لَكَ ، وَأَيِّدْنِي بِكَ لَكَ ، وَاجْمَعْ بَيْنِي وَبَيْنَكَ ،
وَحُلْ بَيْنِي وَبَيْنَ غَيْرِكَ

اللهُ اللهُ اللهُ ،

إِنَّ الَّذِي فَرَضَ عَلَيْكَ الْقُرْآنَ لَرَادُّكَ إِلَىٰ مَعَادٍ ،

رَبَّنَا آتِنَا مِنْ لَدُنْكَ رَحْمَةً وَهَيِّئْ لَنَا مِنْ أَمْرِنَا رَشَداً ،

O Allah send Your blessings upon him from whom burst open the secrets, and from whom streamed forth the lights, and in whom ascended the realities, and upon whom descended the sciences of Adam, by which all creatures fall stupefied in wonder, he before whom human comprehensions are feeble and who thus has never been truly understood, neither by those past nor present. It is He who thus splendours the gardens of the heavens with his resplendent beauty and the sacred grounds of the World of Dominion gush forth with his light. There is nothing that is not dependent on him, because if there were no intercessor then everything interceded for would

disappear, as it is said. Bless him with a prayer that is befitting of You, from You, to him, as he deserves.
O Allah indeed he is Your all-encompassing secret that leads, by You, to You and he is Your Greatest Veil standing directly before You.
O Allah join me to his line and actualize me on his account and let me know him, and by such knowledge be saved from the wellsprings of ignorance, and through it drink from the wellsprings of virtue.
Carry me on his path to Your Presence, a journey encompassed all the way by Your Aid, and hurl me at falsehood so that I may destroy it and plunge me into the seas of Oneness, yet save me from the stormy states of Unicity, then drown me completely in the source of the Ocean of Unity until I neither see, nor hear, nor perceive, nor sense, except through It.
O Allah make the Greatest Veil the life of my soul and his soul the secret of my reality and his reality the entirety of my inner worlds (soul, mind, spirit) through the realization of the Foremost Truth.
O First! O Last! O Manifest! O Hidden!
Hear my cry just as You heard the cry of your servant Zakariyya and grant me victory through You, for You and support me through You, for You and join me to You and come between myself and anything other than You.
Allāh! Allāh! Allāh! [Hold each "ā" approximately 12 seconds]
Indeed He, Who ordained the recitation [Quran] upon you,
O Lord grant us from Yourself Mercy and grant us guidance as to our affair.
Indeed Allah and His angels send blessings upon the Prophet.
O you who believe, send blessings on him and greet him with peace.
May the benediction of Allah, His peace, greetings, mercy, and blessings, be upon our Master Muḥammad, Your Servant, Prophet and Messenger, the Unlettered Prophet and also upon his family and companions.
Upon him be peace to the count of all even and odd numbers (infinitely) and by the infinite number of the perfect and blessed words of our Lord.

Dua Nāṣirīyah

The Dua Nāṣirīyah was composed by Shaykh Muḥammad bin Nāṣir al-Darʿi (d. 1674 CE), founder of the Nāṣirīyah Ṭarīqa in the ancient city of Tamegroute. Today the Shaykh's zāwiyah still stands in the desert in all its splendour, as it has for centuries. At its height, the Nāṣirīyah was a huge Ṭarīqa responsible for a revival of Sufism and Islam in Morocco.

The dua itself is a precious inheritance from this sacred heritage and unsurprisingly remains very popular in gatherings around Morocco. Generally translated as "The Prayer of the Oppressed", it was composed by the Shaykh during a difficult period in Moroccan history, when the country suffered great losses at the hands of its enemies. Andalusia had been in the hands of the Christians for over a century due to corrupt leadership and the balance of power was swinging towards the Europeans, leaving Morocco, at Europe's door, particularly vulnerable. The prayer is a powerful entreaty to God to save the pious from the oppression of their enemies, both domestic and foreign.

يَا مَنْ إِلَى رَحْمَتِهِ الْمَفَرُّ   وَمَنْ إِلَيْهِ يَلْجَأُ الْمُضْطَرُ

وَيَا قَرِيبَ الْعَفْوِ يَا مَوْلَاهُ   وَيَا مُجِيبَ كُلِّ مَنْ دَعَاهُ

بِكَ اسْتَغَثْنَا يَا مُغِيثَ الضُّعَفَا   فَحَسْبُنَا يَا رَبِّ أَنْتَ وَكَفَى

فَلَا أَجَلَّ مِنْ عَظِيمِ قُدْرَتِكْ   وَلَا أَعَزَّ مِنْ عَزِيزِ سَطْوَتِكْ

لِعِزِّ مُلْكِكَ الْمُلُوكُ تَخْضَعُ   تَخْفِضُ قَدْرَ مَنْ تَشَاءُ وَتَرْفَعُ

وَالْأَمْرُ كُلُّهُ إِلَيْكَ رَدُّهُ   وَبِيَدَيْكَ حَلُّهُ وَعَقْدُهُ

وَنَحْنُ قَدْ رَفَعْنَا أَمْرَنَا إِلَيْكَ   وَقَدْ شَكَوْنَا ضَعْفَنَا إِلَيْكَ

فَارْحَمْنَا يَا مَنْ لَا يَزَالُ عَالِمًا   بِحَالِنَا وَلَا يَزَالُ رَاحِمًا

وَانْظُرْ إِلَى مَا مَسَّنَا مِنَ الْوَرَى   فَحَالُنَا مِنْ بَيْنِهِمْ كَمَا تَرَى

قد قل وفرنا و قل جمنا　　وانحط ما بين الجموع قدرنا
واستضعفونا شدة وشوكة　　وستنقصونا عدة وعدة
وَنَحْنُ يَا مَنْ مُلْكُهُ لاَ يُسْلَبُ　　لُذْنَا بِجَاهِكَ الَّذِي لاَ يُغْلَبُ
إِلَيْكَ يَا غَوْثَ الذَّلِيلِ نَسْتَنِدْ　　عَلَيْكَ يَا كَهْفَ الضَّعِيفِ نَعْتَمِدْ
مِنكَ الْعِنَايَةُ الْتِي لاَ نَرْتَجِي　　حِمَايَةً مِنْ غَيْرِ بَابِهَا تَجِي
أَنتَ الَّذِي تَهْدِي إِذَا ضَلَلْنَا　　أَنتَ الَّذِي تَعْفُو إِذَا زَلَلْنَا
يَا وَاسِعَ الإِحْسَانِ يَا مَنْ خَيْرُهُ　　عَمَّ الْوَرَى وَلاَ يُنَادَى غَيْرُهُ
وَسِعْتَ كُلَّ مَا خَلَقْتَ عِلْمًا　　وَرَأْفَةً وَرَحْمَةً وَحِلْمًا
وَقَدْ مَدَدْنَا رَبَّنَا الأَكُفَّا　　وَمِنكَ رَبَّنَا رَجَوْنَا اللُّطْفَا
فَأَبْدِلِ اللَّهُمَّ حَالَ الْعُسْرِ　　بِالْيُسْرِ وَامْدُدْنَا بِرِيحِ النَّصْرِ
وَاجْعَلْ لَنَا عَلَى الْبُغَاةِ الْغَلَبَهْ　　وَاقْصُرْ أَذَى الشَّرِّ عَلَى مَنْ طَلَبَهْ
وَانْصُرْ حِمَانَا يَا قَوِيُّ نَصْرا　　وَاقْهَرْ عِدَانَا يَا عَزِيزُ قَهْرا
وَاعْكِسْ مُرَادَهُمْ وَخَيِّبْ سَعْيَهُمْ　　وَاهْزِمْ جُمُوعَهُمْ وَأَفْسِدْ رَأْيَهُمْ
وَعَجِّلِ اللَّهُمَّ فِيهِمْ نِقْمَتَكْ　　فَإِنَّهُمْ لاَ يُعْجِزُونَ قُدْرَتَكْ
وَكُنْ لَنَا وَلاَ تَكُنْ عَلَيْنَا　　وَلاَ تَكِلْنَا طَرْفَةً إِلَيْنَا
يَا رَبِّ يَا رَبِّ بِكَ التَّوَسُّلُ　　لِمَا لَدَيْكَ وَبِكَ التَّوَصُّلُ
يَا رَبِّ أَنتَ رُكْنُنَا الرَّفِيعُ　　يَا رَبِّ أَنتَ حِصْنُنَا الْمَنِيعُ
يَا رَبِّ يَا رَبِّ أَنِلْنَا الأَمْنَا　　إِذَا ارْتَحَلْنَا وَإِذَا أَقَمْنَا
وَاجْعَلْ بِصَادٍ وَبِقَافٍ وَبِنُونْ　　أَلْفَي حِجَابٍ مِن وَرَائِنَا تَكُونْ
بِجَاهِ لاَ إِلَـهَ إِلاَّ اللهُ　　وَجَاهِ خَيْرِ الْخَلْقِ يَا رَبَّاهُ
وَجَاهِ مَا بِهِ دَعَاكَ الأَنبِيَا　　وَجَاهِ مَا بِهِ دَعَاكَ الأَوْلِيَا
وَجَاهِ كُلِّ مَن رَفَعْتَ قَدْرَهُ　　مِمَّن سَتَرْتَ أَوْ أَشَعْتَ ذِكْرَهُ

وَجَاهِ آيَاتِ الْكِتَابِ الْمُحْكَمِ   وَجَاهِ الاسْمِ الأَعْظَمِ الْمُعَظَّمِ
رَبِّ دَعَوْنَاكَ دُعَاءَ مَن دَعَا   رَبًّا كَرِيماً لاَ يَرُدُّ مَن سَعَى
فَاقْبَلْ دُعَاءَنَا بِمَحْضِ الْفَضْلِ   قُبُولَ مَنْ أَلْقَى حِسَابَ الْعَدْلِ
وَامْنُنْ عَلَيْنَا مِنَّةَ الْكَرِيمِ   وَاعْطِفْ عَلَيْنَا عِطْفَةَ الْحَلِيمِ
وَانشُرْ عَلَيْنَا يَا رَحِيمُ رَحْمَتَكْ   وَابْسُطْ عَلَيْنَا يَا كَرِيمُ نِعْمَتَكْ
وَخِرْ لَنَا فِى سَائِرِ الأَقْوَالِ   وَاخْتَرْ لَنَا فِي سَائِرِ الأَحْوَالِ
وَاجْمَعْ لَنَا مَا بَيْنَ عِلْمٍ وَعَمَلْ   وَاصْرِفْ إلى دَارِ الْبَقَا مِنَّا الأَمَلْ
وَانْهَجْ بِنَا يَا رَبِّ نَهْجَ السُّعَدَا   وَاخْتِمْ لَنَا يَا رَبِّ خَتْمَ الشُّهَدَا
وَأَصْلِحِ اللَّهُمَّ حَالَ الأَهْلِ   وَيَسِّرْ اللَّهُمَّ جَمْعَ الشَّمْلِ
وَاقْضِ لَنَا أَغْرَاضَنَا الْمُخْتَلِفَهْ   فِيكَ وَعَرِّفْنَا تَمَامَ الْمَعْرِفَهْ
يَا رَبِّ وَانصُرْ دِينَنَا الْمُحَمَّدِي   وَاجْعَلْ خِتَامَ عِزِّهِ كَمَا بُدِي
وَاعْفُ وَعَافِ وَاكْفِ وَاغْفِرْ ذَنْبَنَا   وَذَنْبَ كُلِّ مُسْلِمٍ يَا رَبَّنَا
وَصَلِّ يَا رَبِّ عَلَى الْمُخْتَارِ   صَلاَتَكَ الْكَامِلَةَ الْمِقْدَارِ
صَلاَتَكَ الَّتِي تَفِي بِقَدْرِهِ   كَمَا يَلِيقُ بِارْتِفَاعِ ذِكْرِهِ
ثُمَّ عَلَى الآلِ الْكِرَامِ وَعَلَى   أَتْبَاعِهِ الْغُرِّ وَمَن لَهُمْ تَلاَ
وَالْحَمْدُ لِلهِ الَّذِي بِحَمْدِهِ   يَبْلُغُ ذُو الْقَصْدِ تَمَامَ قَصْدِهِ

O You to Whose mercy one flees! You in Whom the one in need and distress seeks refuge!
O Master, You Whose pardon is near! O You Who help all who call on Him!
We seek Your help, O You who help the weak! You are enough for us, O Lord!
There is nothing more majestic than Your immense power and nothing mightier than the might of Your force.

Kings are humbled to the might of Your domain and You lower or elevate whomever You wish.

The entire affair returns to You, and the release or conclusion of all matters is in Your hand.

We have presented our affair before You, and we complain to You of our weakness.

Have mercy on us, O You Who know our weakness and continue to be merciful.

Look at what we have experienced from people! Our state among them is as You see.

Our troops are few and our wealth is little. Our power has declined among groups.

They have weakened our solidarity and strength and diminished our numbers and our preparation.

O You Whose kingdom cannot be pillaged, give us shelter by Your rank which is never overcome!

O Succour of the poor, we trust in You! O Cave of the weak, we rely on You!

You are the One on Whom We call to remove our adversities, and You are the One we hope will dispel our sorrows.

You have such concern for us that we cannot hope for protection which comes through any other door.

We rush to the door of Your bounty and You honour the one You enrich by Your gift.

You are the One Who guides when we are misguided.

You are the One who pardons when we slip.

You have full knowledge of all You have created and encompassing compassion, mercy and forbearance.

There is no one in existence more lowly than we are nor poorer and more in need of what You have than us.

O you of vast kindness! O You Whose good encompasses all mankind, and no other is called on!

O Saviour of the drowning! O Compassionate! O rescuer of the lost!
O Gracious Bestower!
Words are lacking, O Hearing, O Answerer! The cure is difficult, O Swift!
O Near!
To you, our Lord, we have stretched out our hands and from You, our Lord, we hope for kindness.
Be kind to us in what You decree and let us be pleased with what pleases You.
O Allah, change the state of hardship for ease and help us with the wind of victory.
Give us victory over the aggressors and contain the evil among those who asked for it.
Overpower our enemy, O Mighty, with a force which disorders them and crushes them.
Overturn what they desire and make their efforts fail, defeat their armies and unsettle their resolve.
O Allah, hasten Your revenge among them.
They cannot stand before Your power.
O Lord, O Lord, Our protection is by Your love, and by the might of Your help.
Be for us and do not be against us.
Do not leave us to ourselves for a single instant.
We have no power of defence nor have we any device to bring about our benefit.
We do not aim for other than Your noble door, we do not hope for other than Your encompassing bounty.
Minds only hope for Your blessing by the simple fact that you say "Be" and it is.
O Lord, O Lord, arrival is by You to what You have and seeking the means is by You!
O Lord, You are our high pillar of support! O Lord, You are our impregnable fortress.

O Lord, O Lord, give us security when we travel and when we remain.

O Lord, preserve our crops and herds, and preserve our trade and make our numbers more!

Make our land a land of the deen and repose for the needy and the poor.

Give us force among the lands as well as respect, impregnability and a polity.

Appoint it its might from the protected secret, and grant it protection by the beautiful veiling.

By ṣād, qāf and nūn, place a thousand veils in front of it.

By the rank of the light of Your noble Face and the rank of the secret of Your immense kingdom,

And the rank of 'la ilaha illallah' and the rank of the Best of Creation, O our Lord,

And the rank of that by which the Prophets prayed to You and the rank of that by which the awliyā' pray to you,

And the rank of the power of the Quṭb and the Awtād and the rank of the Jaras and Afrād,

And the rank of the Akhyār and the rank of Nujabā and the rank of the Abdāl and the rank of the Nuqabā,

And the rank of every one worshipping and doing dhikr and the rank of everyone praising and giving thanks,

And the rank of everyone whose worth You elevated, both those who are concealed and those whose renown has spread,

And the ranks of the firm āyats of the Book and the rank of the Greatest Supreme Name,

O Lord, O Lord, make us stand as fuqarā before You, weak and lowly.

We call to You with the supplication of the one who calls on a noble Lord who does not turn aside those who call.

Accept our supplication with Your pure grace, with the acceptance of someone who sets aside the fair reckoning.

Bestow on us the favour of the Generous, and show us the kindness of the Forbearing.

O Merciful, extend Your mercy over us and spread Your blessing over us, O Generous.

Choose for us in all our words and select for us in all our actions.

O Lord, make it our habit to cling and devote ourselves to the resplendent Sunna.

Confine our manifold desires to You and grant us full and complete gnosis.

Combine both knowledge and action for us, and direct our hopes to the Abiding Abode.

O Lord, make us follow the road of the fortunate and make our seal the Seal of the martyrs, O Lord!

Make our sons virtuous and righteous, scholars with action and people of good counsel.

O Allah, remedy the situation of the people and, O Allah, make the reunification easy.

O Lord, grant Your clear victory to the one who takes charge and empowers the Deen,

And help him, O You Who are forbearing, and help his party and fill his heart with what will make him pleasing to you.

O Lord, help our Muḥammadan deen, and make it end mighty as it began.

Preserve it, O Lord, through the preservation of the scholars, and raise the minaret of its light to heaven.

Pardon, grant well-being, make up for our deficiency and forgive our sins and the sins of every Muslim, O our Lord.

O Lord, bless the Chosen one with your perfect prayer of blessing.

Your prayer is that which grants success in his business as befits his lofty worth.

Then bless his noble family and glorious Companions and those who have followed them.

Praise belongs to Allah by whose praise those with an aim completely fulfil that aim.

Translation by Aisha Bewley

Jawharat al-Kamāl

اللّهُمَّ صَلِّ وَسَلِّمْ عَلَى عَيْنِ الرَّحْمَةِ الرَّبَّانِيَّةِ وَالياقُوتَةِ المُتَحَقِّقَةِ الحَائِطَةِ بِمَرْكَزِ الفُهُومِ والمَعَانِي،

وَنُورِ الأَكْوَانِ المُتَكَوِّنَةِ الآدَمِي صَاحِبِ الحَقِّ الرَّبَّانِي، البَرْقِ الأَسْطَعِ بِمُزُونِ الأَرْبَاحِ المَالِئَةِ لِكُلِّ مُتَعَرِّضٍ مِنَ البُحُورِ وَالأَوَانِي، وَنُورِكَ اللاَّمِعِ الذي مَلأْتَ بِهِ كَوْنَكَ الحَائِطِ بِأَمْكِنَةِ المَكَانِي،

اللّهُمَّ صَلِّ وَسَلِّمْ عَلَى عَيْنِ الحَقِّ التي تَتَجَلَّى مِنْهَا عُرُوشُ الحَقَائِقِ عَيْنِ المَعَارِفِ الأَقْوَمِ صِرَاطِكَ التَّامِّ الأَسْقَمِ، اللّهُمَّ صَلِّ وَسَلِّمْ عَلَى طَلْعَةِ الحَقِّ بِالحَقِّ الكَنْزِ الأَعْظَمِ إِفَاضَتِكَ مِنْكَ إِلَيْكَ إِحَاطَةِ النُّورِ المُطَلْسَمِ صَلَّى اللهُ عَلَيْهِ وَعَلَى آلِهِ، صَلاَةً تُعَرِّفُنَا بِهَا إِيَّاهُ

O Allah, send benediction upon and salutations on the Essence of Divine Mercy, the Accomplished Ruby encompassing the centre of comprehensions and meanings, the Light of all created universes, the Adamic who possesses Lordly Truth; the all-filling Lightning in the rain-clouds of gains that fill all the intervening seas and receptacles; Your Bright Light with which You have filled Your creation and which surrounds all possible places. O Allah, bless and salute the Essence of Truth from which are manifested the thrones of realities; the Essence of the Most Righteous Knowledge, Your Complete and Most Straight Path. O Allah, bless and salute the Advent of the Truth by the Truth; the Greatest Treasure, Your Outpouring from Yourself to Yourself; the Encompassment of Talismanic Light. May Allah bless the Prophet and his household, a prayer which brings us to knowledge of him.

Dalāʾil al-Khayrāt

Dalāʾil al-Khayrāt (The Evidences of Virtues) is easily the most famous poem in all of Morocco. It is also lengthy, frequently requiring a whole week to recite from start to finish. Gatherings of the recitation thus generally split it up into portions and recite it in this way.

Dalāʾil al-Khayrāt was composed by the founder of the Shādhilī Jazūlī Ṭarīqa, Muḥammad ibn Sulaymān al-Jazūlī (d. 1465 CE). Legend has it that he was inspired to compose the poem after an incident in which he came by a well and had trouble drawing the water without a bucket and rope. Suddenly, a young girl appeared and spat in the well, and the water began gushing from the recesses until it overflowed at the top. Amazed, al-Jazūlī inquired how the girl achieved this miracle, to which she replied it was a result of her sending prayers upon the Prophet ﷺ. Thereafter al-Jazūlī decided to compose a great prayer for the Prophet ﷺ, and the *Dalāʾil* was born.

Ḥizb al-Baḥr

بِسْمِ اللهِ الرَّحْمٰنِ الرَّحِيمِ يا عَلِيُّ يا عَظِيمُ يا حَلِيمُ يا عَلِيمُ أَنْتَ رَبِّي وَعِلْمُكَ حَسْبِي فَنِعْمَ الرَّبُّ رَبِّي وَنِعْمَ الحَسْبُ حَسْبِي تَنْصُرُ مَنْ تَشاءُ وَأَنْتَ العَزِيزُ الرَّحِيمُ نَسْأَلُكَ العِصْمَةَ فِي الحَرَكاتِ وَالسَّكَناتِ وَالكَلِماتِ وَالإِراداتِ وَالخَطَراتِ مِنَ الشُّكُوكِ وَالظُّنُونِ وَالأَوْهامِ السَّاتِرَةِ لِلْقُلُوبِ عَنْ مُطالَعَةِ الغُيُوبِ فَقَدِ ﴿ٱبْتُلِىَ ٱلْمُؤْمِنُونَ وَزُلْزِلُوا۟ زِلْزَالًا شَدِيدًا ۝ وَإِذْ يَقُولُ ٱلْمُنَٰفِقُونَ وَٱلَّذِينَ فِى قُلُوبِهِم مَّرَضٌ مَّا وَعَدَنَا ٱللَّهُ وَرَسُولُهُۥٓ إِلَّا غُرُورًا﴾ * فَثَبِّتْنا وَانْصُرْنا وَسَخِّرْ لَنا هٰذا البَحْرَ كَما سَخَّرْتَ البَحْرَ لِمُوسَى وَسَخَّرْتَ النّارَ لِإِبْراهِيمَ وَسَخَّرْتَ الجِبالَ وَالحَدِيدَ لِداوُودَ وَسَخَّرْتَ الرِّيحَ وَالشَّياطِينَ وَالجِنَّ لِسُلَيْمانَ وَسَخِّرْ لَنا كُلَّ بَحْرٍ هُوَ لَكَ فِي الأَرْضِ وَالسَّماءِ وَالمُلْكِ وَالمَلَكُوتِ وَبَحْرَ الدُّنْيا وَبَحْرَ الآخِرَةِ وَسَخِّرْ لَنا كُلَّ شَيْءٍ يا مَنْ

بِيَدِهِ مَلَكُوتُ كُلِّ شَيْءٍ ﴿ كٓهيعٓصٓ ﴾ (٣) أُنْصُرْنا فَإِنَّكَ خَيْرُ النّاصِرِينَ وَافْتَحْ لَنا فَإِنَّكَ خَيْرُ الفاتِحِينَ وَاغْفِرْ لَنا فَإِنَّكَ خَيْرُالغافِرِينَ وَارْحَمْنا فَإِنَّكَ خَيْرُ الرّاحِمِينَ وَارْزُقْنا فَإِنَّكَ خَيْرُ الرّازِقِينَ واهْدِنا وَنَجِّنا مِنَ القَوْمِ الظّالِمِينَ وَهَبْ لَنا رِيحًا طَيِّبَةً كَما هِيَ فِي عِلْمِكَ وانْشُرْها عَلَيْنا مِنْ خَزائِنِ رَحْمَتِكَ وَاحْمِلْنا بِها حَمْلَ الكَرامَةِ مَعَ السَّلامَةِ وَالعافِيَةِ فِي الدِّينِ وَالدُّنْيا وَالآخِرَةِ إِنَّكَ عَلَى كُلِّ شَيْءٍ قَدِيرٌ اللَّهُمَّ يَسِّرْ لَنا أُمُورَنا مَعَ الرّاحَةِ لِقُلُوبِنا وَأَبْدانِنا وَالسَّلامَةِ وَالعافِيَةِ فِي دُنْيانا وَدِينِنا وَكُنْ لَنا صاحِبًا فِي سَفَرِنا وَخَلِيفَةً فِي أَهْلِنا وَاطْمِسْ عَلَى وُجُوهِ أَعْدائِنا وَامْسَخْهُمْ عَلَى مَكانَتِهِمْ فَلا يَسْتَطِيعُونَ المُضِيَّ وَلا المَجِيءَ إِلَيْنا ﴿ وَلَوْ نَشَآءُ لَطَمَسْنَا عَلَىٰٓ أَعْيُنِهِمْ فَٱسْتَبَقُوا۟ ٱلصِّرَٰطَ فَأَنَّىٰ يُبْصِرُونَ ۝ وَلَوْ نَشَآءُ لَمَسَخْنَٰهُمْ عَلَىٰ مَكَانَتِهِمْ فَمَا ٱسْتَطَٰعُوا۟ مُضِيًّا وَلَا يَرْجِعُونَ ﴾ ﴿ يسٓ ۝ وَٱلْقُرْءَانِ ٱلْحَكِيمِ ۝ إِنَّكَ لَمِنَ ٱلْمُرْسَلِينَ ۝ عَلَىٰ صِرَٰطٍ مُّسْتَقِيمٍ ۝ تَنزِيلَ ٱلْعَزِيزِ ٱلرَّحِيمِ ۝ لِتُنذِرَ قَوْمًا مَّآ أُنذِرَ ءَابَآؤُهُمْ فَهُمْ غَٰفِلُونَ ۝ لَقَدْ حَقَّ ٱلْقَوْلُ عَلَىٰٓ أَكْثَرِهِمْ فَهُمْ لَا يُؤْمِنُونَ ۝ إِنَّا جَعَلْنَا فِىٓ أَعْنَٰقِهِمْ أَغْلَٰلًا فَهِىَ إِلَى ٱلْأَذْقَانِ فَهُم مُّقْمَحُونَ ۝ وَجَعَلْنَا مِنۢ بَيْنِ أَيْدِيهِمْ سَدًّا وَمِنْ خَلْفِهِمْ سَدًّا فَأَغْشَيْنَٰهُمْ فَهُمْ لَا يُبْصِرُونَ ﴾ شاهَتِ الوُجُوهُ (٣) وَعَنَتِ الوُجُوهُ لِلْحَيِّ القَيُّومِ وَقَدْ خابَ مَنْ حَمَلَ ظُلْمًا*

﴿ طسٓ ﴾ ﴿ حمٓ ۝ عٓسٓقٓ ﴾ ﴿ مَرَجَ ٱلْبَحْرَيْنِ يَلْتَقِيَانِ ۝ بَيْنَهُمَا بَرْزَخٌ لَّا يَبْغِيَانِ ﴾

﴿حمٓ﴾ ﴿حمٓ﴾ ﴿حمٓ﴾ ﴿حمٓ﴾ ﴿حمٓ﴾ ﴿حمٓ﴾ ﴿حمٓ﴾ ﴿حمٓ﴾ ﴿حمٓ﴾ ﴿حمٓ﴾

حُمَّ الأَمْرُ وَجاءَ النَّصْرُ فَعَلَيْنا لا يُنْصَرُونَ ﴿ حمٓ ۝ تَنزِيلُ ٱلْكِتَٰبِ مِنَ ٱللَّهِ ٱلْعَزِيزِ ٱلْعَلِيمِ ۝ غَافِرِ ٱلذَّنۢبِ وَقَابِلِ ٱلتَّوْبِ شَدِيدِ ٱلْعِقَابِ ذِى ٱلطَّوْلِ لَآ إِلَٰهَ إِلَّا هُوَ إِلَيْهِ ٱلْمَصِيرُ ﴾

﴿ بِسْمِ اللَّهِ ﴾ بابُنا ﴿ تَبَارَكَ ﴾ حِيطانُنا ﴿ يسٓ ﴾ سَقْفُنا ﴿ كٓهيعٓصٓ ﴾ كِفايَتُنا *
﴿ حمٓ ۝ عٓسٓقٓ ﴾ حِمايَتُنا

﴿ فَسَيَكْفِيكَهُمُ ٱللَّهُ وَهُوَ ٱلسَّمِيعُ ٱلْعَلِيمُ ﴾ (٣) سِتْرُ العَرْشِ مَسْبُولٌ عَلَيْنا وَعَيْنُ اللّهِ ناظِرَةٌ
إِلَيْنا بِحَوْلِ اللّهِ لا يُقْدَرُ عَلَيْنا ﴿ وَٱللَّهُ مِن وَرَآئِهِم مُّحِيطٌۢ ۝ بَلْ هُوَ قُرْءَانٌ مَّجِيدٌ ۝
فِى لَوْحٍ مَّحْفُوظٍۭ ﴾ ﴿ فَٱللَّهُ خَيْرٌ حَـٰفِظًا وَهُوَ أَرْحَمُ ٱلرَّٰحِمِينَ ﴾ (٣) ﴿ إِنَّ وَلِـِّۧىَ ٱللَّهُ
ٱلَّذِى نَزَّلَ ٱلْكِتَـٰبَ وَهُوَ يَتَوَلَّى ٱلصَّـٰلِحِينَ ﴾ (٣) ﴿ حَسْبِىَ ٱللَّهُ لَآ إِلَـٰهَ إِلَّا هُوَ عَلَيْهِ
تَوَكَّلْتُ وَهُوَ رَبُّ ٱلْعَرْشِ ٱلْعَظِيمِ ﴾ (٣) بِسْمِ اللّهِ الَّذِي لا يَضُرُّ مَعَ اسْمِهِ شَيْءٌ فِي الأَرْضِ
وَلا فِي السَّماءِ وَهُوَ السَّمِيعُ العَلِيمُ (٣) أَعُوذُ بِكَلِماتِ اللّهِ التَّامّاتِ مِنْ شَرِّ ما خَلَقَ (٣)
وَلا حَوْلَ وَلا قُوَّةَ إِلّا بِاللّهِ العَلِيِّ العَظِيمِ (٣) وَصَلَّى اللّهُ عَلَى سَيِّدِنا مُحَمَّدٍ وَآلِهِ وَصَحْبِهِ وَسَلَّمَ
تَسْلِيمًا وَالحَمْدُ لِلّهِ رَبِّ العالَمِينَ *

In the name of God, the Merciful, the Compassionate. Blessings of God and peace be upon our master Muḥammad and his family.
O God, O Exalted One, O Gentle One, O All-Knowing One,
Thou art my Lord, and Thy knowledge is sufficient for me.
What an excellent lord is my Lord! What a wonderful sufficiency is my sufficiency!
Our plea to Thee is for protection, in movements and moments of rest, in words, desires, and passing thoughts, from doubts, suppositions and fancies, they, over hearts, occluding sight of the unseen.
The faithful were tried; they were severely shaken.
Then the hypocrites would say, with those of disease-ridden hearts, "God and His Messenger promised us only delusion." (Q. 33:11–12)
Even so, make us firm, aid us, and subject to us this sea, as Thou did subject the sea to Moses, and the fire to Abraham, and the mountains and iron to David, and the wind, the Satans, and the jinn to Solomon.
Put in subjection to us every sea of thine in earth and heaven, in this domain

and the celestial, the sea of this world and the sea of the next. Render subservient to us everything, "O Thou, whose hand holds sovereignty over everything." (Q. 23:88)

Kaf ḥā yā ʿayn ṣād

Kaf ḥā yā ʿayn ṣād

Kaf ḥā yā ʿayn ṣād

Help us, for Thou art the best of helpers.

Open to us the hand of mercy, for Thou art the best of openers.

Pardon us, for Thou art the best of pardoners.

Be compassionate toward us, for Thou art the best of those who show compassion.

Sustain us, for Thou art the best of sustainers.

Guide us and rescue us from the unjust people.

Send us a gentle breeze, as Thou dost know how to do, and let it blow on us from the storehouses of Thy mercy. Let it bear us along as if by miraculous intervention, with security and well-being, in religion, worldly affairs, and the hereafter.

Thou art powerful over all things. God, facilitate for us our affairs, with ease of mind and body, with security and well-being in religious and worldly matters. Be a companion for us on our journey, and a substitute for our households.

Blot out the countenances of our enemies, and transform them where they stand, disabling them from leaving or coming to us. "If We willed, We would blot out their eyes. Yet, they would race forward to the path. But how would they see? If We willed, We should transform them where they stand. Thus, they would be unable to leave or return." (Q. 36:66–67)

"Yā sīn! By the Wise Quran!

Surely thou art one of those sent on a straight path! A revelation sent down by the Mighty, the Merciful, that thou mightest warn a people whose fathers had not been warned. Yet, they do not take heed.

The declaration has been confirmed against the greater part of them. Yet they do not believe. We have circled their necks with chains up to the chin, but they hold their heads high. Before them have We placed a barrier, and behind them a barrier, and We have obscured their vision; so they see not." (Q. 36:1–8)

May their faces be deformed!

May their faces be deformed!

May their faces be deformed!

"Let their faces be submissive before the Living, the Self-Subsistent, for he who is laden with wrong has already met frustration. Tā sīn, hā mīm, ʿayn sīn qāf." (Q. 27:1)

"He has released the two seas that meet; yet between them is a barrier [barzakh] that they do not overpass." (Q. 55:19–20)

"Ḥā mīm, ḥā mīm, ḥā mīm, ḥā mīm, ḥā mīm, ḥā mīm, ḥā mīm!" (Q. 40:1)

The affair has been decreed. The triumph has come. Over us they shall not triumph.

"Ḥā mīm! [It is] the sending down of the Scripture from God, The Mighty, the All- Knowing, Forgiver of sin, Receiver of penitence, Severe in punishing, Forbearing. No god is there except Him. To Him is the returning." (Q. 40:1–3)

In the name of God (bismillah) is our door. May [God] bless our walls.

Yā sīn (Q. 36:1) is our ceiling.

Kāf ḥā yā ʿayn ṣād (Q. 19:1) is our sufficiency.

Hā mīm ʿayn sīn qāf (Q. 42:1) is our shelter.

So God is sufficient for thee against them, for He hears all, knows all.

[Repeat this thrice]

The veil of the throne has been dropped over us, and the eye of God is gazing at us.

"God is behind them, round about. Indeed, it is a glorious recital [Quran], inscribed on a guarded tablet [lawh mahfūz]." (Q. 85:20–21) [Repeat this thrice]

"My Protector is God, Who revealed the Book (from time to time), and He will choose and befriend the righteous." (Q. 7:196) [Repeat this thrice]

"My sufficiency is God. No god is there except Him. In Him have I put my

trust, For He is Lord of the majestic throne." (Q. 9:129) [Repeat this thrice]
In the name of God, with whose Name nothing in the earth or sky can do harm, for He is the All-Hearer, All-Knower. [Repeat this thrice]
There is no force and no power except with God, the High, the Mighty.

Translation by Elmer H. Douglas

Glossary

Ālim: Scholars of the Islamic sciences; authorities in Islam.

Awtād: The "Pillars". In the hierarchy of sainthood the Awtād is the third highest rank after the Quṭb and the Abdāl.

Badl/Abdāl: Literally meaning "Substitute(s)", the Abdāl are the second highest ranking saints after the Quṭb(s). They are called the Substitutes because when a Qutub dies they are replaced (substituted) by one of the Abdāl.

Baraka: Spiritual "grace" or "blessing(s)". Baraka is sought at holy sights, on holy nights, through pious action, and especially from saintly figures.

Darbūz: A large decorative box or marble slate built directly over the tomb of a saint to mark the grave.

Ḍarīḥ: A mausoleum.

Dhikr/Adhkār: The principle spiritual practice associated with Sufism. Meaning literally "Remembrance (of God)", dhikr involves the ritual chanting of phrases or names of God.

Dhimmi: A historical term for non-Muslims living in an Islamic state with legal protection.

Grand taxi: Grand taxis are taxis that only drive a certain route with set fares, pick up and drop off points. After the driver has gathered enough customers to fill up all the seats (two in front, 4 in the back) he departs. Customers pay by the seat only and save money. These taxis are used for longer routes and often serve between cities.

Ḥabus: Government fund set up to cater to religious projects.

Haqiqah: The "Truth" or "Reality". Used frequently in Sufism to denote mystical or gnostic knowledge, as well as the spiritual unveiling of the Divine.

Hilloulah: Death anniversary of a Jewish saint.

Karāmah/Karamāt: The miracles of the saints, as distinct from the miracles of prophets.

Khalwa: A period of spiritual retreat and isolation marked by ascetism and religious practice.

Khatīb: Orator. One who delivers the Friday sermon.

Madh: Devotional song.

Madrasa/Madāris: Islamic school.

Matn: The actual text of a book, as distinguished from its oral explanation, chain of transmission or commentary.

Medina: Literally meaning city, in the context of Morocco the medina now refers to the old quarters of a city.

Medina Jedid/Jedidah: A reference to the recently constructed modern portions of the cities in Morocco.

Muftī: A scholar authorised to issue legal opinions.

Muqaddam: The leader of a zāwiyah, and in most cases the representative of the ṭarīqa in that region.

Murīd/Sālik: Terms both denoting the spiritual initiate and/or seeker.

Petite taxis: Petite taxis are just normal taxis using a meter.

Qabr: Literally, tomb.

Qadiriyyah: The spiritual fraternity associated with the teachings of the famous medieval saint ʿAbd al-Qadir al-Jīlānī of Baghdad.

Qubbah: A dome-like structure frequently constructed over the tombs of saints posthumously.

Quṭb: Literally meaning "Pole", this is the highest ranking saint in the spiritual hierarchy of Islam. Like the sun's relationship to the solar system, it is around the Quṭb that the other saints circulate, and from his emanation of spiritual grace that the other saints are illuminated. Not only does the universe have its own Quṭb, but each continent, country, city, etc. has its own, being in each case the most pious believer of the province.

Samaʿ: A Sufi ceremony involving religious songs and sometimes dance. Translated usually as "audition".

Shadhiliyah: The spiritual fraternity associated with the 12th century saint Abū al-Ḥassan al-Shādhilī, who died in Egypt.

Shaykh: Literally "elder", the term shaykh is a reverential term applied to those either authorised to teach or to rule. Thus, a student who completes his or her education becomes a shaykh, a spiritual seeker who completes their wayfaring becomes a shaykh of Sufism, and the governors or princes of a region are sometimes also referred to as shaykhs.

Sufism: The spiritual, inner dimension of Islam. Today Sufism is associated with the practice of formal spiritual brotherhoods (ṭarīqas) that have over time developed their own spiritual practices (wirds or hizbs), followers (murīds), representatives (muqaddams), centres (zāwiyahs), and esoteric teachings.

Tabarruk: Seeking blessings.

Tarbiyah: Literally meaning "child-rearing," used in the context of Sufism to denote the disciplining of a murīd.

Ṭarīqa: A spiritual fraternity, generally associated with the teachings of some major historical saint or another.

Tasawwuf: The "science" behind Sufism. In the classical tradition this is most often associated either with mystical practice and states, or more generally, the science of purfying the "ego-self" (nafs) from its faults.

Tayibiyy: See Wazzānīya.

Tzidiq/Tzidiqim: Jewish saints.

Walī/Awliyāʾ: The Islamic term for saints, literally, the "Friends" of God.

Waqf: A form of charity in which rather than donating money, a person purchases a continual source of income for the object of his charity, such as a plot of date-trees, and the annual profits are donated.

Wazzānīya: Belonging to Wazzān or the Sufi fraternity of Mūlay ʿAbdullāh Sharīf of Wazzān.

Wird: The daily practice or litany of a ṭarīqa, generally a series of chants or recitations praising God practised at specific intervals throughout the day.

Zāwiyah: A spiritual centre of a Sufi fraternity. Similar in concept to a monastery, zāwiyahs are centres for instruction in Islam and Sufism as well as for spiritual retreat, charitable activities, hospitality for travellers, etc.

Ziyārah: A visitation to a Muslim saint.

Bibliography

A'bīdū, Muḥammad, al-Shaykh al-Mūlay 'Abd al-Salām bin Mashīsh: *Quṭb al-Maghrib al-Aqṣā,* Rabāt: Dār Abī Raqrāq Lil Ṭibā'ah wa al-Nashr. Third Edition: 2013.

Abūn-Nasr, Jamil M., *A History of the Maghrib in the Islamic Period,* Cambridge: Cambridge University Press, 1987.

Al-Kattānī, Ja'far Ed. al-Kattānī, Ḥamzah, *Salwat al-Anfās wa Muhādathāt al-Akīyās bi Man Uqbira Min al-'Ulumā wa al-Ṣuluḥā bi Fās.* Rabāt: 2005. https://archive.org/details/Salwat al-Anfas_797

Al-Khatāb, 'Umar, *al-Muṭrib min Ash'ār Ahl al-Maghrib,* Beruit: Dār al-'Ilm al-Jamī'. Waqfīyah.com: 2011.

Al-Kowhen, Muḥammad, *Ṭabaqāt al-Shādhiliyya al-Kubrā al-Musammā Jāmi'a al-Karāmāt al-'Alīyah fī Ṭabaqāt al-Sādah al-Shādilīyah,* Lebanon: Dār al-Kutub al-'Ilmīyah. Second Edition: 2005.

Al-Ṣūm'ī, Aḥmad Ed. Al-Jāwī, 'Alī, *al-Ma'zā fī Manāqib al-Shaykh Abī Ya'zā,* Rabāt: al-Ma'ārif al-Jadīdah: 1996.

Al-Wazzānī, bin Ṭayyib Ed. 'Abd Allāh, al-Targhī, *al-Rawḍ al-Munīf fī al-Ta'rīf bi Awlād Mūlay 'Abdullāh Sharīf,* Tetouan, Jām'iah 'Abd al-Mālik al-Sa'dī: 2009.

Aouni, Lhaj Moussa and El Faiz, Mohamed, *Fes Guide: The*

Thematic Tourist Circuits, Rabāt: Editions OKAD, 2005.

Bazzaz, Sahar, *Forgotten Saints: History, Power, and Politics in the Making of Modern Morocco,* Cambridge: Harvard University Press, 2010.

Ben-Ami, Issachar, *Saint Veneration Among the Jews in Morocco,* Detroit: Wayne State University Press, 1998.

Boyle, Helene N., *Quranic Schools: Agents of Preservation and Change,* New York: Routledge Falmer, 2004.

Burckhardt, Titus, *Fes: City of Islam*, Cambridge: The Islamic Texts Society, 1992.

Cornell, Vincent J., *Realm of the Saint: Power and Authority in Moroccan Sufism*, Austin: University of Texas Press, 1998.

Eickleman, Dale F., *Knowledge and Power in Morocco: The Education of a Twentieth-Century Notable,* Princeton: Princeton University Press, 1992.

Fromherz, Allen J., *The Almohads: The Rise of an Islamic Empire,* London: I.B. Taurus, 2010.

Gaudio, Attilio, *Fès: Joyau de la civilisation islamique,* Paris : Les Presses De L'Unesco, 1982.

Le Tourneau, Roger, *Fès avant le protectorat : étude économique et sociale d'une ville de l'occident musulman,* Rabāt : Editions La Porte, 1987.

Miller, Susan Gilson, *A History of Modern Morocco,* New York: Cambridge University Press, 2013.

Parker, Richard, *A practical guide to Islamic monuments in Morocco,* Charlottesville: The Baraka Press, 1981.

Sanseverino, Ruggero Vimercati, *Fès et sainteté, de la fondation a l'avènement du Protectorat (808-1912): Hagiographie, tradition spirituelle et héritage prophétique dans la ville de Mawlay Idrīs,* Rabāt : Centre Jacques-Berque, 2014.

Skali, Faouzi, *Saints et sanctuaires de Fes*, Rabāt : Marsam, 2007.

Photo Credits

Introduction – Fes Camel pic: Vince Gx (Unsplash)

1 – Fes: The Jewel of the Maghreb

Taxis waiting for fares on a busy Fes road: Bjørn Christian Tørrissen

The train station in Fes Ville Nouvelle: Bjørn Christian Tørrissen

A

Arabic Language Institute in Fes (ALIF): Arabic Language Institute in Fes (ALIF)

2 – Fes Bali: The Qarawiyyin Quarter

The courtyard or sahn of Zawiyah of Mulay Idris II; looking west towards the mausoleum entrance: Houssain Tork

Al-Qarawīyīn University gate: Matthias Bethke

The tomb of Moulay Idris II in the mausoleum: Jamil Chishti

The courtyard and minaret of Bou Inania Madrasa: Bjørn Christian Tørrissen

The Bab Bu Julud, also known as The Blue Gate, leads into Fes's old medina: Bjørn Christian Tørrissen

Ain al-Kheil, also known as Al-Azhar Mosque in Fes el-Bali's Ain Allou neighbourhood: Satanoid

The Western side of the Al-Atarine Madrasa courtyard, looking towards the entrance: Robert Prazeres

The tomb of Shaykh Ahmad Tijani: Jamil Chishti

The famous coloured baths of Fes' tanneries, in which leather skins are softened or given a new tan: Vince Gx (Unsplash)

3 – The Andalusian Quarter

The main entrance of the al-Andalus Mosque, or Mosque of the Andalusians: Robert Prazeres

A town square that is home to Fes' copper and brass workers – Mike Prince

4 – Fes Jdid and the Mellah

Tombstone of Sol Hachuel in Morocco with inscriptions in Hebrew and French: Mathieu Ravier

Bab Semmarine, the main southern gate of Fes al-Jdid. From here a street goes south towards the entrance of the Mellah, which was oriented towards this gate: Sambasoccer27

The tombs of Jews buried in the Jewish cemetery of the Mellah: bobistraveling

The main gates of the Royal Palace: Michal Osmenda

Interior of the Al-Fassiyine Synagogue or Slat Al-Fassiyine: Yamen

The Merinid Tombs of Fes overlook the main medina: Josep

Renalias

The main avenue of the gardens at Jnan Sbil: Robert Prazeres

The Merinid Tombs of Fes: Mx. Granger

5 – La Ville Nouvelle: The French New City

6 – Bab al-Futuh Cemetery

Bab al-Futuh cemetery, with Borj Sud visible in the distance on the right: Robert Prazeres

The Bab al-Futuh cemetery. On the left of the image, one of the larger mausoleums, the Mausoleum of Sidi Harazem was under restoration: Robert Prazeres

The Mausoleum of Sidi Harazem in the Bab al-Futuh Cemetery, pictured in 2014, while it was under restoration: Robert Prazeres

7 – Visiting Outside of Fes

The simple and humble tomb of Sheikh Abdul Assalaam Ibn Mashish: Morocco2U

The indoor patio chamber to the north of the mausoleum of Sidi Amar Hassani in Meknes, with a central fountain and marble columns: Ben Bender

The Mausoleum of Idris I, noticable by its green roof, in Moulay Idris: Umer Al-AmerikeeGenistrus